PELICA

# WITCHCRAFT

Pennethorne Hughes taught history for five years at a
leading English public school, and then joined the B.B.C.,
originally as a producer. He held a number of senior
appointments, being Director of Programmes in the West
of England, Director, Middle East, and Director, New
Delhi, during the war; then he became Director of the
Eastern Service, and for a number of years was in charge
of Staff Training in London. He retired to have more time
for writing, and lives in Wiltshire.

His published works include a wide variety of articles,
short stories, poems, and book reviews on historical and
anthropological subjects. He has also written a history of
Modern Europe, a book about Egypt in wartime, *While
Shepheards Watched,* and one about the origin of surnames,
*How You Got Your Name*. He has broadcast extensively on
both sound and television.

# WITCHCRAFT

*Pennethorne Hughes*

*Penguin Books*

Penguin Books Ltd, Harmondsworth, Middlesex, England
Penguin Books Inc., 7110 Ambassador Road, Baltimore, Maryland 21207, U.S.A.
Penguin Books Australia Ltd, Ringwood, Victoria, Australia

—

First published by Longmans, Green 1952
Published in Penguin Books 1965
Reprinted 1967, 1969, 1970

—

Copyright © Pennethorne Hughes, 1952, 1965

—

Made and printed in Great Britain
by Cox & Wyman Ltd,
London, Reading and Fakenham
Set in Monotype Garamond

# Contents

# List of Plates

# Foreword to the Pelican Edition

It is sometimes a merit to be able to say of a book which is being re-issued that it has been completely revised and re-written. I do not believe that it is necessary for this work (although certain references date a little) simply because no new facts about the history of witchcraft have emerged since I first compiled it. Approaches have veered, as I suggest they always will, but anything fresh in the records of witchcraft is only likely to endorse arguments already set out and attitudes already adopted. Certainly this is true of H. C. Lea's three industrious volumes of *Material Toward a History of Witchcraft*, edited by Arthur C. Howland and newly issued here in 1957. Russell Hope Robbins's *Encyclopedia of Witchcraft and Demonology* (1959) does not claim to quote from new sources.

It does, however, represent a swing in the pendulum. Dr Margaret Murray's thesis, with which I deal fairly fully, was that witchcraft represented, in some respects, a continuation of an old pre-Christian fertility belief. This new approach was important, and still is. Unfortunately it led to wild extravagances, with almost every occupier of the English throne, up to the Hanoverians, a hidden leader of the cult, and promoted a devoted search for 'clues' which would have done justice to the craziest Baconians.

Dr Robbins therefore, and a new set of no-nonsense pragmatists, swing right round and suggest that witchcraft was the invention of the seventeenth-century demonologists: a horrifying hoax.

Meanwhile, on the journalistic level, *soi-disant* witches from Cornwall, the New Forest, or the North London suburbs crop up every now and again on the radio or in the Sunday papers. Individual white witches do of course exist, and so do societies. They claim a religious pre-Christian basis, but their understandably rare revelations of their practices smell of

9

undigested book-learning, and sometimes of organized nasti- ness as well. No doubt they help to fill some spiritual vacuum, and I have received many letters from would-be witches asking to be put in touch with these groups, and a rather charming one from a woman who said she belonged to two covens in the country, but could I put her in touch with a smart West End one? The picture is further confused by hooliganism in churchyards, whilst the romantic 'o-tell-us-a-witch-story' school still peddles industriously.

This is a historian's book, probably displeasing to all the vested interests. I hope, however, that it may continue, and in this edition even more widely so, to interest the general reader.

P. H.

# I

## *The Approaches to Witchcraft*

THIS is a serious book, on a serious subject. It was only the
original approach which was, perhaps, flippant.

At Oxford University, in 1928, a few of us founded a witch-
group. One paper only was read – by a young undergraduate
from Lady Margaret Hall who became a distinguished politi-
cian – in the half-light of a room which our host had garishly
decorated for the occasion with murals of startling colour and
obscenity. There were black candles, and afterwards we ate
passion fruit. To subsequent meetings the late Montague
Summers was or was not invited to come – I forget which, but
it was anyhow projected – and certainly at one of them a
puppet representing Mr Peter Fleming was allegedly, and
quite pointlessly, burnt. It was all extremely childish, and
distressing to those who were seriously yearning after historical analysis of the occult, with perhaps a little academic
pornography thrown in as well. Very soon it petered out. We
had flattered ourselves that, as a result of the pre-publicity
won (by sherry) in the undergraduate papers, a priest in
Oxford had spent the day of our first meeting guarding the
sacrament lest we should try to steal it for diabolical rites. This
was almost certainly untrue.

But the legend went on, and it was during the same generation and at the same university that a strapping hockey girl
from one of the women's colleges was said to have asked for
late-night leave to attend the Black Mass. It was to have been
in Berkshire, she said, but leave was denied, and in the end she
went instead, I believe, to the Playhouse, which in those days
must have been quite as uncomfortable.

Undergraduates are useful barometers, and there is no
question that witchcraft obtained more readers in the twenties
and early thirties than read about it very seriously. The vogue

perhaps dates from the publication, in 1921, of *The Witch-Cult in Western Europe* by Professor Margaret Murray. At all events anthropology was one of the first studies to make a popular recovery after 1918, as again in 1947. The repressed romanticism of a generation determined to be astringently scientific accepted the witch gladly. She had haunted their childhood's reading with the full trappings of the cockeyed picturesque. She could be debunked – and debunking, then, seemed an intellectual necessity for war survivors – and it stirred any remaining romantic memories as well. And so the devil got a good Press, particularly when the Catholic orthodox, the nineteenth-century hangovers, ghost-peddling magazine writers, and other vested interests, joined in. True study, however, was confined to a dilettante, limited-edition public, for the subject was unattractive, and largely inaccessible, to the earnest and worthy student. The co-cultural boggled. It was, moreover, if treated seriously, too shocking for ordinary subscription-library readers. But it went on. To show what the main approaches became, the best way is perhaps to tabulate them briefly, with a note on their survivals today.

First of all, there is the Orthodox Diabolic Belief of naïve acceptance, which postulates the authentic and effective validity of the traditional witch rites and worship. This only remains fragmentarily in folklore, in the conviction of Peacock's Mr Toobad, and among self-deluded eccentrics of the school of the late Mr Aleister Crowley.

Secondly, there exists its variant, the Catholic Orthodox approach. This represents the standard attitude towards the phenomenon of witchcraft held by the Church in the Middle Ages. Its creed was that witchcraft was the direct evidence of Antichrist. Witches were his servants, in league with him against Christendom, and witchcraft was the parody of Christianity. The Devil gave his agents supernatural powers of evil as doctrine attested and evidence confirmed. Holy Church alone, it was felt, could combat their powers, and 'Thou shalt not suffer a witch to live'.

This view, with modifications or intensifications to taste, has usually been accepted by the public exponents of the

Roman Catholic faith. It has until recently been presented, with a battery of quotation and full vocabulary of horror, in a series of works about different sorts of witchcraft, and translations of some of the stock authorities, by the Reverend Montague Summers. Official Catholic publications are more cautious, but Dr Summers has still seen the devil in our midst, seeking with great wrath whom he may devour, or transform into werewolves and vampires. The excesses of the rationalists and the special pleading of the anthropologists give the orthodox view plenty of debating points. Witches existed, and do exist, they claim, to tempt man and defy God. It is worth noting at once that, although Protestant orthodoxy was quicker to accept rationalism, the reformed Churches of the Reformation were as fierce witch-hunters as the Catholics had ever been. Of course they became a bit muddled sometimes, as when Milton wrote of the Vaudois as 'slaughtered saints', when a less partisan and more particular study would have proved them to be anything but satisfactory Christians. Yet, even in predominantly Protestant countries, popular feeling has always been that the Catholic priest was the safest disinfectant against the powers of darkness, and it is the Catholic exorcists who have been invoked, rather than Protestant ones.

Next there arose the stage of what may be called Rationalist-cum-Scientific Disbelief.

With the rise of rationalism, and the disbelief in a personal god, came a corresponding disbelief in his opposite, the Devil. By the middle of the eighteenth century, comparatively few educated people believed in either personification with any profound conviction, although John Wesley accepted them both with evangelistic fervour. A decline in the acceptance of miracles meant a decline in the acceptance of spells. The clear light of reason, later to be focused on the subject by Mr Lecky, looked down on witchcraft and saw it as bunkum, and priestly bunkum at that. The evidence of the witch-trials was laughed aside or put down to torture, and witches were seen as hysterical crones. By the beginning of the nineteenth century, this was the recognized analysis of the subject accepted by educated men in most civilized countries. The discredited witch had become another useful agent in the campaign to clear the world of popery, nonsense, superstition, and non-acceptance generally of the profits basis of a bourgeois world. By 1840 Nuttall's Dictionary dismissed witchcraft as 'a kind of pretended magic, or sorcery, in which our ancestors believed'.

The no-nonsense, 'pack-o'-lies' school still holds the allegiance of many stockbrokers and hard-headed businessmen. The more intelligent ones are beginning to hear of the anthropological school as well.

By the middle of the nineteenth century sentiment had swamped, however, much of the simple affirmation of the historians that witches had not existed and did not exist, and the climate of opinion favoured a romantic–rationalist approach. The enormous popularity of Scott's works meant that the anecdotal style of his *Letters on Demonology and Witchcraft* set the pace for hundreds of pseudo-historical romances. Along came Harrison Ainsworth and the Lancashire Witches, and away went the increasing thousands of the reading public, down the shelf which was perhaps to end with *Dracula*.

Whilst this was happening, the popular conception of the witch had grown up.

This saw her – it was always 'her', never a man – either as a hostile and wicked old woman or as a misunderstood and martyred old woman.

The subject of the first of these visions was illustrated by the conventional accoutrements of Macbeth's witches. She had nutcracker jaws, rags, and a hat like an Eisteddfod advertisement. She possessed a cat (in spite of the fact that the domestic cat as we know it was not introduced into England until the sixteenth century) and a cauldron. She was given to the preparation of hellish brews from toads and herbs, and to association largely with corpses. She spat and poisoned, and would cackle about on a broomstick. She lived in the heart of a forest, in a little hut with small children in the oven, and her name was Old Mother Something.

It was all a little hazy, and tied up with Grimm's *Fairy Tales* and 'The Hand of Glory' from *The Ingoldsby Legends*.

The other sort of witches were, by this popular estimate, not witches at all, but poor harmless old women living on the outskirts of the village, and hated because they were deaf. The brews they made were not hellish, but tremendously beneficent and packed with traditional wisdom.

In either case, the women were incredibly old, and were, after a ducking, burnt alive at the stake. Few had bothered to look back at the evidence and so discover that witches, when women, were nearly as often young as elderly; or to ascertain that in fact and in law no witch in England had ever been burnt alive at all – unless it were for witchcraft combined with husband-murder or heresy.

This tradition has more recently received the confirmation of Mr Walt Disney, and a whole new generation has grown up to dream of those long cruel fingers, the poisoned apples, and the cute little cottage in the woods.

A further reaction towards romantic half-belief set in with the 1890s. It came from two directions. First there were the diabolists. These were often recruited from what in literature are known as the decadents, who, on their soul-sick path to and from Rome, discarded Victorian propriety and the mufflings of Victorian religious morality, to come out strongly for the exotic. Some took to Surrey Buddhism. But a number went back to Mani and the earlier dualistic religions of the East. Eliphas Levi had published works on magic in Paris, and the adolescent temptation to be hellishly wicked combined with a genuine intellectual attraction towards the Mediterranean cults in their more elaborate forms. Heresy and mystical experiment were applied to the romantic stage appurtenances of the witch, and spiritually weary intellectuals devoted time to such exercises as sitting in a dark room trying to put a soul into a cat. It is easy to make fun of the posturing of the decadents, but there is no doubt that if they had not preferred parlour magic and physical excitement to more reasoned analysis, they were intellectually equipped to contribute extensively to the study of witchcraft.

From the other wing came the later Celtic twilight school.

Their derivations were from Sir Walter Scott and the old-fashioned ghost story. Soon, however, they joined the black-cat exploiters, and achieved a curious approach which in turn became mixed with psychology and spiritualism. The result was a cast of mind, very common among Edwardians, which combined a love of the earlier Yeats and the earlier stories of Algernon Blackwood with popular psychology, with much high talk of ectoplasms and elementals. It had a different pedigree, however, in that the Celtic races have, historically, preserved traces of the witch tradition after it died out elsewhere. Their peoples do, in some families, possess more than usual sensibility on the non-rational plane: second sight.

This tradition filtered on into the whimsy novelist's approach to witchcraft. In the second generation, however, it more usually broke up into specialized and diffused groups of Freudians, spiritualists, or ghost raconteurs. It finally wilted before the advance of science and the findings of Professor Margaret Murray. Her anthropological approach was the best thing that had happened for generations to what had become folk-lore – that rather charming but often disparaged interest. Folk-lore had developed into antiquarianism with an Anglo-Saxon bias, and witchcraft seemed a genteel amalgam of most of the estimates mentioned above, with an understanding smile for the fortune-telling tent on the lawn at fête day.

Now Professor Murray, an acknowledged authority on Egyptology, suddenly in 1921 excited students with the scientifically arrayed reminder that witchcraft had been a genuine cult, the remnant of an extensive fertility belief possibly first condensed in Egypt. She claimed that witches had indeed been organized in covens, that the evidence of the witch-trials must be treated seriously, and that the credulity of disbelief was perhaps quite as inaccurate as the credulity of belief had ever been.

Other writers followed Professor Murray. Some were good. Some were bad, and merely quoted the more sensational examples of her research, among the ordinary catalogue of charms and legends. Yet the idea of a scientific approach had caught on, and is still there, the basis for most contemporary treatment of the subject. I myself owe my first interest to Miss Murray, who was courteous about this book, and what my subsequent reading prompted me to believe, although she may have had private reservations about it. By this time, of course, there was *The Golden Bough* to draw on as well – a bible for a whole new generation.

The odd thing was that, in spite of Sir James Frazer and Professor Murray, there was no very considered attempt to relate witchcraft in Europe to the parallel activities of the contemporary African or Polynesian witch-doctor. A few travel writers perfunctorily explained that West Indian voodoo was so called because it was a corruption of Vaudois,* and because the Haitian rites were at first thought to be similar to those of the Vaudois heresy. But they did not pursue the idea, preferring to plunge on into subjective accounts of their trips and a few dark hints of savage diabolism with which the white man should not meddle. Superstition, they felt, was the same all the world over, but worse in the lower cultures – besides, savages were such mimics that they had incorporated a few burlesques of Christianity as well. The idea of a common origin or a continuous tradition was not clearly worked out anywhere.

The latest – neo-conscious – treatment of the subject, is usually indebted to the theories of Gerald Heard, Aldous Huxley, and others of the colony of English writers for some time probing masochistically in California.

These writers analyse the development of the individual consciousness and character, and show how, in gaining various mechanical and logical powers, men have lost the original other-consciousness which at one time they believe existed, and which still exists, in a debased form, in certain 'savage' tribes today. Their recommendation for the regeneration of humanity is a conscious return to this plane, with a corresponding shedding of materialism and false values. It leads them to a sympathetic study of Yogi and contemporary mystery religions.

They see witchcraft, as did Professor Murray, to be the historical survival of the old fertility religions, whose rites and

* Which it is not; it is an African word meaning 'the gods'.

organization fight on – largely through the women – as an undertone to the dominant materialism of the main-stream of Western development. They are therefore sympathetic to the underlying faith of the witches. They understand the expression of it which intrigues Professor Murray and has made her see the medieval sabbat as the joyful festival of escapists from a mainly penitential age. Perhaps it has been as well that others have re-introduced complications. Miss Murray's blinding light, for all its value, left too many dark shadows still unexplored.

My own approach is eclectic and historical. This book is an essay, and in no way an exhaustive treatment, for which I am not equipped. I have no axe to grind, and am neither a theologian, an occultist, nor a materialist. The essay is the result of wide reading rather than deep and specialized research. It has been made over a number of years by a historian who has studied the subject more intensively, and has thought more deeply about it, than when we burnt Mr Peter Fleming, and the floor (which was above the Dean's study) cracked and scorched in the fashionable diabolism of the flaming twenties. Examination since then has made it evident to me that witchcraft has represented something early and essential in human experience. This makes it necessary to start with a number of chapters of somewhat extensive background.

On the other hand there will be no 'witch stories': no whimsy about the Screaming Skull: no ghostly anecdotes: and I have exercised a studied avoidance of poltergeists and ectoplasms. There will be no tips on astrology, nor lists of precious stones. And there will not even be exclamation marks, to show which bits are particularly interesting.

And yet some of them should be.

*Part One*

# THE SETTING

## 2

# *The Religious Background up to Classical Times*

CERTAIN observers claim to have watched the great apes of tropical Africa gyrating ecstatically to the light of the full moon. But there is no clear evidence that any animals, birds, or insects have a process which could be properly described as religious perception. Their emotional processes are instinctive undifferentiated reactions, unrelated to an external force. Only man has a religious instinct. And no known society of men has been without what can be held to be a religious belief or practice of some sort.

Witchcraft is the degeneration of one of the earliest stages of religious belief and practice. In its history it has added parodies of the various later religions which have challenged it, and which, after generations of struggle, have usually swamped it. The story of the witch cult is only comprehensible against the background of religious development as a whole.

Prehistory, more especially in its less material phases, is a peculiarly inexact science. When the Ancients invoked the Golden Age, when Rousseau invoked the Noble Savage, or even when Adam Smith evolved the Economic Man, these unhappy dummies were accepted as useful formulas without historical pretensions. Nowadays, however, anthropology and archaeology have combined to produce evidence of evolutionary history so wide and various that it can easily be drawn upon by almost any writer who has a thesis to prove and a library subscription to provide him with an arsenal. Religion is derived by some writers from dreams directed by God, by others from dreams provoked by psychic indigestion, and by others again from the frivolous and superficial perception of ghosts and marvels. It is far too easy to dogmatize, and immensely difficult not to induce the beginnings of the religious sense from rationalization of existing taboos. If, moreover, you postulate a directing evolutionary sense, a god or a life-urge, anything further is reduced to a rehearsal of processes. It may be less artistically attractive than that of the Greeks, if perhaps not always so contradictory as that of the Hebrews in the book of Genesis.

A contemporary anthropological explanation is, very briefly, this: the animal – the proto-human anthropoid animal – is primarily affected by the preoccupations of food acquisition, sex release, and self-preservation (not as yet self-continuation, immortality being a later development). These dominants are felt in common by the community, and create an emotional nexus which satisfies itself by joint action to achieve the required ends. The most highly developed machinery for this is perhaps that of some insects. Certain primates, however, owing probably to climatic good fortune, developed the hand, an immensely useful new technical asset. Others, partly through being confined to the forests, remained stationary, or degenerated.

At this stage the communal emotional bond became so intense that individuals separated from the group might die, even if given identical food and amenities.* If one member of this sort of group undertakes to obtain, say, food, the others will sometimes move in sympathy. An ape tries to reach a banana just out of reach. The others stretch out their hands and strain with him, to help, without necessarily moving from where they are. It is the human reaction of treading on an imaginary brake to help the driver in a motor-car emergency, or punching the air to help a boxer whom one supports, in the ring.

* Ants obviously communicate at great distances, and so possibly do some of the anthropoid types. They have at all events telepathic or similar means of communication. T. H. Huxley writes of ducklings which had no idea of a particular danger until their mother was allowed near them, when she immediately communicated fear to them all. Where electric wiring has been introduced to fold pigs, and subsequently taken away, it is often difficult to force young pigs to cross the line where it has been. Klaatsch comments how primitive tribes today seem to have as yet unexplained means of communication over distances – subconscious ones, as well as the much publicized systems of whistling and drumming.

These sympathetic movements some anthropologists see as the beginning of the dance. At all events, the dance is an extremely early expression of the emotional and rhythmic unity of the group. In it, the full force of the nervous identification is released, and later, when individuality has appeared, it provides the means, again, of losing that painful acquisition, and becoming once more a part of the general group release. Religion – the relation of the individual to the cosmos, at first only seen as the group – grows with the dance. As religion develops historically into the long struggle between the rationalizing ascetic and the emotional erotic, the dance becomes almost a dividing line. It will be seen later how the dance is identified with the fairies and the witches and the old fertility beliefs, and is therefore often bitterly attacked by the Catholic Church, and even more fiercely by the Puritan. Today, dancing is still seen conventionally as a physical release, and is frowned on as a wasteful emission of energy by ascetic individuals, and sometimes as self-indulgent individualism by the authoritarian state, which prefers the gyrations of drill.

Originally, then, proto-palaeolithic man is a group thing, with a group sense, motivated mainly by these desires for food, sex, and self-preservation, and exercising the sense of psychological unity mainly in the dance.

Gradually, over some incomputable period of time, the sense of personal individuality begins to develop. With this the machinery of the group alters, and from being a matriarchate, dominated by women, it becomes for the first time a patriarchate, dominated by the males. But the process is an enormously lengthy one. It is not necessarily the same wherever the scattered patches of human experiment exist, separated by hundreds of miles of swamp and forest, and in the narrow belt of the biologically habitable world.

In any case, the old matriarchal ideas go on: that of the mother round the fire – the cauldron, which symbolizes home and food and warmth, and the idea of the fire itself. Fire myths still continue.

Individuality provokes loneliness and fear. From this fear of personality, the individual flies back to the group, and to the known release – the ecstasy of the dance, organized by the elder males or the elder females of the group, as the case may be -- the first priests, magicians, adepts.

The dance was originally connected with the acquisition of food, and its movements mimicked the stalking or slaying of game. But personal loneliness, and the attempt to resolve it by a re-identification with others, means a preoccupation with sex. The personal sexual motive is added to the group interest in fertility as a necessary means to increasing the cattle. The fertility dance becomes an emotional experience for the person – an individual release and solution – as well as a group prac- tice, a communal exercise, for the achievement of a general end.* The one who can call the dance and direct it is the priest and the magician and the medicine man. The machinery of religion is there, although the transcendental side is still to come.

By this time, the developing consciousness of the external world has led to animism and the worship generally of the phenomena of nature, including ancestor-worship, perceptible in apes as a temporary boycotting of the women and effects of a dead group-patriarch. Man is still part of nature, but fears that he is escaping from it, and tries by any means to remain identified. He makes offerings to trees, and more particularly he tries to identify himself with the animal world from which he is escaping. He has self-knowledge and sexual consciousness and tries passionately to return to Eden. In the dance and the religious exercises, for a time he does so. Increasingly, though, it becomes a trick. When it has become too consciously a trick and competes with a later system of belief, it has become a superstition, and scrabbles into history as magic.

For the time being, however, it is a trick closely guarded by the magician, himself a member of the group, who has

* Individual sexuality is still probably undeveloped, however, at this cultural level. The savage is still nearer the primitive sexual periodicity, and the 'sex-dance' and 'sex-orgy' witnessed by shocked contemporaries may be a necessity for him to achieve sexual tumescence at all. Even the 'civilized' Negro takes normally three times as long as the European to achieve ejaculation. The wild animal, too, is far less sexually athletic than the domestic or caged members of its species.

rationalized the movements and is busy turning consciousness into conscience. The thing has to be increasingly organized as the group expands from the original size. It will be shown later that the most effective psychic field seems to be about a dozen – the apostolic circle, the witch coven, the knights of the round table, and even the teams in many organized games.

For a period in world history, phallic religions, with fertility rites led by the magicians – who can rationalize the need for the dance which reunites the lost individual to the psychically contented group – dominate the early religious exercises of mankind. The woman's position remains all-important, both as the repository of tradition, the guardian of the home round the fire, and the symbol in herself of sexual fecundity.

Animal cults form so important a part of the witch background that it is worth making a special note about them here, although they will reappear in detail as part of the paraphernalia of the cult practised in the Middle Ages.

Palaeolithic man probably played jackal to the large mammals, and ate what was left by such remaining physiological freaks as the sabre-tooth tiger; or he may, in hyena-like herds, have followed the wild horse. In the far north, the Mousterians were 'reindeer men', as dependent on the movements of the reindeer as the historic Eskimoes have been on the seal, or the North American Indians on the buffalo.* Later in history, whole societies have existed whose economic existence depended upon the tunny-fish or upon sheep.

When animals see men for the first time, they are often comparatively tame and unsuspicious, and can be exterminated as easily as were friendly natives in the eighteenth century. It is possible that the hunting methods shown in palaeolithic and bushmen's wall paintings, of men disguising themselves to resemble animals for the purpose of killing them, may have been effective.

But the relationship with animals was far closer than this.

* There were also bear people, who put aside bear-skins for religious protection, as the Hairy Ainu of Japan do today. The Mousterian culture is considered to have prevailed for some thousand years beginning about 13,000 B.C. But all early dating is on a sliding scale with the end broken off.

There was a real psychic affinity between the human group and the animals with whose lives their own was bound up. There was even a greater physical intimacy than we can immediately understand. Klaatsch gives examples of the way in which the women of primitive races, today, will suckle the young of, for example, baboons. It makes a little less repulsive that story, so terrifying at school, in the sober pages of the *Cambridge History of Modern Europe*, about the pre-revolutionary Russian aristocrats who made the peasant women suckle their baby wolfhounds.

The strength, agility, or other desirable qualities of the totem animal might be acquired by drinking its blood. This was particularly effective when the animal – now a symbol of godhead – was sacrificed. Bathing in its blood, as did the heroes Siegfried or Mithras, was desirable as a prophylactic. The ox-roasting celebrations and ram-roasting feasts carried on in the country until today (the B.B.C. broadcast in 1938 about the ram-roasting at Kingsteignton in Devonshire, although the custom naturally died out during the war) are survivals. The fortunes made by proprietors of essences with beef ingredients and bullocking publicity are equally illustrative.

In the caves into which he retired from the cold of the approaching fourth ice-age, palaeolithic man fashioned or depicted the animals upon whom he lived – an aesthetic expression of an economic purpose. The combination became a religious exercise. At his dances, the festival of the bull or the stag or the goat was celebrated in the skins of the appropriate animal. The dance was led by the priest-god, who was now identified with that animal, whose skins he wore, and whose head in effigy covered his own; whose behaviour he mimicked. The worshippers themselves became the animal – the phenomenon is observable today in some tribes in Australia and elsewhere – barked, grunted, or cried, and later coupled in sympathetic magical affinity to the totem animal. The godhead was finally slain.

Fear of animals, observation of the natural danger-warning of birds, and other forces – all contributed to the totem stream. But the psychological and economic bond remained the real reason for the animal totem – the most evident expression of early religion.

The magical side was developed and cultivated in Egypt, which also raised the totem to supreme godhead – a conception which united the symbol of an immensely advanced system of nervous and psychological control with a simple physical reality which could appeal to the ordinary man in the temple. In spite of the rise of an ascetic priestly rule, of the introduction of the idea of immortality, and of the immature challenge of Akhnaton and monotheism, the animal cults and taboos lasted for thousands of years. Farther away from the Egyptian orbit, they stayed on in even more primitive forms – the festivals of early religion and folk-lore, belief in lycanthropy and shape-lifting generally, and particularly as a component of the witch cult.

Originally, then, man had a psychic sensitivity which was lost, for the ordinary individual, in the course of material civilization and the development of the intelligence. Just as do some native peoples today (although with them it is in a degenerate form), under particular stimuli he threw off this individual personality and merged again into the group or universal consciousness in a condition which may roughly be called hypnosis.

There cannot have been many men living, say, 25,000 years ago. The habitable world, a strip between the tropics of Africa and southern Asia, and the glacial and sub-glacial areas of Europe and northern Asia, was too small. Evidence, such as it is, goes increasingly to show that there was communication between the scattered groups of true men, whether or not they mated with declining evolutionary sports – neanderthalers and others – who remained either as actual contemporaries or legendary ogres. The ice receded, and the dark hairy little palaeo-men left the caves to follow their herds across the new grasslands. As they did so, sea-shells travelled between them, flints travelled, and so did cultures. Although the actual details of the taboos might differ, and the cults might be dedicated to different animals, they sprang from similar processes and created similar psychic conditions.

But the world grew larger. Cultures separated still further. And above all, individual personality became increasingly defined. The reattainment of psychic release was more and more dependent upon organized exercises. This may be called *religious* where carried out in good faith for an unselfconscious end. It became *magic* when procured consciously as an individual release. Religion, which gives, became increasingly differentiated from magic, which takes.

In Egypt, the highest of the early cultures achieved its apex. Contemporary with the hunting and herding communities elsewhere, or evolving from them, there grew up in the Delta of the Nile, as in the deltas of other great rivers all the habitable world over, a society centred on the idea of cultivating crops. It was therefore a settled culture. The arts flourished and the individual further developed, although the great mass of the people were still slaves – a mass without intense personal life, though without, on the other hand, the old group unity. Their psychological focus was the god-king, the Pharaoh, and their psychological compensation was priestly religion.

Round the Pharaoh ruled the hierarchy of the adepts – the ascetics, preaching above all the doctrines of immortality: that this world was a necessarily uncomfortable journey to the next. Yet, even so, they were sufficiently in touch with the old phallic emotional centres of feeling and tradition to elaborate their processes into a code of astonishing comprehension. By means of this they retained their power. By the time of their decline their system had spread again throughout the inhabited world.

The Egyptian priestly control can be summarized under three heads. These divisions have actually been quoted somewhere as applying to French West African magic, which was a late and degenerate memory of the common original.

The first is totemistic: a control over animals.

Historically, Egyptian religion evolved from the combination of the totem cults of a number of different tribes. For long, Horus, the hawk-god, emblem of one of the most powerful tribes, remained pre-eminent. But before long he, like all the others, became inextricably mixed in the welter of sun-gods,

sky-gods, serpent-gods and the whole anthropomorphic confusion of mersion and compromise. The Nile itself, and the
moon, became all-important symbols, just as Osiris and Ra,
different tribal manifestations of the sun, were variously
supreme. The gods and goddesses were assorted into triads, of
which in the latest period the most important was that of
Osiris, Isis, and Horus, and finally Isis herself, the embodiment
of the old maternal sex-concept.

Yet the animal symbolism remained. The priests, on occasion, wore the animal masks; the totem animal – the bull, the
pig, the goat, or the serpent – remained sacred, and the
Pharaoh on state occasions wore a bull's tail on his girdle.
Festivals timed to coincide with the mating times of animals
still competed with festivals coinciding with the sowing or
reaping of crops.

With this identification went a power over animals. Not, as
it had been in the early days, or as it remained in the culturally
less advanced civilizations, a direct communication: but a preoccupation with animals and their processes, particularly their
fecundity, and a ceremonial regard for animals as objects of
sacrifice creating a psychic field. There were tricks, too: the
Oriental snake charming, or the capacity to make a serpent go
rigid, as the court magicians did before Pharaoh. Moses could
do even better, though with him (if you accept Christian
tradition and Professor Freud and consider him a historical
personage) it was even more a trick, a magic. For he belonged
to the new monotheism, and deplored the symbol of the
golden calf, even if he enforced the sacrifice of the spotless
lamb.

In the later cults the form that animal festivals took was
often the form which had first been regularized in Egypt.

The second of the priestly controls was physiological: the
hyper-normal control of the body. The miraculous power is
by far the most striking evidence of the Egyptian system. It
was the tradition of the ancients that it did exist in Egypt, and,
historically, most of the other systems in the world seem to
owe much to Egyptian practice. The power consisted princi-
pally in obtaining, by psychic means, hyper-normal control of

the body, anaesthesia, suspended animation, and abnormal resistance to injury.

These powers exist today. They are the delight of the spiritualist (rather illogically, as one would have supposed) and the despair of the photographer. In certain ecstatic states, however, there can be no doubt that the body does become immune to physical harm. There is no doubt that this is often the result of purely mechanical trickery, or a peculiar pathological condition (two stomachs or an abnormal skin). It is hard to believe in the spiritual intensity of many Oriental exhibitors of marvels. It is impossible to credit the mystical purity of that magnificent character 'The Fireproof Lady of Bartholomew Fair', who in 1814 delighted the curious by putting melted lead in her mouth, thrusting her arm in the fire, and washing her hands 'not only in boiling water but also in boiling lead and aquefortis'.

But the power of obtaining temporary immunity to fire or pain, without mechanical aids, obviously exists. It is employed by the native in his supernatural frenzy. It was employed by the Christian saint who endured torture for his faith, and has helped the martyrs of every religion. It stimulated, no doubt, the fire-fighting activities of the originals of Shadrach, Meshach, and Abednego. It even makes one wonder whether there may not have been a good rational basis to a people who had faith, in the ordeal by fire. Witches and their proof against torture will be dealt with in due course, but it is possible to quote, as other examples, the Essenes, who astonished the Romans by their ability to undergo frightful pain; the Sufi dervishes, who plunge knives in and out of their cheeks and thighs with apparent pleasure, or the feats of juggling with white-hot iron or incandescent iron balls, dancing in flames, stirring boiling water with the hands, smelling ammonia, and eating broken glass, all undertaken, with even more remarkable operations, by the voodoo addicts of the West Indies.

The point of all this is that auto-intoxication is a stage produced by the subject, usually voluntarily, sometimes by the help of the witch-doctor or magician, as an escape into a mystical non-personal world. It is an induced state of release from self – back into the other-world. It is the religio-magical formula for escape from humanity into a common sub-human consciousness. It is not just physical stoicism.

In discussing the witch sabbat, the parallels with other phenomena of the same sort will become more apparent. Here it is enough to underline that the means to this release were codified and transmitted by the priests of Egypt. They had power of hypnosis, telepathy, and auto- and hetero-suggestion. They were able even to operate at a distance, as is the African witch-doctor or was occasionally the Christian saint. They could no doubt achieve by remote control the stigmata, or the appearance upon the body of the effect of whipping. In a world becoming increasingly remote from the subconscious, super-conscious animal, and a society progressively more rationalistic, they pinned down and manipulated the formulas for achieving ecstasy and release into another field of consciousness.

The third control formulated in Egypt was specifically psychological: detached consciousness.

As well as having its external manifestations, the Egyptian system was also a mystical one for sublimating the body and isolating the spirit. It resembled the Yogi systems of today, with their combination of intense spiritual discipline and acute physical perception. Thus, the activity and importance of the ductless glands, for example, a comparatively new discovery to Western medicine, have for long been catalogued in the Far East as Centres of Light or Lotus Flowers. So, too, the spinal ganglia are whimsically described as the Coiled Serpent. The alchemical and astrological systems derived from Egypt, also, to quote Gerald Heard, 'more than once disguised knowledge of the endocrine system and how, by breath control and concentration, to release harmonic charges which not only changed the energies and powers of the body, but profoundly altered the quality and extent of the consciousness'. For these were systems in which the body was made actively to serve the ends of the soul. They postulated a spiritual conception, and, as such, were as remote from the medieval terror of the body as from those muscular contemporary codes in which a 'clean mind' is rather naïvely related to ordinary good health.

So far then it has been indicated, as much as is relevant, how man emerged into religious consciousness. This consciousness he resolved by exercises regulated in deference to natural phenomena and the animal world around him. The exercises were probably more or less common wherever communities of true men existed. This was partly because they came from a natural evolutionary process, and partly because the number of early men was probably extremely small and more or less intercommunicating.

The habitable world extended. Parts of it were covered by the newly formed seas. Communities were cut off. Some were possibly drowned. Others, probably nearer the original centres, settled and formed static agricultural communities. Here, though the true psychic unity became lost, or was diluted into the heroic sublimate of the slave empire of the priest-king, the machinery for artificially invoking psychic release was developed to an incredible degree. This happened particularly in Egypt.

Subsequently this knowledge of the Egyptian passed back in greater or lesser quantities, and more or less garbled forms, to the outside world again.

It is impossible to enter here into the controversy as to whether 'civilization' grew up independently in different parts of Europe, Africa, and Asia, or whether it proceeded from Egypt. The literature of mummification, circumcision, cephalic indices, culture drift, and the rest of it, is juggled by the authorities with quite the dexterity, and almost the same improbability, as is employed by the publicists of British Israel. Scientific rationalists tend to favour spontaneous cultural ignition in different centres, whilst for scientific romanticists every cultural stream is an inverted tributary of the Nile.

It is, however, certain that the 'arts' of Egypt found their way, by one route or another, over most of the world.

It is not easy to say when the permeation first began. There can, after all, be no doubt that the Egyptians did send colonists to Western Europe and much of Asia, and over and round most of Africa. Egyptian armies reached the Caspian Sea. As Winwood Reade described it in the proud plush of his explorer's Victorian prose, long caravans of Egyptian camels brought 'the gums of Arabia Felix, the pearls of the Persian Gulf and the carpets of Babylon, the pepper and ginger of Malabar, the shawls of Cashmire, the cinnamon of Ceylon, the fine muslins of Bengal, the nutmegs and camphor and cloves of the Indian Archaepelago: and even silk and musk from the distant Chinese shores'. And in turn Egypt exported, as well as Egyptian culture, the elements of Egyptian religion and magical practice.

Then the settled phallicism of the Mediterranean world was challenged by the new peoples from the North, who had largely deserted the old animal cults in favour of wind gods and rain gods and sky gods. They were masculine and had passed the matriarchal stage: their sex ideal was a dominant one, positive and possessive, not passive, female, and sensual. They attacked the Mediterranean world, invaded Greece, sacked Crete, filtered into Asia Minor. Static and exhausted, Egypt itself crumbled.

And then the Egyptian, Mediterranean tradition, the dark voluptuous culture which centuries had ordered into a code, took on the additional attraction of the illicit. Refugee phallicism spread down into Africa, and up through the newly suppressed peoples of Europe; out through the chaos of the Near East into Asia.* It reinforced the older phallic fertility tradition it found there, and its traces continued in a variety of forms down into history.

It has been said that 'studies of the magic and ritual of Africa have in the last few years established with some certainty that all the systems for the disturbance of consciousness practised by the African Negro are derived from ancient Egypt'. Thousands of Africans were transported to the New

* The Near East had been subject for thousands of years to these incursions of wild nomadic herdsmen. It was why its magical system (in spite of tremendous astronomical discoveries) never settled down quite as fully as the Egyptian, with which it was in close contact.

World, and many of those who went to Haiti, from 1512 onwards, were from the finest African stocks, and perhaps carried with them a synthesis of the cults then existing on the Congo. It is easy to show how close the parallels are between the voodoo they practised and medieval witchcraft.

The mysteries of Delphi and Eleusis, or the Roman cults, probably had the same origin. The ritual of the Druids copied that of Osiris: some of the Druids were known as adders, and there seems to be an affinity with the snakes entwined on the Pharoahs' caduceus. Odin himself is believed by some authorities to be merely a frosty version of Osiris. Witchcraft, almost everywhere, had two main derivatives to which its other formative influences became attached – the fertility cults persisting from the indigenous inhabitants of any area, and the later 'magical' practices derived through direct or distorting channels from the centralizing Egyptian source.

# 3

## Classical Witchcraft and the Coming of Christianity

WITCHCRAFT, as it emerges into European history and literature, represents the old palaeolithic fertility cult, *plus* the magical idea, *plus* various parodies of contemporary religions.

When man's increasing interest in reason and civilized progress caused a diminution in his earlier ability to connect with the world of other-consciousness, this declining ability was condensed and formalized by the priests of the Egyptian and other hierarchies – notably of Babylon, with its divination and study of numerology, to become so important to the Biblical Hebrews. It became magic – a reservoir of occult power which could be drawn on for individual benefit, although it no longer represented a primal religious instinct and communal release.

When, in the second millennium B.C., the peoples who were to settle on the northern shore of the Mediterranean world as Greeks and Romans came down from the north, they brought, as has been said, their own gods with them. These gods were patriarchal. They represented ideal and heroic virtues – courage, strength, truth. Although they still expected animal sacrifices, they dated from a later culture-stage than the palaeolithic phallic animal-cults. They were the deities of a late development of animism, already agricultural, rather than hunting or food-gathering. These gods were what is inaccurately called Aryan: infinitely clean-limbed and simple symbols, given to an anthropomorphic lack of self-control, and a tendency to al-Raschid expeditions into human sex-relationships, followed by low-comedy recriminations with their legal partners. They had expansive passions, no minds, sensuous preoccupations, and billowed athletically on the clouds above

Olympus. It was an unsophisticated idea of divinity, and, very early, all but the most unsophisticated Greeks and Romans grew out of it. The Greek genius found other intellectual and emotional outlets, while the Romans' practical trend made them so indifferent to spiritual values that it has been said that we derive the very word 'religion' from perhaps the least religious race that ever lived. *

The gods of the invaders, however, never successfully conquered the Mediterranean. Nor for that matter did the invaders themselves, who rarely reached, except as travellers, the real centres of earlier Mediterranean life: Egypt and the Near East. The older cults surged up everywhere, particularly through the women, so large a part, even in occupied territories, of slave households. The Near Eastern philosophies early tempered the rectitude of the infiltrating tribes. These adapted themselves to the culture of the Minoans or the Etruscans, and identified, with their own gods, those of the peoples they ruled. Zeus, Poseidon, Apollo, Ares, Dionysius, Dione, Hestia the Hearth goddess, and Demeter the barley mother came from the North. But Athena, Aphrodite, Artemis, Rhea, and Hephaestus the Smith were all Minoan gods.

As with the greater gods and goddesses, so with the lesser. The rites and beliefs of the Mediterranean merged with those of the North, and the mystery religions, the mother goddess cult, and the dark practices of the older peoples became more and more mixed with the less exacting devotions of their masters. Diana, the virgin huntress, was, by turns, Tanit-Astarte, the female sex-symbol. So even was Demeter. In the later period of independent Greek history, the stock figures of Olympus had become merely orthodox conceptions of conventional characteristics and mythology, regarded much as a pious Christian today regards the bearded representation of God-the-Father employed by Victorian illustrators: the portrait is not one which the ordinary man bothers to denigrate, but it has no spiritual content for him either. Their gods had even less awe-inspiring qualities for the Greeks, both as these

* It is also stated, significantly, that when Rome was founded she possessed more gods than inhabitants.

gods were in themselves more human, and in their dogma far less definitive, than the Protestant Jehovah.

In Greece the spirit of the people was analytical and speculative. As a result of this and of the social system there, the sixth century B.C. saw one of the great revolutions in human history – the scientific, amoral, rationalizing efflorescence of the human mind. * The philosophies covered every field of human intellectual experience, and paved the way, in the West, for immense practical developments of the world's resources as well. However, it was essentially an individual revolution. Man had come of age. The old super-conscious relationship with nature, which could create non-human fields of consciousness, was lost. The precarious balance of the priestly hierarchies was on the decline.

Driven into opposition, however, the old tradition fought on. The philosophers themselves contributed to it, in some cases by including in their systems, like Pythagoras, ideas derived from the wisdom of the old order. The machinery, even of the most advanced ideas, was caught up in the earlier symbolism – the pursuit of the Golden Fleece, of the solar ram. And, since philosophy is an individual exercise which can never appeal to the majority, and the old Olympian conception was a worn-out mythological formula, the people slipped increasingly into a somewhat shamefaced acceptance of the cults.

When the Roman state had absorbed Greece, Greek religious ideas were soon introduced to bolster the indigenous pantheon. It became almost a ritual, as every threat to the state was met by the hasty incorporation, on the advice of the Sibylline Books, of yet another paid-off Olympian. In addition, the Greek-cum-Mycenaean deities Athena, Artemis, Hera, and Aphrodite, for instance, were identified, and soon polished and vulgarized, into Minerva, Diana, Juno, and Venus. More important still, the whole underworld of the Greek religion, the Orphic and Eleusinian mysteries, the machinery of ecstatic pythonesses and inspired mutterings across the Styx, and the

* It was, independently or not, happening in the East and Far East as well.

processes generally of the old Mediterranean cults, were successively included in the list of approved deities. The dark Etruscan myths were there already. All roads, for discredited mythologies, led to Rome.

As the empire became more sophisticated and eclectic, the gods of each new conquest were included in a state pantheon which had become entirely outside the central control of the Pontifex Maximus. The Carthaginians and the Egyptians lent their peculiar religious conceptions to bewilder and terrify, and iconoclasm and scepticism among the educated classes increased, while for the others the prodigious batteries of available gods and goddesses declined individually into little more than charms. For all Romans there was the formal recognition of the divinity of the Emperor himself. For emotional expression there were the salvationist religions of sacrifice, redemption, or solar monotheism: Isis, Baal, Mithras, and the rest. Attempts were made to stop the new depravities. Between 59 and 48 B.C. five attempts were made to repress the worship of Isis in the empire. But it was no good. The Oriental religions had come to stay, and by the time of Vespasian, Isis worship was officially recognized throughout the empire.

It may be said, then, that whilst the intellectual revolution in Greece had cut off Mediterranean man from the palaeolithic cult-unity, the 'mysteries' – the exercises to promote other-consciousness and its effects – had, after some centuries when they were overthrown by political forces, seeped back to be the dominant religious expression in an age of advanced scepticism.

Soon they were to be challenged again, this time by the greatest of the monotheist salvationist religions, Christianity.

In the meantime, however, whilst discredited, much of their force had escaped through the safety-valve of witchcraft.

Unfortunately, the records of classical witchcraft are those of the literate and professed sceptics, and the witch, when we first read about her, was already a 'her' – a woman – and a literary creation. Witchcraft was mixed up with the whole process of general superstition, and tales of the *strigi* are lumped with rites and practices for curing warts, and votive offerings for ensuring safe travel at sea. But obviously the Roman provincial believed firmly in the arts of witches – particularly the witches of Thessaly. *The Golden Ass of Lucius Apuleius* is the supreme example of a current belief, expressed by a writer who was himself a sceptic, a mystic, and a literary genius. Its hero ultimately escapes from the donkey metamorphosis into which his lust and folly have allowed witches to transform him, to the haven of Isis worship.

Witchcraft was already black magic as opposed to white – it represented an attempt to harness the powers of the Unseen without the medium of the established priesthood. It was to the orthodox priest, even if he himself worshipped at the shrine of Isis, much as unqualified bone-setting is to the surgeon today. This is another reason for its rites being recorded, so far as they are, with every circumstance of horror and exaggeration. Moreover, witchcraft was already credited to the political opposition, and Pliny upbraided the Persians for introducing it into Greece. Magicians had a habit of making astrological predictions about the demise of a ruler to the benefit of his opponents. The three Magi, it will be recalled, had to avoid Herod. Pythagoras was accused of being a foreign and un-Greek magician, just as, in the Koran, Moses is accused of witchcraft.

The Thessalonian sorceresses were the terror of those ancients who remained unsophisticated. They were perennially charged with attempting to draw down the moon from the sky – which means that they were unlicensed devotees of the moon goddess – Isis or Nut – and of having a homicidal knack with herbs. This was probably true, as traditional palaeolithic knowledge of the qualities of the vegetable world was always one of the cult secrets, and, with or without the intent to harm and the accompanying ritual which makes it black magic, it has remained so until today. There is an elaborate description of the proceedings of witches in the Esquiline country, with bare feet, loose hair, and robes tucked up round their waists, gathering bones and herbs in a cemetery by the light of the new moon. To a people raised on the myths of notable shape-shifters like Circe or Medea, it must have been extremely alarming. The Romans, moreover, were prodigiously super-stitious. There was constant legislation, and all astrologers and magicians had been banished from Italy in A.D. 16. Wizards were, from time to time, thrown from the Tarpeian rock. Yet Augustus himself wore a seal skin as protection against lightning, with the simple faith of those who today carry lockets of seaweed or elephant-hair, and he studied his dreams with introspective devotion, whilst, as compensation, he burnt two thousand books of 'curious arts' in one day. Even he, however, only attempted to purge Italy itself.

Classical witchcraft then cannot be perceived through any-thing but a haze of literary and professional jealousy. So far, however, as we can recognize it from tradition, Apuleius, and the comments of the Early Christian Fathers, its practice seems to have been this:

The dates of the big festivals were those of the old hunting ceremonies, and the times of the mating of animals. The witches would gather at the full moon, naked or in black robes, to pick herbs at midnight. These had to be reaped with a bronze sickle – which must have been a late accretion. They danced and indulged generally in the ecstatic practices, howled unintelligibly like dogs or wolves, and shouted nonsense rhymes. They tore a black lamb into pieces to summon the dead.

On 15 February, the date of the Lupercalia, even more elaborate ceremonies took place, with devotees from farther away, and young men covering their bodies with goat-skins as they danced. Goats were sacrificed, and women were whipped with straps made from the hides. Masks were worn, images and round balls were hung up on trees, and spells, repeated three times, were cast on enemies. As well as poisons, aphro-disiacs were manufactured – not always successfully, for Lucretius, for example, is said to have died from an overdose of love potion. Preparations were made which the chroniclers catalogued with horrid pleasure – sloughed skins, saliva, tubercles from the forehead of a new-born foal, and all those animal by-products the handling of which gave an intimacy with nature now felt only by guilty schoolboys and professional zoologists. By sympathetic magic, rivals could be bewitched so that their hair fell out, and undesirable competitors could be made impotent. This was possible particularly by sticking a pin into the liver of a wax model of the one to be bewitched, for the liver was considered to be the seat of the sensual passions. The genitalia of hares prevented barrenness. And so on through innumerable and intricate processes of associatory magic. The ordinary exercise of such sympathetic magic as sticking pins into images or burning them, to provoke comparable results on the living characters they represented, was carried on as it must have been for thousands of years already.

A rhombus, or magic wheel, was whirled, which may have been that universal palaeolithic symbol which is still a toy in Germany, the bull-roarer.

Leaving on one side the romantic and symbolical trappings of hell-hounds, coiled snakes, and moons suffused with blood, it is clear that the witch-cult in classical times contained, as one would expect, a number of the features which afterwards became apparent in medieval Europe. We should expect to find the rites being conducted near cemeteries, because the burial grounds of one people are frequently used for the same purpose by an invader, so that the primitive death and renewal ceremonies, going on in the old places on the old dates, became cemetery rites. They were so in the Middle Ages. It is the same with most of the other features. The animal symbolism is sufficiently obvious, even if it did not link up with the worship of Apollo or Zeus Lykaios, whose devotees were primitive lycanthropes, howling like wolves and wearing wolf masks. The goat, the horned god, is particularly noticeable. The dance is the fertility dance on its way to becoming the dance of the sabbat. The masks, specifically stated as being worn, are important in view of the fact that it will be shown that the medieval devils were often masked. The dexterity with poisons and the tradition of levitation are there too.

It would be ridiculous to pretend that medieval witchcraft descended directly from classical witchcraft. It would be ridiculous to pretend that it descended directly and unbroken from anything. But the classical witch represented various palaeolithic fertility and totem cults, crossed with the magical tradition borrowed from Egypt and the East. So did the medieval witch, although by then the cult stream had been muddied by other tributaries, driven in places underground, in others canalized, or used as a sewer. Meanwhile the Catholic Church was busily and mercilessly mopping up what still flowed on.

The system of the ancient world, its discredited gods and underlying witch-cult, deriving from the older mystery faiths, was complicated by the arrival of Christianity.

In Rome itself, the Christian religion had numbered 100,000 converts (most of them slaves or other disreputable persons) by about A.D. 250. It was officially tolerated in A.D. 313 by the Edict of Milan, and a Jewish heresy became the state religion of the civilized world. There were positive and negative reasons for this.

First, the Roman world was in a state of psychic collapse. The educated classes were openly sceptical or had interested themselves in later Hellenic thought, seeking Eternal Truth or Some New Thing. But the ideas of intellectuals have never been effective unless directed by a political force, or diffused by a common emotional one. Later Greek thought was subject to neither impulse.

The uneducated classes were deprived of intellectual leadership. The old Roman virtues, the abstractions of Olympus, had become private charms or had relapsed into the muscular attitudes of public statuary, and the mystery religions were dark, foreign, and nostalgic.

In the provinces, the new additions to the empire kept their beliefs unaffected by the central authority, and only slightly tinged by the cults of the legions which occupied them. But the heart of the empire was Rome, and it was Rome which adopted Christianity.

Socially, too, the empire was top-heavy, and Constantine's main motive in recognizing the Christian Church was probably the hope that it would prove a unifying force.

Then, positively, Christianity offered much more than any other religion to many more classes of society. It offered redemption of sins, salvation, immortality, and the assurance that those benefits were the equal reward of the slave or the patrician. It was particularly addressed to women. It had symbols which were easy to comprehend and in its saints an extremely high standard of personal conduct. For it may be said that most of its early members whose names survived without grave reflections upon them, subsequently qualified for canonization. It was, moreover, as only the Jewish faith was, exclusively monotheistic.

In its earliest form, Christianity was a charitic religion. The emphasis of its founder was upon the Kingdom of Heaven within the individual. The expression of this was not, however, a sterile and selfish process. It involved good conduct, faith, and 'the Spirit' – an emotional release which was particularly achieved in the Agape, the group unit of thirteen, which sat in a circle, creating a psychic field in which the worshippers were in a state of hyperaesthesia, and from which they emerged with a sense of unity and release. There was no emphasis on vulgar salvationism, and extreme asceticism was reprobated.

It is doubtful whether Christianity in this extreme form could have developed into a world religion. Probably it would have declined into another minor offshoot of Judaism in the Near East, and been swamped by the Mithraism which was quickly becoming so fashionable.

The genius of Paul prevented this. His prodigious energy welded the dissolving and disheartened Christians into a powerful Church which included Gentiles as well as Jews. He combined with the philosophical Hellenic trend the Jewish standards of conduct, and the Roman genius for organization. He taught the idea of redemption of sins through a Saviour who would rise from the dead. Pauline Christianity captured the tired Roman world, and later converted the barbarians who were clumsily learning to inherit it.

Much of the old mystery religion found its way into Christian belief and practice. But for a time, in spite of heresy and persecution and constant adjustments in its own attitude, the new revelation swept through the Mediterranean and outwards to the utmost confines of the Imperium. The story was gladly inscribed of the sign which had gone out from the pagan world when Christ was born. Olympus was scaled, and the gods and goddesses were revealed as withered and immoral fancies: the ancient world was gone, and with it the dark and sinister practices of the cults. And (it was a wistful but satisfactory reflection, in the security of the cloister and the enthusiasm of a new faith) Pan was dead.

Yet he was far from dead: merely buried.

# 4

## Early Christianity and the Surviving Cult Worships

THE emotional charitic character of Christianity – the love-feast and the common circle of a few believers (so obviously a convenience as well as an ordained exercise when Christians were scattered in cells among the pagan orthodox) – did not last long. The teaching of St Paul only increased the contemporary tendency to asceticism. What had been a doctrine of love and fellowship (if indeed of apostolic simplicity) soon threw off sects which devoted themselves, on the contrary, to self-laceration and seclusion from their fellows.

It would be ridiculous to accuse Christianity of responsibility for the pathological misfits who constituted the saints of the Thebaid. Indeed, monachism was pre-Christian in origin, and represented the mass tedium and defeatism, only slightly reoriented by the acknowledgement of the Gospel, which was part of the general psychic ennui of the Ancient World. It was the promotion of spiritual escapism into a physical field, and thousands upon thousands, particularly in Egypt and Syria, sought to flee to the discomforts of the desert from the temptations and horrors of a civilization disintegrating before successive waves of barbarians.

There were soon five thousand cenobites on the mountain of Nitria alone. Near Suez, the abbot Serapion governed ten thousand, and a single town on the Nile housed ten thousand shaggy monks and twenty thousand god-dedicated virgins. It was even estimated that there were soon as many monks in the deserts as there were inhabitants of all the cities of Egypt. Every cave had its quota of masochistic and ulcered perverts, hung with chains and crawling with lice, living on dried peas and feats of insanitary piety to the Glory of God and the wonder of the Infidel. They reduced the rebellious flesh by flagellation, and the proud spirit by such renunciations, dear to the annalist, as that of the monk who destroyed unread a packet of letters from his relations which reached him after fifteen years of solitude in the wilderness. Continence was, of course, essential, and the only excuse that could be found for the sacrament of marriage, even for non-monks, was that it at least had the creditable effect of generating new virgins. The ultimate pitch of piety was attained by the Stylites, who sat or stood upon pillars. The most celebrated fakir of this sort was of course St Simon Stylites, who died in A.D. 460 at the age of seventy-two years, most of which had been spent either in a pig-sty or on top of a pillar, where the gangrenous devotee undulated his body in the abasement of constant prayer, only ceasing in order to haul up on occasion a little water and dried peas. The last few years he had spent on one leg. He was, not unnaturally, subject to severe temptations.

Fakirism is endemic in the East, and this particularly repulsive outburst is only important here in that its acceptance by the Christian world, as a poster to holiness, reveals the ascetic cast into which a religion of love had in many places subsided. The Church of St Peter projected the discipline of St Paul, and conscious anti-phallicism was enthroned.

Naturally, the pre-Christian cults did not just disappear. As Gibbon wrote: 'such was the mild spirit of antiquity, that nations were less attentive to the differences than to the resemblances of their religious worship'. Christianity had come into power through fire and martyrdom. Therefore much of the mildness and toleration implied in its first teaching was lost. It was its singleness and its ferocious refusal to cooperate which had enabled it to supersede its rivals – esoteric and subtle neo-platonism and insipid if accommodating syncretism. But the temper of the people was such that they were only too willing to find parallels, in the new worship, to the features they knew in the old. And the Church, preoccupied with combating its own early heresies, was prepared to meet them. Without doing so it would have foundered. The process had two sides – an inclusion of basic Mediterranean beliefs in the central teaching, and a guerrilla warfare in detail, often ending in compromise, with local cults.

The Inquisitors of the Middle Ages accused the witches of being mere diabolical parodists of Christianity. To an extent they were so, particularly as they found that this gave so much resentment to Christians. But many of the witch 'parodies' were in fact degenerate examples of their common origins with Christian practice itself. So, without going in any detail into the subject, a few of the chief points of cult symbolism adopted by the early Church may be tabulated.

Probably Jehovah himself was originally a sky and thunder god. The whole of the Jehovistic, Old Testament side of the Bible and of Christian dogma appealed particularly to Northern Europe, converted from its own sky and war gods. Some historians (with suspicious facility) see the Reformation and every major impulse in subsequent West European history as the rivalry between Old Testament (Jewish) Christianity and New Testament (Mediterranean) Christianity.

The Jewish religion was itself a compendium of Mesopotamian beliefs with interpolations which seem Egyptian. It even included the common tradition of a sacred stone from Heaven like the Kaabah – the Ark. Its originality lay in its intense nationalism combined with equally passionate monotheism: 'There is but one god.'

Thus the Jewish background of Christianity provided many parallels to all those who already acknowledged Eastern cults – although it might seem retrograde to the philosophic Greek.

The Trinity is, for instance, the old Egyptian triad – at least it was so to a convert from Isis worship, who could quickly substitute for the Gnostic Father, Son, and Spirit conception the old family group, Osiris-Isis-Horus, God-Virgin Mary-Jesus. Later the mother triad, a familiar Mediterranean motive, reappears in the worship of the three Marys, which had a prodigious vogue until forbidden, in its extreme forms, by the Church Councils.

Then the Virgin Mother quickly attained in herself an intermediary power with the Almighty which made her virtually a deity. To her were attached mother-goddess ideas of every sort – the mystic role of virgin and mother, and many of the old fertility ceremonies, although the official Church never gave serious countenance to them.

The story of the Saviour was itself, in many particulars, adapted to a pattern. Many gods of the ancient world had been the offspring of Immaculate Conceptions, had had a childhood of danger, and had undertaken a mission which culminated in sacrifice for their people. They had died and risen again (in some cases as a cultivation rite related to the rebirth of the year) and promised their followers salvation through their blood. The most obvious contemporary parallel was Mithras, from whose story most of the blood symbolism of early Christianity was derived – 'washed in the blood of the Lamb', and so on. There is practically no blood in the histories of the evangelists. The Mithraic cult also included the 'Eating of the God', and the belief in a second coming.

Tree-worship was another form of animism particularly widespread in late palaeolithic and neolithic periods, and it became part of almost every religion – even in territories which had few trees at all. It still exists in primitive cultures today. The very word savage comes from a late form of the word 'silvaticus' – forest man. Dancing round sacred trees was a part of the witch ritual. The Druids and all the peoples of the North notoriously worshipped in groves. The sacred groves were, as often as caves, the centres of Greek cult worship. In some places the tree became an obelisk or a pillar – and so a phallic emblem as well.

In Christianity the sacred tree appeared twice. First, it was the original sacred tree of the knowledge of good and evil of the Old Testament – almost the first property in the whole Semitic religious background. In this it was the parallel to Ygdrasil, the sacred tree of the North, found in different forms all over the world. Secondly, it reappears as the Cross – the sacred tree of the Crucifixion, miraculously renewed throughout time.

There were innumerable other parallels: ritual, the shaving of the heads of priests, lustration, and so on. December the twenty-fifth, the date of Christmas Day, is borrowed from

Mithraism. Christmas, before it became a commercial festival with the additions of Teutonic props and Dickensian sentiment, was a Persian one. It is, like so much else, a complex.

There were, it is true, main themes of the Mediterranean for which Christianity did not cater, and which it strenuously opposed – such as fertility cults, sun and moon worship, human sacrifice (of which the 'eating of the god' was a sublimation), animal totemism,\* and hermetic magic as such. As far as the last were concerned, it particularly opposed trick magic outside the cults – and such competitors as Simon Magus, a demonstrator who worked with an attractive girl partner, the prototype of the blonde in tights of the modern conjurer. Much, though, was included. Christianity was a new religion; but it was also a synthesis.

Until the coming of Christianity, the gods of a defeated culture, if not forgotten, were quickly incorporated into the current pantheon. Often, owing to their common origins, they were, with different names, already there. Christianity, being monotheistic, could not adopt this. Instead, it translated the gods and goddesses which had preceded it to the status of saints or devils.

In the Mediterranean world, the more common practice was for the place-nymphs and elementals, and the local manifestations of the Olympians, to become saints. The Italian peasant still brought his offerings to the health-giving springs of Apollo, but now they were accredited to St Apollinaris, and the temple had been sprinkled with holy water. The saint still cared especially for the crippled, or the traveller, or whatever it might be. Indeed, every human activity was especially the province of one member or other of the hagiocracy. An array of professional saints, of whom St Christopher is almost the sole remaining active practitioner in Protestant Europe today, was headed by St Luke, the patron of painters, St Peter, the patron of fishmongers, and St Valentine, the patron of lovers. St Hubert cured mad dogs, and St Vitus those afflicted with

---

\* The crude Roman caricature of an early Christian worshipping a Christ with an ass's head, hanging from a Cross, is almost certainly an ignorant joke, even though it is significant.

madness and dance mania. St Fiacre – as innocent of the fact that his name was to be applied to a hackney-coach as St Awdrey that the word tawdry was to be applied to the fancy goods first exhibited at her fairs – looked after those suffering from piles. Trees and wells associated with particular gods and goddesses still received reverence, but they were now holy wells. The old shrines and burial grounds had become Christian churches and cemeteries. A minority of worshippers remembered their old associations. The majority justified the wise latitude of the Church, and, after a few generations, although the old practices dallied on under the indulgent eye of the parish priest, the worshippers had become Christian. Even the purveyors of magic – the wise women and poisoners of La Vecchia: 'the old religion' as witchcraft is still known in Italy – no longer particularly clung to the sacred places, but declined into lonely practitioners of white or black magic, with, as far as evidence can show, little organization.

In Northern Europe it was different.

Witchcraft, in any organized form, as opposed to a general magical tradition, particularly survived in Northern Europe and in Africa.* The African form was, in spite of great powers of hyperaesthesia and magical control, degenerate, as is most African culture. Here we must narrow down the canvas to a more direct treatment of Europe north of the Mediterranean basin.

In Britain, northern France, and Germany, the magical tradition of Egypt and the Near East was naturally not so strong. The old palaeolithic fertility practices, however –

---

* It was, as is the whole theme of this book, a widespread survival of palaeolithic emotive religion, of which there are traces everywhere. Curiously, for instance, Mexico, when first visited by the Spaniards (the Inquisition was especially primed to notice these things at the time) had a demon Tlazolteote who was depicted wearing a peaked hat and riding through the air on a broomstick. Mexican witches smeared themselves with ointment, like medieval European ones, and had familiars. The whole cult seems to have flourished there. There are parallels, too, in the Far East. The horned god appears in India in the earliest times. To attempt any sort of examination of these more exotic evidences is, however, quite impossible here.

particularly those which included animal totemism – were stronger. The magic which in that stage of culture was associated with the matriarch – or sometimes the patriarch – wizard had, moreover, been reinforced by the magical system developed in the far north, particularly by the Lapps.

This cruder, older religious form was naturally frowned upon far more severely by missionary Christianity, especially as those who practised it had also a completely different social culture from the Latin races who had now made Christianity – and especially New Testament Christianity – their own. In Britain, for instance, Augustine was an Italian, Theodore came from Asia Minor, and his assistant Hadrian was a Negro. Thus in the north, although an enormous number of pagan gods became saints, a far larger number than in the south were regarded as devils.

For long the enforcement of anything like Christian ortho-doxy was virtually impossible. Whole provinces, like Britain, were partially converted and then relapsed into the paganism of new invaders before being revisited by Christian mission-aries. These then found a distressing lack of information on points which had been approved by Rome in the meantime – about the correct date of Easter or the use of the tonsure. The people themselves had often adopted Christianity as an act of reluctant political necessity. The royal households might be Christian, but the people were pagan. St Olaf made his sub-jects choose between baptism or death, and Charlemagne conducted mass baptisms of Saxons by the vigorous expedient of driving them with swords through a river previously blessed upstream by his bishops. (The Saxons held their sword arms out of the water, that they should not be enervated by Christian effeminacy.) But, as Francis Thompson wrote: 'You cannot label men for God, and save them by the barrel-load.' Later converts had a habit of reappearing periodically for baptism for the sake of the baptismal robes awarded them as part of the ceremony – meanwhile, like Redwald, King of the East Saxons, keeping one altar for God and a little one for devils. The old gods did not lack adherents.

It would be hopeless to try to enumerate them. Every tribe

had its own totems and particular practices. Moreover, the names under which they are described are those formalized into mock Latin by the Christian chroniclers, or, more simply, identified with the classical gods and goddesses whom they most resembled. Often they were really the same, although to accept this too glibly is to forget that huge cultural divisions lay between Freya of Jutland and, for instance, Diana of the Ephesians. Palaeolithic fertility and animistic totems were overlaid by neolithic and agricultural symbols: both were in places tutelary to the war gods of the north – the nursery parade of Tuesday, Wednesday, Thursday, and Friday: the whole confusion was complicated by late adaptations from Roman and Greek mythology and the legends of local heroes.

The first representation by man of any anthropomorphic deity whatever, is perhaps that of a horned figure, wearing a stag's head and apparently dancing, hidden in the inner darkness of a cavern in Ariège. It is a palaeolithic painting. It is hard to determine how long ago it can have been executed. It would perhaps be as unprofitable to know its age as it would be to calculate how frequently it has been reproduced. But it serves as a pointer to the argument that a horned figure – the priest as the god, or the god as the priest – was perhaps the commonest factor in the worship, the dance-release, of the palaeolithic peoples. Other figures, carved on ivory, painted on walls, or scratched on rock, show the same motive.

The horned god naturally appeared less shaggy and more resplendent with the first civilizations. In Mesopotamia, the number of horns for long indicated the relative importance of the god. The Lamp with Seven Horns, in the Book of Revelation, borrows the symbolism. The demon Eukidon, one of the types of the Christian devil found in illustrations, possessed not only horns but hooves and a tail as well. In Egypt, many goddesses had horns, and Osiris, the greatest of all the gods, wore the horns of fertility. So, of course, did Isis.

Pan, a local Greek manifestation who condensed in his myth the phallic theme of earlier times and the mystery of the Egypto-Greek compromise, was horned. He was a goat. But goats and bulls and rams and heifers (not quite so many stags, for stags do not widely exist in the temperate zones) dance through or preside over all the important stages in the development of religious history up to Christianity. The Old Religion went on, and every new religion found that the ordinary worshippers accepted most easily the god who revealed himself as an animal. Theseus, the sacrifice to a Mediterranean god, fought a priest who was half Minos, the sacred bull. Mithras himself was in part the bull he had slain.

In the north of Europe, the Old Religion persisted in spite of the coming of Christianity. Courts and courtiers might be Christian, but the forests were true to the phallic cycle and the old magicians. They had already absorbed the paganism of the Baltic and the North East. It seemed for long as if they might even challenge successfully the religion of the higher culture which was now coming up from the Mediterranean. It must have been very gradually indeed that the old worshippers were driven farther and farther into the woods, or across the water to the outlying western islands of the Continent.

As well as Odin and Thor and the evil Loki, and the other warrior gods of Scandinavia, and as well as the local gods of the groves, the wells, and the rivers, the Early Fathers found the horned god. He had innumerable forms. And because each missionary dealt with only a limited area, and noticed only particular aspects of local religious idiom, he was given innumerable names. He was just bulls. Or, because he had two faces, he was Janus. Or he was the female counterpart Diana-Hecate, who also had two faces. Or he was the mystery of the Druids. He was indeed a common denominator in the fertility theme which lay behind the cult practices involved in all these manifestations.

A frequent name for the god is Cernunnos, a clothed and bearded figure with two stag antlers on his head, whose figure is found on an altar-stone dug up in Paris, and dating from perhaps 500 B.C. There is a Jupiter Cernenus on a tablet at Pesth, and another, squatting between Apollo and Mercury, at Rheims. But it would be tedious to rehearse all the archaeological evidence. The horned figure appears all over Europe at this period, from Jutland to the borders of Africa. It reappears in the history of the witch-cult and in the law courts (when the wearer of the horns finds the mask a legitimate cover for attempted rape) or in folk-lore ('an interesting old Stafford-shire survival') until the twentieth century.

This permanence of the central figure of the Old Religion emphasizes how strong it must have been in the first ten centuries of this era. King Edgar, A.D. 900, was regretting that it was even at that date more common in England than worship of the Christian God. This may have been pious horror at the wickedness of the world, but equally it may have represented a truth. The list of injunctions against devil worship trails down the centuries. In 681, the Council of Toledo, repeating the decrees of earlier councils, admonishes 'the worshippers of idols, those who venerate stones, who kindle torches, who celebrate the rites of springs or trees'. In the seventh century, the Archbishop of Canterbury prohibits sacrifice to devils and eating and drinking in heathen temples, and in a famous injunction proclaims that:

If anyone at the kalends of January goes about as a stag or a bull; that is, making himself into a wild animal, and putting on the heads of beasts; those who in such wise transform themselves into the appearance of a wild animal, penance for three years because it is devilish.

There are special penances for charming, making love philtres, poisoning, or 'making vows at a clump of trees, at a spring, at certain rocks, or at a spot where boundaries meet'. In the same century, St Caesarius of Arles deplores that 'some dress themselves in the skins of herd animals; others put on the heads of horned beasts; swelling and madly exulting if only they can so completely metamorphose themselves into the animal kind that they seem to have completely abandoned the human shape'.

In the ninth century, a general council decried 'certain wicked women' who 'reverting to Satan, and seduced by the illusions and phantasms of demons, believe and profess that they ride at night with Diana on certain beasts, with an innumerable multitude of women, passing over immense distances, obeying her commands as their mistress, and evoked by her on certain nights'. The injunction was all very well in Italy, but up in Scotland a Celtic peasantry was dancing round a phallic symbol in 1282, led by its village priest. He was allowed to keep his benefice, and in 1343 the very Bishop of Coventry himself was accused before the Pope of doing homage to the Devil. For hundreds of years a fat buck was led up to the altar of Old St Paul's, where once had been a temple of Diana.

The evidences of survival are innumerable, even where they are not tied up with witchcraft. But it is significant that the penalties for flirtation with devilry were not at first particularly terrifying – they were penance, penitence, fasting, and the paying of wer, wite, lah-sib, or as a more severe measure, cxx days in prison. Christian dogma and practice were not strong enough to do more than skirmish with the Old Religion, until Christian culture had made this a psychological anachronism. Magicians were punished, and even put to death. But this was, as it had been in the classical world, for their crime against man, not for their offence against God.

The cult of the horned deity lived on: and with it the vestiges of palaeolithic other-consciousness, released through the dance, were still at war with asceticism and rationalism.

# 5

## *The Medieval Background*:
## *Reaction into Heresy*

'THE Middle Ages' is the most unsatisfactory of historical labels, especially in minds for which it extends backwards loosely, if generously, to include the undocumented maelstrom of the Dark Ages as well. The generations, and the beliefs, between A.D. 400 and 1500, provide ample evidence to support the prejudices of any historical student or journalist. They are therefore a battleground for sectarian historians and their camp-followers, whose acrimony, starting imposingly in expensive double-deckers, declines respectably into papers in the historical quarterlies, sometimes to decline finally into the mausoleums of expensive and privately printed pamphlets. The rival schools of thought assail each other with records, to prove and refute not only the habits, morals, and beliefs of their period, but the equally indefinable problems of how many people actually lived then at all. Catholic medievalists, assuming that virtue lies in numbers, claim that in Britain, for instance, there were perhaps some six or eight million contented Christians. Protestant opponents explain that the complacent slaves or oppressed anti-clericals of this unhappy period numbered at most a pitiful and scorbutic four million. The two views are invoked as required by what is known as the Ordinary Reader.

The charitable hold that the Middle Ages presented 'a many-coloured pageant'. They see a foreground in which the soldiers fought for Christendom and the monastic orders prayed for it, while the people in the background lived mainly in contentment. For them the large-scale blessings of unity and authority in Europe were relieved by a feudal detail of villages gathered round the benevolent – or, at all events, protective – despot of the castle, whose wimpled wife relieved their afflic-

56

tions, although the monks in the hospital of the near-by abbey (good, but jolly, men) were always ready to do the same. Every few days there was a holy day, given over to song and dance round the maypole, more in the manner of the village of Happy-Go-Lucky at the beginning of a pantomime than of the younger Breughel. Knights, very refined and Christian, went off to the Crusades, and their wives, very resigned and beautiful, stood silhouetted on the battlements, singing and sighing. There was a gay peripatetic population of troubadours, strolling players, Chaucerian pilgrims, and friars of orders grey, with of course gipsies, and, for sport, Jews. Deeds of chivalry, hawking, and knightly jousting, with bards, bowers, and battles, made up a picture of romantic glamour in which defeat was the lot only of the pagans, the High Sheriff of Nottingham, and, in infinitely creditable circumstances, of Richard Cœur de Lion. For full measure, there were jesters as well.

This exquisitely vulgar convention is more particularly found in Great Britain, and is presented in rather different (if equally glowing) colours in the Catholic countries of Europe. It derives much from a diluted memory of Sir Walter Scott's romantic antiquarianism, ignoring the fact that his genius missed the religious temper of the Middle Ages, and that his detail was usually picturesquely inaccurate. Other popular influences have been Froissart (although the motives of his characters are shown by the author as frankly economic), Malory, Alfred Tennyson, and Hollywood.

The alternate view is expressed in the bitter journalism of, for instance, Mr H. G. Wells, writing of a Middle Ages*

. . . when Western Europe, superstitious, dirty, diseased and degenerate, thrashed by the Arabs and Mongols and Turks, afraid to sail the ocean or fight out of armour, cowered behind the walls of its towns and castles, stole, poisoned, assassinated and tortured, and pretended to be the Roman Empire still in being. Western Europe in those days was ashamed of its natural varieties of speech

* For Mr Hilaire Belloc the same years (the twelfth to fifteenth centuries) are 'the four great centuries in which our race attained the summit of its happiness and stable culture'.

and talked bad Latin: it dared not look a fact in the face but nosed for knowledge among riddles and unreadable parchment. . . .

The passage goes on with mounting repugnance, and represents very fairly much else that is written today, when scientific study has reinforced Protestant rancour, and it is possible to add to generalizations, such as Froude's about 'the long night of ecclesiasticism', specific material charges of bad teeth, rickets, and an endemic lack of the proper vitamins.

For those who prefer this attitude, the pageant is not of courtly knights on their way to the Crusades, but of such Crusaders as those at the taking of Jerusalem in 1099, who, in the words of one of their own number, wept with joy as they sang slaughtering through the streets, which 'ran with blood to their horses' hocks'. They fought as fiercely among each other as they did against the pagan, with whom indeed they often intrigued in self-interest. They were illiterate barbarians who horrified the Eastern Church they claimed that they had come to save. They cared nothing, if they could win estates for themselves, that the misguided and fanatical peasantry, who preceded them, were murdered in heaps all over the Near East. In all they were credulous, dirty, and eventually unsuccessful. At home, a starving populace, frequently decimated by plague, was bled to pay the ransoms of lords who could not even speak the same language, and was forced to work for a rapacious (and again generally illiterate) priesthood. They were ruled from a castle inhabited by a fading foreign woman condemned in her husband's absence to the constriction of an insanitary chastity belt, and to the discomforts of an ill-built and windswept edifice which, if of stone at all, was liable to be pulled down by the king.

The peripatetic population, by this analysis, is of down-at-heel soldiers. It includes male and female penitents proceeding from church to church to be flogged naked as an interlude in the sacred mysteries. There are branded and mutilated outlaws the Church had condemned to death by starvation, since no man might help nor take them in, footpads, and papal officers peddling pardons, relics, and pieces of the inexhaustible Cross. The procession moves slower than that of the Catholic sympathizers, however, because it is pointed out that, in spite of some Roman roads being still only half decayed, much of the country was bogged and impassable. The people, except perhaps in Italy, trembled under a religion which was built on fear, and a political system which was based on selfish force. The whole period was, with only minor exceptions, one of physical, moral, and intellectual degradation and atrophy.

This all derives from the sceptics of the eighteenth century, Gibbon and Voltaire, and in English-speaking countries and more recently, from the Protestant historians of the nineteenth century, and (of course) Hollywood again.

It is not cheap to mention the influence of the cinema here. For that medium represents the lowest common denominator about anything. It condenses in its overdressed productions the two ideas of the Middle Ages – the romantic and the statistically realistic, merged into entertainment with a sort of gutter-snipe devoutness: Notre Dame and Sanctuary, and Quasimodo being whipped, all for 1s. 9d. On their rather higher levels, few readers are much more happily adjusted.

It has been shown that religion is an attempt to provide a system and a practice to defeat loneliness and the fear of individuality. The Catholic Church of the Middle Ages, although ascetic and widely differing from the teachings of its founder, did, for the majority, provide some such solution, more or less successfully. It is impossible for those who have not shared the benefits of this release to recognize its force, just as it is perhaps impossible to estimate the real attractions of totalitarianism if one does not live under, and accept, totalitarian rule.

For the Faithful, it was an Age of Faith and, as such, all-embracing. Criticism was madness, and heretics and witches were lynched with the terrified cruelty with which animals will dispatch one of their own kind which suffers from a deformity. If Totality admits toleration, its case is lost. There was a conception of Universality: of unity and authority and law. God's viceregents ruled on earth, the Pope ruled men's souls, delegating to the Holy Roman Emperor and his vassals the care of their bodies. Or, if you followed the Emperor, the authority was in reverse order.

This theoretical position, however, was not all. The classical world had possessed a variety of religions, but a universal law. The Middle Ages in Europe possessed ideally a religion of universality, but a heterogeneous welter of legal systems. The arts and the ordinary standards of living were lower than they had been for hundreds of years over a large part of the civilized globe. There was profound, unrelieved, and wilful ignorance of the simplest facts of medicine, geography, natural science, and literary scholarship. Kings who could neither read nor write were celebrated for learning. A large number of priests found it impossible to grasp even the dog Latin of the Lord's Prayer, and the infatuated hordes who formed the first Crusaders slaughtered the citizens of Hungary, whom they thought Saracens since they spoke an unknown language. The best minds of the age were concerned with theological quibbles and doctrinal absurdities – and so were many even of the worst. There was, in every class, a tendency to hysteria and violent emotionalism,\* and naturally, with this instability, there went also a gross brutality. Few stories are more horrible than that of St Dominic plucking a sparrow alive for the edification of his admirers and the discomfiture of the Devil. There was no sort of social freedom, and there was a level of semi-starvation, particularly in winter – when there was no meat – so bitter as even to provoke sporadic cannibalism.

This situation was the result of an ascetic religion which was both all-powerful and profoundly pessimistic. This world was held to be a vale of blood and tears preparatory to the next, which was, for the majority, to be one of eternal torture and damnation. It was, indeed, a culpable heresy to hold that more than a tiny minority were likely ever to escape hell fires. 'How shall I laugh, how shall I rejoice?' asked Tertullian, and orthodoxy agreed that such behaviour was inviting the fires of

---

\* Soldiers 'cried like women in travail' when their scurvied gums were cut by the barbers, and Crusaders wept regularly whenever they won a battle, whilst congregations, applauding popular preachers, would clap and give ecstatic cries of 'Orthodox!' and 'Thirteenth Apostle!'

Eternity. 'He who fees a joculator,' it was held, 'fees the Devil.' The body was an ass, and too conscious care of it was another short cut to hell. Roman hygiene gave way to pious dirt, and it was with a strong sense of the miraculous that Christians learnt that St Bridget had been vouchsafed in a vision that they might without offence wash twice a month. Ideal behaviour for women was that of the virgin saint Asella, who had lumps on her knees 'like those on the legs of camels' from kneeling on hard stones, and flattered herself at the age of fifty that she had never in her whole life spoken to a man. The followers of St Thomas à Becket – even the less initiated – were able to extol his grime and the number of lice to which he was host. Fasting, flagellation, and maceration of every kind were sought willingly. The end of the world might come at any moment, and preparation for it was the only useful occupation of a mankind driven desperate in search of salvation. Oneness with nature was gone. The formula of the Christian Church was adopted with furious gratitude in an attempt to attain, through penitence and absolution, the substitute of a oneness with God. There was no time to be lost, for the Second Coming was hourly expected. 'Babylon the Great is fallen,' read the Apocalypse, '. . . surely I come quickly.' The whole life of medieval Europe was rocked when, from time to time, it was concluded that the hour was even now at hand. Wars ceased and the ordinary practices of life were suspended in Christian Europe and the East, as all men strained their eyes to Heaven, in expectation of the delayed millennium. Even Sir Thomas More, by the time of the high Renaissance, orthodoxly believed the last stage of the world to be imminent. Round humanity clustered devils, for ever seeking to clutch men and to drag them down to hell. The ascetic preoccupation had indeed made a religion of love into one – in many hearts – of terror.

Naturally, the Church tried many times to correct, in detail, the depressive preoccupation of its high theory. It has already been shown how the natural festivals of earlier religions were incorporated into the practices of Christianity. There were, indeed, fairs, and bards, and pageants. There were, indeed, expressions of love and charitism in the lives of many of the saints. With the twelfth-century Renaissance came a blossoming of the arts, and a revival in the study of Aristotle and some of the ancients, mainly in Arabic translations. Greek thought, ornamented by Aubekr, Avicenna, or Alfarabi, was turned into dog Latin and copied with incredible zeal and some inaccuracy. The Crusaders brought back with them from the Near East, as well as venereal disease and other unpleasantness, higher standards of living – cushions, muslins, and spices – and also a sense of new intellectual fields. There was everywhere an impulse towards speculation. But the results were not universally happy, and induced a defensive persecution by the forces of ascetic orthodoxy.

By the twelfth century, even without extraneous vices from the East, the backslidings from conventional morality appalled a succession of chroniclers. Among peasants, sexual self-restraint has always been almost impossible, since sexual satisfaction is almost the only emotional outlet for the very poor, and the lower the standard of living, the more the population always increases. The tendency throughout the Middle Ages was always for population to increase, in spite of war, famine, epidemics, and the tremendous infant mortality. Moreover, the periods of abstinence imposed by the Church were not backed by employers of the serfs, who naturally wanted to encourage fecundity, as later did slavers, in the interests of good economics. The middle classes formed a comparatively small part of the population until the later Middle Ages, and, in any case, were notoriously less devout than the peasants, perhaps as a result of copying their morals from the wealthy. The wealthy were soldiers, whose occasional feats of pious romanticism were normally compensated by feats of athletic self-indulgence (the statistics are carefully noted in the chronicles), or they were clergy; and the clergy were corrupt. Moreover, since the structure of Catholic Europe was largely institutional, homosexuality, the besetting vice of segregated institutions, was also the besetting vice of the Middle Ages.

The corruption of the clergy was agreed by all contemporary writers, whether devout or merely cynical. There must have been innumerable pious and good priests, worthy monks, and devoted nuns. But a string of reformers claimed that these were not the majority. The higher Church officials were venal and openly licentious, and it was apparently impossible to restrain parish priests from concubines or monks from nunneries. The enormity of the papal scandals has given unhealthy satisfaction to generations of writers of Protestant tracts. Archbishops were as bad. In 1100, the Archbishop of Tours pardoned the adultery of Philip I, and, in return, the See of Orleans was given to a frail youth, whom the Archbishop had taken over from his predecessor, and with whom he was for the moment in love. This young man was known as Flora, after a contemporary courtesan, and ribald songs were sung to him openly in the streets. His election was formalized on the Feast of the Innocents. In 1198, the Archbishop of Besançon was accused by his chapter of perjury, simony, and incest with the Abbess of Remiremont. He suffered a comparatively mild penalty. Bishops were almost the worst of all. A typical example is that Bishop of Toul who was 'wholly abandoned to debauchery and the chase' and whose favourite concubine was his own daughter by a nun of Épinal.

These examples would be valueless if they did not seem to represent the general standard among the higher clergy by the twelfth century. In the emancipated south of France it was a common expression to say 'I had rather be a priest than do such-and-such' when elsewhere Europe said 'I had rather be a Jew. . . .'

The lower clergy were, like their superiors, extortionate as well as immoral, and there is a story of two laymen, meeting in the market-place in what must have been an intimate conversation, who discovered that the same priest had sentenced one of them to a severe monetary penance for lying with his wife during Lent, and the other for abstaining from his, and so running counter to the divine purposes of procreation. In their own derelictions, clergy were above the law. It was no wonder that in many parts of Europe they were almost universally despised.

The result of this situation – a religion of ascetic dogma and corrupt practice – was reaction. It was of three main types. First there were the orthodox ascetics who wished to reimpose the old purity and were welcomed by the Church for this purpose. These men, the Franciscans and the other Holy Orders who attempted to elevate current practice by both precept and example, have no direct connexion with witchcraft, except when, as in the example of the Inquisitors, they were specifically employed to combat it. They can therefore be ignored here. The second reaction was that of the heretics who tried to reform standards with the help of beliefs which the Church held to be, and which often were, imported from non-Christian sources. The third was a reaction towards the old pre-Christian system which still lingered amongst the less cultured peoples, crossed with the magical formulas of the 'intellectuals'. This was witchcraft, and the manifestation it now took is the subject of this book.

These heresies are worth noticing very briefly because in the minds of the Inquisitors they were closely allied with witchcraft, and did have features in common with the cult. Just as the right-wing Inquisitors of Nazism spoke comprehensively of Jews, intellectuals, and Marxists, so the Churchmen of the Middle Ages and of the Renaissance period spoke comprehensively of Jews, witches, and heretics. Their list also included lepers, who were held to be part of the general diabolic conspiracy, and were sometimes persecuted accordingly. Today there are few physical lepers in Europe, but their name has passed into the general vocabulary of political disapprobation.

After the early suppression of the Arian heresy, and the clearing up of the errors of peoples who had been converted by early missionaries and then cut off, like the British, organized heresy shrank. The energies of Christendom were directed outwards, towards combating the pagans from the east or north, and a certain fighting unity was achieved, in spite of occasional bogus Christs and subjective visionaries. (One of these poor freaks, who achieved a following and subsequent martyrdom, was the thirteenth-century Rudolphus, who thought that Nemo – the 'No Man' of 'No man hath ascended into Heaven' – was a god.) There were unorthodox teachers like John Scotus Erigena or Abelard, and many gnostic sects carried on an underground existence. However, there was little scepticism, and there were only a few magicians and astrologers, although Pope Sylvester II, for example, had a sinister reputation in the tenth century, and Italy, particularly, still had its memories of occult processes deriving from the east and reinforced from the south. With the twelfth century, however, the increased speculation and the exposure of clerical scandals meant a mushroom growth of sects which spread, with the trade routes, all over Europe.

The Waldenses, or poor men of Lyon, were the simple-living followers of Peter Waldo of Lyon, who had the misfortune not to be recognized by the Church, as was St Francis in his generation. It has frequently been pointed out that the Waldenses were burnt for the practices for which the Franciscans were canonized. They were poor, simple, and evangelical, although no doubt their tenets became mixed with those of the multifarious other heresies of the thirteenth century. Of these, many derived from the teaching of Peter of Bruys, who was burnt in 1125 after a life of proto-Protestant reformation. He and his adherents attacked clerical vices and led a mild Jacquerie which included the scourging of priests, the enforced marriage of monks, the burning of crosses, and iconoclasticism generally.

Much more important were the dualistic teachings which originated in the teaching of the Persian Mani, who had been crucified as early as A.D. 276. Of course, however, the idea of a God whose two sides, Good and Evil, strove for mastery in the soul of man was a far earlier one. The Manichee heresy flared up particularly in the south of France. Here, the soft flexible culture of the Languedoc had absorbed a racial mixture of Iberians, Vandals, Phoenicians, Greeks, Franks, and Saracens who had settled into a lazy prosperous community more tolerant – and in many ways more advanced – than anywhere else in Europe. Here, even Jews were tolerated, and the conventional idea of a romantic Middle Ages came nearest to reality. There was indifferentism and latitude, and only priests were hated. But, because of this hatred, the various heresies made many converts, and Albi became so notorious that many of the different heresies were labelled, in the north, as Albigensian. The sects themselves, however, had many names, and were variously known all over the south and east of Europe, whilst a few spread into the north, into Holland, Germany, and even England. In the west of France they were known as Tisserands, because they found many adherents among the weavers. Elsewhere they were Cathari, Patarins, Bogomils, or just Manichaeans. In many lands they were known as Bulgars, because dualistic teaching had long smouldered in Bulgaria. For some reason this particular name became associated with the homosexual practices which the heretics were held to encourage, since they did not believe in procreation into a world dominated by the evil principle. Hence they were known as Bulgari, Bugari, Bulgri, or Bougres, a word which, as it is delicately put, 'has been retained with an infamous signification in the English, French, and Italian vernaculars'.

Apart from their dualistic teaching, the chief outstanding quality of the Cathari (although almost the only evidence is that of their enemies) was their piety and charity. They were divided into two sections: the ordinary lay believers, and the Perfecti, who believed in complete abstinence and even the logical end of all asceticism – the Endura – a passionate disavowal of physical humanity which led them to starvation and even apparently to mass suicide. They adopted most of the Christian teaching and dogma of the New Testament, mixed with gnostic ritual, using asceticism as an end to visions and other-consciousness. They were so loyal to their beliefs that a John of Toulouse was able to plead before his judges, in 1230, to assure them he was not an Albigensian, 'Lords: hear me. I am no heretic; for I have a wife and lie with her, and have children; and I eat flesh and lie and swear, and am a faithful Christian.' Many of them seem, indeed, to have lived with the barren piety of the saints. They were accordingly accused of sexual orgies and sacrilege, and burned, scourged, and harried. Nevertheless, the heresy flourished, and Cathari were even able to hold conferences on equal terms with orthodox bishops.

In 1208 the Albigensian Crusade was preached by Pope Innocent III, and the vigorous, greedy cavalry of the north, led by Simon of Montfort, uncle of the hero of the text books, pillaged the south and brought flames and desolation to the valleys of Languedoc. The Holy Inquisition of St Dominic was deputed to move in, with the full powers of the later black-coated police of totalitarianism, to stamp out the heresy which remained. The Cathari and the Waldenses showed bravery in defence of their tenets. There is the story of a beautiful girl rushing headlong into the flames in which her lover was being burned, and the usual heroics of any large-scale persecution. But the process went on, and orthodoxy and dull resignation gradually superseded the Courts of Love and the twanging of the troubadours.

With persistence and with pious thoroughness the Inquisition did its work, and then turned north to grapple, aided by increased experience, with the manifestation of Satan in the north: witchcraft. For the Church, now reasonably secure against outside invasion, could concentrate upon loose thinking inside its own structure.

There are many instances in the examination of the Cathari, and of the Templars, who were accused, perhaps unjustly, of being influenced by the heresy, of conceptions which were to become more apparent in the evidence of the witch trials. For instance, the devil was held to appear to them as a black man, sometimes with two or three faces. This is as one would expect in a dualistic religion, although there are instances in the trials of the Templars, where the excessive number of Satan's legs and arms makes it appear that he may there have had Indian affinities. The figure thirteen, that of the witch coven, which may too have been derived from the Agape, seems to have been a popular number for the inner circle of believers. Salt was not eaten by the Cathari: and there are other parallels. It may well be that the Master Devils of the witches, who often were educated men, had a knowledge of the Eastern cults which were incorporated in these throwbacks into increased asceticism. If so, it would account for the fact that the palaeo-lithic memories of the witch-cult coincided so conveniently for the Inquisitors with the external practices of the very different heresies of the south. But a skilful Inquisitor can manufacture many parallels.

It is witchcraft in the north, the other reaction from the Catholic State of the Middle Ages, that we must now consider.

*Part Two*

# MEDIEVAL WITCHCRAFT

# 6

## *The People who Became Witches*

IT was not until the fourteenth century that the existence of
a definite sect of witches was finally accepted by the Church
as an imminent danger, although the earliest detailed account
is that of Nider, writing as early as 1137, when he also men-
tions earlier manifestations. By the fourteenth century, the
Inquisition, confirmed in its now carefully adjusted machinery
for the extermination of heresy generally, had turned to in-
vestigate more closely what had previously been held to be
only individual error or, in some localities, a regrettable
tendency to revert to periodic paganism. The districts on the
perimeter of the Catholic State, and those which, for various
topographical or economic reasons, remained as only partially
converted pockets within it, could be coordinated. In the first
centuries of Christendom it had been enough to demand a
nominal conversion, and wisely to overlook rites and beliefs
of earlier religions, particularly if these could be attached to the
name of recognized saints. But now that Christian Europe had
attained manhood, it was felt that minority anachronisms must
be destroyed.

Investigation showed, however, what had been already
claimed constantly by horrified parish priests, particularly in
the north, that in some parts the Old Religion was hardly a
minority one at all. The ancient palaeolithic cult worship, so
much of it associated with the rites of the horned god, still
kept adherents everywhere, particularly in the country districts. It is almost impossible, today, to realize the inaccessi-
bility of many regions during the period following the break-
down of the Roman system, although, even until 1939, the
village of Imber, on Salisbury Plain, used to receive its
patronizing paragraph in the national Press every year, whenever cut off by a heavy fall of snow. (It is now confiscated by
the Army.)

In England, for instance, the Fen district still isolated the eastern counties, which in any case felt for centuries the results of their devastation after the defeat of Boadicea in A.D. 61. The Weald still separated southern England from the Gallic sophistication of Kent, although that culture was confined for some time to the dominant Norman minority, or to the priestly caste, recruited from the conquered, but by definition non-reproductive. Yorkshire was a waste devastated by William of Normandy. Wales and Cornwall spoke a Celtic language, and used a Celtic culture for centuries at war with Norman–British procedure. Independent Scotland, given up to high-born brigandage and a low regimen, looked culturally to the Scandinavian north or to France. All dialects were probably incomprehensible outside a very narrow circle, although this was immaterial, as the majority of the population were attached to the soil on which they were born, and on which they spent their lives – which were, until after the Black Death, forfeit if they tried to leave. The scattered hamlets and villages, most of them self-contained units, miles apart from each other, lay off the ridgeways which the Romans had adapted into military highways, and were surrounded by swamp, forest, and devils. It was not surprising that the beliefs they had brought with them when their ancestors first settled there should persist, only superficially affected by the culture of their overlord and the inexplicable doctrines of his religious compatriots. The obvious comparison is those communities of the recent past and of today – for instance in the West Indies or Africa – in which missionary and colonial influence extends from the capital to the towns and large villages, whilst the interior remains true to voodoo and the goats.

There is, of course, a reverse side to this picture. As the Middle Ages proceeded, travel of every sort increased. Norman adaptability helped to spread and organize society, and the Church itself, in spite of every sort of difficulty and individual incompetence, secured the adherence, and often the passionate adherence, of all classes. Without it, there was only extermination – physical if heresy was openly avowed, spiritual and eternal if cherished secretly. Throughout the period, and even, perhaps, down into the seventeenth century, there were other groups of villages. These, not usually on the main trade routes, uncritically accepted both religions as occasion dictated, and still remained attached to the old practices.* Until now, their beliefs had been recognized as surviving paganism. From the eighteenth century onwards, the remaining traces, disguised as custom and folk-lore, were to be tolerated as amiable antiquarianism. But, for some four centuries, the organized asceticism of Christianity suppressed with blood and fire the scattered, degenerate, but still persistent organization of the cults, and successfully purged their challenge as a rival faith.

This Old Religion – of the horned god and the emotional reunion with nature through the dance and the practice of long-established taboos – was not, of course, pure. The ordinary Christian in a European country today could give, on the spur of the moment, only the most sketchy and inaccurate account of his creed and the history of the faith to which he claims to belong. A minority opinion is always more passionately and more consciously held, but the adherent of the medieval cults, in their degenerate thirteenth-century form, would have been even more inarticulate and ill-informed in his beliefs – a jumble of phallic-Druidism, the dregs of Mediterranean ritual, Scandinavian magic, and, before long, Christian parody. Yet this does not invalidate the fact that the beliefs did exist, and the extraordinary feature is how far the evidence of trials, even as late as the seventeenth century, shows this.

The practitioners of the cult were originally merely the people of those racial fringes of Europe which still represented palaeolithic culture. The worshippers were known variously as witches or fairies.

This identification has been expanded at length by Miss Margaret Murray, who has collected, set out, and certainly not underestimated, the evidence. But the idea is anything but new. It was, of course, recognized very early that the

---

* Arras was almost the only *town* held to have a strong witch party, and in this case the evidence was very possibly trumped up for purposes of private jealousy.

witch beliefs were – many of them – survivals from earlier religions. Even in the first half of the eighteenth century this was perceived by one Girolamo Tartarotti of Rovereto, as Montague Summers points out (apparently with the conviction that the fact that this author is discredited also discredits all work today which reaches any similar conclusions). In the same way it is a truism that the tradition of fairies, whenever it is found, often embalms race-memory of earlier peoples. Even Robert Burton, writing the *Anatomy of Melancholy* in 1621, identified fairies and devils, cataloguing 'Terrestrial devils, Lares, Genii, Fauns, Satyrs, Wood-nymphs, Foliots, Fairies, Robin Goodfellows, Trulli &c.' This identification is almost as well recognized as the Freudian revelation that nursery rhymes have only too often a phallic significance – a discovery which has given so much excitement that it is said that the British Broadcasting Corporation once received protests under this head when nursery rhymes were being broadcast.

But the very identification of witches and fairies, as being names equally given to the submerged races – more particularly in Europe – is a major theme of Sir Walter Scott's *Letters on Demonology and Witchcraft*. As the point is an important one, however, it may be worth repeating some of the evidence.

In the popular mind today, fairies are associated chiefly with *A Midsummer Night's Dream*, somewhat unsuccessful astral photography by admirers of the late Sir Arthur Conan Doyle, pantomime sopranos, and a gauzy little creature called Tinker Bell. They sit upon mushrooms, and their principal preoccupations are acorns and thistledown. They are known as the Little Folk,* and are often associated with Sussex teashops. But fairies were originally far more than this. They represented various constants in human belief – dreams and hallucinations of little people, used by the subconscious for expeditions of Lilliputian self-expression, finding an outlet in literary nympholepsy. Also, they represented belief in ghosts and nature spirits, and the lesser deities of the Teuton and the Celt. But, more particularly, they were race-memories of the stocks which had inhabited Europe before the coming of the Celts,

* Under this name they have, in Ireland, a whole folk-lore of their own.

with their iron culture, in the first two millennia before Christ. In the same way, the people of Africa and India identify with monkeys the peoples they have supplanted.

The palaeolithic peoples of Western Europe were small dark cattlemen, living on the animals with which, as has been shown, they were so closely identified in a psychical as well as a physical sense. As the various waves of invaders came, equipped with a higher economic standard and a higher mechanical efficiency and armoury, they retreated into the swamps and the islands, loathing with passion the agriculture, iron, and church bells which were their defeat. Some of them intermarried with the invader, particularly when the Celts were themselves in turn pushed westward by newer Nordic tribes. The original inhabitants of Scandinavia, later known as dwarfs, were, as is pointed out by Sir Walter Scott, who had not even heard of the Diffusionist theory:

originally the diminutive natives . . . who, flying before the conquering weapons of the Asae, sought the most retired regions of the north, and there endeavoured to hide themselves from their eastern invaders. They were a little, diminutive race, but possessed of some skill probably in mining or smelting metals, with which the country abounds. Perhaps also they might, from their acquaintance with the changes of the clouds, or meteorological phenomena, be judges of weather, and so enjoy another title to supernatural skill. At any rate, it has been plausibly supposed that these poor people, who sought caverns and hiding places . . . were in some respects compensated for inferiority in strength and stature by the art and power with which the superstition of the enemy invested them. These oppressed yet dreaded fugitives obtained, naturally enough, the character of the German spirits called Kobold, from which the English goblin and the Scottish bogle, by some inversion and alteration of pronunciation, are evidently derived.

In the north the dark little Lapps were less interbred than the mixed Romano-British-Iberian peoples who inhabited the rural districts of much of Britain, Brittany, and the forest districts of western France and Germany. But, in all these places, the racial minority lived on, largely with its own customs and beliefs. And in all these places, these customs and beliefs, the magic of the physically defeated but mysterious Little People, became the superstition, and often the justified fear, of the dominant race.

As the racial distinctions became less, the earlier practices continued, but those who used them were no longer a people physically apart – Little People, Elves, Leprechauns, Trolls, and Fairies. They were the peasant majority, fairly innocently celebrating round a maypole or dancing the Furry Dance at Helston – or they were the consciously bedamned, the witches. Nevertheless, the people who until the late Middle Ages were called fairies by one name or another were often those who, until the seventeenth century or so, were called witches. Even after Shakespeare, a sceptic, had laughed at the countryman's fears of the Little People and had turned Robin Goodfellow from a devil into a beneficent footman to Oberon, the old fear of fairies went on in some places, and, in Scotland particularly, witches and fairies were commonly identified.*

The qualities of the fairy people, as observed and feared until the seventeenth century, were all those of the early dwarf races. They were, for instance, particularly associated with fairy mounds and caves. These fairy mounds were almost certainly barrows. Here, and at the stone circles, the witches used to meet. In the same way, they were accustomed to dance round fairy trees, and, at her trial for witchcraft, Joan of Arc was accused particularly of dancing round the Fairies' Tree at Domrémy. She denied that she had seen fairies there, but her godmother, the wife of the Mayor, had done so. (There was, by the way, no notion whatever in France at this time, any more than in Ireland or Scotland, of the fairy being of much less than human size.) These fairy trees were, of course, the contemporary parallels of the groves of the Druids, the Ygdrasils of the north, the phallic obelisks of Egypt, or the Cross of the Christians. They were, at all events, actual traditional points, and neither the imaginary conception of an inquisition nor the properties of the fairy kingdom of whimsy.

* A whole theory could be built about Bottom, with his ass's head, sitting in the middle of a witch ring, surrounded by fairies.

The palaeolithic peoples,* dark, shy, small, and swift, probably had the property of moving quickly to escape detection. Fairies are always supposed to have had the quality of appearing and disappearing at will, and this is probably the result of their mobility, combined with the belief in their capacity for levitation and shape-shifting. It may also have been due to their habit of appearing to be swallowed by the earth as they retired into the ground – for caves, from Mendip to the north of England, like those of the Pyrenees and elsewhere, show evidences of having been continuously inhabited from the time of the Fourth Ice Age until the late Middle Ages. They are equally associated, in folk belief, with the fairy cattlemen and the witch-cult. In Northumberland, for instance, there is a Bull Cave of the Witches which includes both conceptions.

Fairy bulls, like fairy horses, were, indeed, as famous in the British Isles as fairy reindeer were in Scandinavia. The Little People were pastoral, and elf-bulls would be part of their ordinary economic life. At all events, there is the evidence of that Isobel Gowdie, who, at her trial in 1662, claimed to have gone into a fairy hill, and that 'there were elf-bulls routing and skoyling up and down there and affrighted me'. These may have been the ordinary cattle of the Little People: they may have been, as Miss Murray suggests, some of the fierce dogs of the Chow type which the Neolithic peoples employed as watchdogs: or they may have been members of the cult – though this does not sound so likely – dressed in their masks for the occasion, and identifying themselves with their particular local aspect of the horned god. The animal forms of the cult were, of course, extremely numerous, and it is perhaps significant that horses should have been so important a feature of fairy mythology when it is remembered that the early peoples were such great horse-breeders.

* Miss Murray, in discussing the same subject, calls these people 'Neolithic and Bronze-age'. I prefer 'palaeolithic' as suggesting the earlier psychical stream. But chronologically, as far as these terms can be chronological, and in terms of material culture, neolithic is of course more accurate.

It is natural that these palaeolithic throw-backs should have a knowledge of medicine and poisons and material forms of power, as well as the remembered ability to create states of hypnosis, and to provoke magical effects upon those made suggestible by belief in the taboo, or by fear of this. Knowledge of poison may account for the fatal effects which were known to be produced by elf-bolts or elf-arrows. These are the stone arrow heads still found from time to time on open heaths and downs. They are insignificant weapons, and, being projected only by very small bows, or a catapult process with the fingers, could hardly have produced death or paralysis unless they had been dipped, as are the darts of the African pygmies, in poison. There are, indeed, records of fairy arrows made of bog-weed, tipped with white flints and dipped in hemlock. Isobel Gowdie, who had been frighted by the fairy bulls, explained that the Devil made them himself with his own hands. But palaeolithic stone, and the marvels of neolithic bronze, could not compete with the mastery of iron, which therefore acquired a capacity in superstitious belief for baffling fairies and witches. In some places it was feared. It is unlucky today, among such nursemaids as survive changed social conditions, to give a knife or a pair of scissors as a present. In most places iron was a protection, and the horse-shoe combined great magic in being at once the moon shape of the Mother Goddess, the attribute of the sacred horse, and being composed in itself of the sovereign metal.

The fairy people wove their own clothes, which often appear to have been green, although they did not possess the loom, and it was a constant accusation that the women would come down and use the looms of the 'mortals' in their absence. In the same way, they were supposed to steal new-born children and carry them off, substituting, as changelings, their own puckish children. This is still said to be done by racially suppressed minorities in different parts of the world – although the story might also be a convenience for those too mortal women whose children, upon maturity, bore an embarrassing resemblance to a member of the suppressed and servant race.* Adults who were so unwise as to sleep on fairy mounds were also liable to be kidnapped. John Walsh, of Netherbury in Dorset, stated in 1566 that 'there be three kinds of fairies, the black, the white, and the green, of which the black be the worst'. It will be seen that the Devil was usually dressed in black, and the colours may have represented some sort of uniform.

Evidence everywhere is insistent on the hoods which the fairies wore. The little green and red hoods of the gnomes are still remembered, which the seven dwarfs share with the witch of caricature, in her high hat with the elf locks peeping from under it. In Germany, the local hobgoblin was called Hoode-kin, or Hutkin, and Robin à Hood may be another manifestation of the devil king of the fairies.

Robin Hood, before Scott re-created him and he became the property of the cinema athletes and a legend of sturdy freedom, had indeed affinity with Rob Roy and Robin Goodfellow, or Puck. He was the king of the peoples of the woods, the down-trodden and the oppressed minority. By late medieval times this minority was identified, in a world ruled by Normans, with the Anglo-Saxons. But when the far older legend began, the oppressed minority must have been pre-Anglo-Saxon. Robin's followers wore hoods, and were dressed in the fairy colour, green. Their weapon was the arrow, with which they were deadly. It may well have been the elf-arrow, for the story begins centuries before the introduction of the long-bow. They met, as did the witches and the fairies, round a great oak or oaks. They opposed particularly the Christian Church. As well as Robin himself, there were twelve chief companions – the thirteen of the witch coven. The only priest in the company was a renegade. Two other characters in the story seem familiar: Maid Marian, the consort of the king, the Virgin goddess of the woods, and Little John, who may be the English version of Jannicot, the Little John of the Basque country, one

---

* Until recently it was customary, in some country places, to put iron and salt (neither fairies nor witches would touch salt) at the bed foot of a new-born child. This would defeat the Little People, and also that almost conventional witch, the fairy godmother.

of the names of the two-faced Janus, who was one of the gods called upon by the witches.

The legend of Robin Hood was never entirely localized in Sherwood Forest. It appears up and down the country, sometimes with episodes attached to parallel heroes such as Rob Roy* or Herne the Hunter (an obvious incarnation of Cernunnos, horns and all), but usually under the name of Robin. And the legend appears throughout many centuries. It may well be that there were, locally, particularly famous and even historic Robins. But it appears at least equally probable that Robin Hood – traditionally acclaimed round that folk memory of his Druidic oak, the maypole – was a constant name, in many places, for the devil king of the fairy witch people.

King Arthur was another leader of the oppressed who dealt in magic, lived surrounded by twelve knights, and never died. His legend, although poetized and adopted by the Church – perhaps because the story became identified with a particular Christian prince of the dark days in Britain – contains many parallels. In Somerset, until the other day, men still sang primitive songs and danced round the trees of Arthur's native Apple-land, Avalon. And apples have always been associated with witchcraft, Satanism, and physical release, even in the Authorized English translation of Genesis. Merlin, Arthur's chief counsellor, was the son of an elf.

That there were kings and queens of the fairies is incontestable. Quite apart from the general folk stories to this effect, which were the basis for Oberon and his Titania, there is the account of Bessie Dunlop, accused of witchcraft and sorcery on 8 November 1576 in remote Ayrshire. She had been familiar with a Thorne Reid, who claimed that his interest in her was the result of his orders from the Queen of Elfhane, who had visited her when she was in childbirth many years before. The Queen was 'a stout woman who came into her and sat down on the form beside her and asked a drink at her and she gave it'. It hardly seems the picture which imagination would prompt to satisfy inquisitive judges. In the same way, Alesoun

* Another folk hero who, incidentally, disguised himself with goat-skins 'to resemble the Highland Satyr'.

Peirson, of Fifeshire, was 'convict for haunting and repairing with the good neighbours and Queen of Elfhane, and she had many good friends at that court which were of her own blood, who had good acquaintance with the Queen of Elfhane'. One Andro Man was husband of the 'Queen of Elphen', and had several mortal children by her over a course of thirty-two years, which sounds equally remote from misty romance. Jean Weir, the sister of the notorious Major Weir of Edinburgh, 'took employment from a Woman to speak in her behalf to the Queen of ffarie, meaning the Devil'. Innumerable marriages are chronicled between mortals and the Good Neighbours – more permanent arrangements than the casual intercourse of the ecstatic sabbat.

It certainly appears that the suppressed peoples kept some of their beliefs and their organization into the seventeenth century, and that the king and queen, though perhaps ordinary enough to the uninitiate, were revered and obeyed by those who belonged to the cult, much as are the king and queen of the gipsies today.

As with the gipsies, the king and queen would be proud of their birth, and of the magic control with which it endowed them. It was never considered, until the great persecutions of the thirteenth century onwards, to be in any way reprehensible to have fairy blood. The Angevins were supposed to have fairies, or devils, for their ancestors, and Miss Murray believes William Rufus to have been a master-devil. Charlemagne was descended from a swan-maiden, and, indeed, most of the kings of the north were proud to claim ancestral kindred with seals, bears, pigs, or whatever it might be. That dreary couple, Hengist and Horsa, whom it is now again becoming fashionable to consider historical figures, may have been the leaders of a race who believed that they derived from the horse. Enemies might be accused in a general way of descent from Satan, as the Huns were said to be the offspring of incubi, but warlords were the lineal descendants of the totem god. The divinity of kingship, however much it became a theoretical dogma of the Christian Church, lay – for its more humble adherents – very much in the position of the king as the totem head of his people – the divine goat, the sacrificial bull, the priest-king.

Witches, then, were early known as fairies, and until the later Middle Ages represented the remaining pockets of pre-Nordic peoples which Christendom still contained in its valleys, behind its swamps, or living in the lonely islands which Rome had never reached and where the converts of Rome, except as colonial exploiters or consciously adventurous missionaries, had barely penetrated. These people still retained the old customs, totems, and festivals which belonged to the pre-agricultural peoples, and something of the palaeolithic fertility system – the other-consciousness, and the power to manipulate it, which material advance had made increasingly rare and increasingly mysterious to peoples in a later stage of development. To Christian priests, bred in a tradition of pietistic asceticism, it was all both incomprehensible and disgusting. A complete lack of historical training made these beliefs seem appalling to the orthodox, especially when it had become less obvious that they represented an earlier religious system. They appeared as obvious manifestations of Satan's diabolical interference in human affairs, and as obscene parodies of the Christian practices – which in fact they often anticipated.

As time went on, the racial distinctions became less. The Lapps, the Welsh, and communities of this sort became more closely merged with their neighbours. National states had not yet grown up, nor a general unifying culture superseded the local variations. The Church, particularly, became a constant throughout Europe, exercising an occasional wise tolerance towards local festivals. The beliefs of the earlier religions became the superstitions of the majority, and the admitted tenets only of a few – the surreptitious sect of witches. These, in turn, found that the magical side of their formula was that most readily acceptable to converts, and the intellectual leaders were now infected with the far more advanced beliefs of gnosticism and the Hebrew Kabbalah. Gradually even the Little People consented, and became the worshippers of both religions.

In the meantime, however, many of the ordinary peasants,

reacting from asceticism and the horrors of a system which credited salvation only of a few, and a life and death of hell for the majority, found an escape in the witch-cult. When any aberration from the severities of ecclesiastical dogma would mean a flaming eternity, it might be as well to be hanged for a sheep as a lamb – for goat-worship as cattle stealing. It was only necessary to make a compact with the Devil to have the promised benefits of material prosperity, the witnessed advantages of a full herbal pharmacopoeia, the tolerable certainty of sexual opportunity, and, at all events, a periodic release from the routine of half-starved feudal servitude. The prospect, for the feebler or the more daring, must have been extremely alluring. In the north, in any case, magic had never been necessarily irreligious, and Odin himself had been a necromancer. The very ferocity of persecution must have increased a belief in the power of the alternative to Christianity. A wave of witchcraft probably did, as the Inquisitors claimed, sweep over Europe. It is by no means improbable, when one remembers that there were dancing, whipping, and other perverted sects which accumulated a considerable following and a satisfactory rota of martyrs. They did this without the same religious tradition, and by little more than force of example acting upon an overwrought populace.

The power and accessibility of the Devil were, of course, as incontestable to the orthodox as the fact of his existence. Many of the saints had possessed the disturbing faculty of being able to see the demons which teemed about mankind. The Blessed Reichhelm of Schöngan, at the end of the thirteenth century, perceived them as rain or as the dust shown in a sunbeam, and statisticians computed the infernal population as consisting of 1,758,064,176 devils, although Jean Wier, physician to the Duke of Cleves, was more conservative, and assessed the number, with equally precise definition, as only 7,409,127, led by seventy-nine princes. The devils were frequently seen by the devout in the delirium of ecstasy, and the legends of the saints are punctuated by anecdotes of how these demons were repelled, often physically, sometimes by exorcism. A favourite story is that of how St Equitius expelled a devil which a nun had inadvertently swallowed, while it was resting on a lettuce leaf. 'What could I have done?' asked the devil. 'I was sitting on the leaf and she ate me.' But St Equitius accepted no excuse. Daily and hourly, devils assailed the souls of living men, and church bells were rung at death – as they still are – to frighten them from the departing soul on its way to purgatory.

It is a truism that there was quite as much evidence for these things, in their generation, as there is for much popularly accepted pseudo-science today. The immediate point is that many people might easily feel that, admitting damnation in the eyes of the Church, they were, in accepting diabolism, not at all necessarily joining the losing side.

Of those who did join the cult, a large proportion were probably women. Fairies, under their various names, were, before being reassessed by the brownie sentimentalists, thought of equally as men or women. But, by the time the racial identity of the Little People had been lost, and the practitioners of their cults had become known as witches, it is natural to find women as the main repositories of the mystery. There are various reasons for this. For one thing, matriarchy had been a dominant practice in the earliest socio-religious systems, and the position of the woman as the hearth mistress, guardian of the sacred fire, and giver of life was probably one of the oldest tenets of the system – older perhaps than the worship of the totem god himself. Wall paintings of the Cro-Magnon culture depict what some anthropologists say are sorceresses. Even as late as classical times this was recognized, and Strabo wrote (with generous overstatement), 'All men allow women to have been the founders of religion.' At all events, their position in early society made it natural that it should be women who employed such knowledge as might exist of herbs and poisons, and, particularly, too, that they should maintain and pass on to the women of the next generation the secrets – essential for cattle, as well as for the conduct of the group ceremonial release – of sexual practice and rituals – whether positive, in stimulating desire and child-bearing, or negative, in inflicting impotence and procuring abortion. Although it may have dwindled into an ignorant composition of weedy hell-broths, country aphrodisiacs, pig-powders, and pre-natal ministrations, aided by auto- and hetero-suggestion, the mystery of the women was passed on from mother to daughter. In converts it could easily be picked up, as lending occult motive to superstitions which existed still among all peasant peoples, although already they were unrelated to remembered belief.

The religion of the conquered races, moreover, would be handed on through the women, even after the men had been exterminated.

The position of woman in medieval Europe was low, in spite of the cult of the Virgin Mary, the romantic protestations of the jongleurs, and many individual and geographical exceptions. This was, of course, inevitable in a consciously ascetic society. Yet it meant that many women probably resented their subjugation, and were, therefore, tinder for a competitive system in which the part of the woman was so important, and which, moreover, made sexual activities a proud mystery instead of drudgery. The cult would serve, too, as a psychological Cave of Adullam for emotional women, repressed women, masculine women, and those suffering from personal disappointment or from any nervous maladjustment which had for some reason not been resolved by the local resources of the Church. For despite all generalizations about racial backwash and theological reaction, the individual motives which persuaded any person to become a witch, other than those for whom it was merely the Old Religion – more natural than the new – must have been extremely complicated.

As well as the remaining Little People – the fairies who became witches and worshipped the old totems and observed the old ritual dating from palaeolithic times – there were, therefore, converts, a majority of whom were women. And, as well as these two components of the movement, there were intellectual diabolists. These men – and they were usually men – represented the other stream into which the original magic tradition had split. This had become highly specialized magic, exported from Egypt, joined with the mystic systems of the Near East, and was constantly outcropping as Manichaeism or one or other form of gnosticism. In the thirteenth century the

Black Book of Solomon passed from the Byzantine to the western world. The Kabbalah was still the secret of the Rabbis, but there were sorcerers and 'learned men', proto-scientists and philosophical heretics. The psychic and alchemical manipulator who sold himself to the Devil became a stock figure – old, bearded, rich, and the possessor of a beautiful daughter and numerous automata contrived in his underground laboratory, from which at night the noise of the furnaces drove away the trembling peasantry. Roger Bacon, Albertus Magnus, several popes, and quasi-mythical Doctor Faustus inspired generations to terror, Marlowe and Goethe to tragedy – and Hoffmann to considerable excesses.

Finally, there were what may be called the customers – those high personages who consulted with witches in order to poison their way to kingdoms, or those peasants who hoped that a local wise woman would help in the recovery of a strayed cow or lover. They were potential witches themselves, and punishable as such by the Church. And there were, all over Europe, even in the Middle Ages, charlatans who had a trick of palmistry or cheiromancy, allied to a glib tongue and a capacity for prompt escape when exposed.

The personnel of the witch movement may therefore be summarized as belonging to one or more of these groups:

(*a*) The surviving worshippers of the Old Religion of the horned god, the totem; the fairy people; the remaining hyperaesthetic stocks of the West.

(*b*) Women, because of the matriarchal stream in this cult tradition, because of their position in society, and because all fundamental beliefs pass always through women, particularly in primitive society and in suppressed racial units.

(*c*) Intellectuals and hyperaesthetic individuals generally, affected by the mystery religions of the East (later Catharism), reacting into parody of Christianity.

(*d*) Political and personal customers or exploiters of the cult.

All these types and persons were reacting from Christian asceticism into the earlier tradition of personal solution in the mass comradeship of the group, released in its worship. The group totem worship was degenerate, scattered, and probably often unsuccessful. It meant torture and frequently death if discovered: it did not even promise immortality. But to thousands it proved an apparently attractive – if ultimately miserable – alternative to Christianity. Although the Church refused to believe it in the face of much evidence, it was a religion, at all events in promise, of joy.

# 7

## Initiation

AT this stage it is possible to examine what seems to have happened when a man or woman joined the witch-cult during the later Middle Ages.

First, however, it may be necessary to say how we know about this, since the evidence is partial, presupposes a mental and material background of which we only have a limited comprehension, and much of it was, in any case, acquired by leading questions under the process of torture. The trials revealed a whole goetic system which public opinion gladly and firmly accepted as true, but which sceptics challenge on several main grounds.

The first of these is that the evidence was given under torture, and so is inadmissible. It is true that many of the witches were neurotic subjects who did not need any aid but their own distorted fancies to claim that they had taken part in hideous orgies. Today they would be writing obscene letters to curates, or practising the emotional masturbation of the Groupists. It also is true that there are few human beings who can resist protracted and hideous torture, without hope of sympathy or release. Sooner or later most people collapse to admit anything the interrogator demands, and to embellish as the maddened nerves and the imagination dictate. They are prepared, too, to implicate – in the hope of the mercy which the thirteenth-century Inquisitor was empowered to promise and then to refuse – as many of their neighbours as the relish of their torturers or the malice of their plight might suggest.

No doubt many of the witches did so break down. Many, perhaps, tormented, sleepless, and questioned, watched, confused, and terrified, convinced even their own minds that their simple village superstitions, their immemorial local customs, and their own personal irritation at the requirements of the Church did constitute sin with the Devil. They were, they might feel, in terrible error, and their neighbours with them. There can be few people of even liberal or mildly humanitarian views today who, under Fascist or similar torture, might not find that they were holders of views approximately Marxist. They would find themselves equally dangerous reactionaries under parallel treatment by a Communist tribunal. The Inquisitors of the fourteenth century were more dangerous than those of the twentieth, for they were more just, if equally cruel, as subtle, and quite as inflexible.

All this will be seen more clearly in discussing the actual processes of the trials.

Yet, in spite of the fact that some of the evidence was the insane screaming invention of the victims of rack and special pleading, and that torture and subtle examiners might even persuade the simpleton that he or she was lost, the evidence in the bulk still stands. For, in England, torture was never legally permitted, and even here the evidence conforms, very largely, with that of the Continent. Many witches gladly testified, in all countries, to the crimes which they were said to commit. Jane Bosdean, for instance, 'confessed freely and without torture and continued constant in it in the midst of the flames in which she burnt'. Witches, as much as their questioners, believed in their powers for evil, and confessed to the organizations which the Inquisitors believed to exist. Torture only muddied the issue by ensuring that a majority, whether guilty or not, conformed to the practices to which untortured members of the witch-cult had freely and even proudly confessed.

It has been mentioned that, like the martyrs of other religions, witches often appeared to resist appalling tortures in a state of some sort of hyperaesthesia which made them insusceptible to pain. Whether this was due to a psychic condition or physical preparations, it at all events argues against technical innocence.

Then it is claimed, in some ways reasonably enough, that the evidence is frankly unbelievable. The credibility of the evidence in the witch trials never worried the medieval world, which accepted miracles. After all, it was an age when the wedding ring of the Virgin Mary could be adored, as it was at

Perugia, without any sense of incongruity. St Sebastian had become multiplied so conveniently that his body was to be found and venerated in four separate places, and his head in two others, quite independently of the body, whilst the grey friars at Angers exhibited his brains – remarkably petrified, as it turned out when the case was eventually opened. The anti-papalists of the Reformation were delighted to draw attention to many such dubious relics. It is obvious that people who were happy – and no doubt did indeed derive strength in their faith – at these things, and revered the exhibition of milk from the breast of the Virgin Mother, or a feather from the Holy Ghost, would not find any difficulty with night-riding on broomsticks, copulation with cacodaemons, spitting of pins, and raising of storms, all of which were at least equally well attested.

Scepticism ever since has refused to accept most of these things. They have been felt to be frankly impossible – outside hallucination. This has been because of a revulsion of feeling and, equally important, of nomenclature. There were witches whose evidence was that of pathological dementia – who were inverted religiomaniacs, or victims of sexual repression and maladjustment. But, as anthropological examination has shown, there is at least a case for believing that many of the phenomena claimed by the witches were actually and literally as they reported them. For instance, when they said that they had copulated with the Devil they meant what we should explain as copulation with the personification of the Devil in the leader of the coven. In intent, and in terms of psychological experience, they had copulated with the Devil, as surely as the Christian had partaken of his god in the Holy Sacrament. The medieval judges were of their age, and more interested in the psychological experience and intention than in quibbling about the physical manifestations of it.

The strong sexual preoccupation of the trials is adduced too, as indicating a kind of hysterical prurience in the witnesses which could not agree with any facts. But this argument is easily refuted: first, because if the witch-cult was a phallic one, obviously its processes would themselves be orgiastic, and its secrets those of the increase or reverse of fecundity secondly, because the Church was by dogma an ascetic institution, and had the horrified fascination of its own repressions.

Then it is sometimes explained that the evidence of the witch trials was, quite simply, manufactured: that it was altogether a ridiculous invention, to which victims were tortured to confess although in fact there was nowhere a basis of fact or belief for the practices admitted.

An answer to this objection is possible, quite apart from the historical fact that so much of the machinery of the witch-cult bore attested connexion with the acknowledged practices of earlier religions and systems. Although there were local variations, the witches themselves, all over Europe, confessed, often freely, to practices which were substantially the same. If they had merely been wishing to commit suicide, or to please their judges, there is no reason why they should not have confessed to any other heresy, or invented quite diverse accounts of Satan and his requirements. That they did not, presupposes that these practices and requirements were, with minor differences, evidences of a general system which did actually exist. One feels this in spite of admitting that there were set patterns of question and answer, which might well elicit the general picture required by the examiners.

The early trials were conducted by sober and sincere men, with the highest regard for truth, as they saw it, and often of great compassion. These had no reason to send any people to a horrible death, other than their sincere belief that by doing so they were stamping out a damnable heresy which threatened the soul of Christendom. This is admitted by intelligent writers of every complexion, including such rationalists as Lecky. It is only the most ignorant and third-hand journalism which has ever pretended that the Inquisitors were cruel from anything but that cruellest of all motives, fanatical sincerity. It was when the cult was already declining, and scepticism had crept in, that we find the admittedly manufactured evidence of the travelling witchfinders and prickers, with their conjurers' bags of collapsible needles.

Finally, it may be pointed out that very much indeed of the evidence given at the medieval witch trials is borne out by the practices of the witches of the West Indies or the Congo today, who can hardly be supposed to have derived their practices from literary sources. There is as good reason to believe in a faith of witchcraft, and its practice, as there is in the belief of the Waldenses or, one might say, the Lollards. They all derive, of course, from the same sources.

The evidence of the trials will recur. But this has all been said to avoid the necessity for justifying each statement as the story proceeds. There were cataleptics, neurasthenics, and cranks, accused by their own folly, the ignorance of their neighbours, or the self-interest of blackmailers. But there were witches also who consciously sought to serve the Devil. Their evidence, suitably sifted, must – in the bulk – be accepted.

In early days, many children would be brought up as witches – members of the old but now illicit religion. Even as late as the seventeenth century, there is evidence from Lille of a girl of fifteen who said that 'her Mother had taken her with her when she was very young, and had even carried her in her arms to the Witches Sabbaths'. The same youthful initiation appears all over Europe, and in some parts was, no doubt, as natural as it was for the girls of St Joan's Domrémy to dance round the fairy tree there. In Britain, it was sometimes evidence of hanging importance that the mother of an accused had herself been a witch. Professor Murray gives several examples of the early age at which initiation took place, including the incident at Forfar in 1661, when Jonet Howat was so young when presented that 'the divell said, What shall I do with such a little bairn as she?' He soon found out, and she is later described as 'his bonny bird'.

Evidence about and by children is always particularly suspect as children's ingenious spite seems to have been responsible for many hideous convictions. But it is only natural that, where the cult was strong, children would be dedicated at birth, or, and this seems frequently to have happened, at the age of puberty, as is customary in all primitive religions. There may even have been, as in Christianity, a ceremony of infant baptism followed by a confirmation at puberty, when the deeper secrets would be revealed.

If not at birth, a witch would be recruited when it appeared to the local officer of the cult that she was in a susceptible frame of mind: or, she might fall to the blandishments of an ordinary member of the coven: or, she might be disappointed and unhappy, requiring the material aid of witchcraft, and seek out the Devil for herself. Even the good Catholic might be led away, for as Nicholas Remy* laments, 'For such as are given over to their lusts and to love he wins by offering them the hope of gaining their desires: or if they are bowed under the load of daily poverty, he allures them by some large and ample promise of riches: or he tempts them by showing them the means of avenging themselves when they have been angered by some injury or hurt received: in short, by whatever other corruption or luxury they have been depraved, he draws them into his power and holds them as it were bound to him.' It is very much the same warning which the opponents of both parties put out, in their early days, against the recruitment methods of the Nazis or the Communists.

There seems to have been a certain amount of blackmail and violence as well, in obtaining new members for the sect. Those who knew too much were liable to be 'carried away by the fairies', and in evidence there are many examples of the Devil twisting necks, burning houses, and threatening families in order to achieve a conversion. 'Therefore,' as Remy ends his chapter about it all, 'we may first conclude that it is no mere fable that witches meet and converse with Demons in very person. Secondly, it is clear that Demons use the two most powerful weapons of persuasion against the feeble wills of mortals, namely, hope and fear, desire and terror; for they well know how to induce and inspire such emotions.'

Naturally, the approach and the ceremonies of admission varied in detail everywhere. The tradition finally expired, as the witch became no more than the lonely exponent of village magic.

It may be interesting, as an English illustration of the later stage, to quote from a witch-tract of 1705,† giving the history

* The quotation is from Dr Montague Summers's edition of *Daemono-latria*.

† The authenticity of this tract is now doubted. It is, however, typical.

of two Northamptonshire witches executed in that year. It shows local bad-women who may or may not have been approached by a remaining representative of the cult. Being so late, it may only show the effect of local malice and persecution on two women who became crazy. But the account of their initiation at least represents what was usually felt to happen and to have happened on these occasions.

To proceed in order, I shall first begin with Ellinor Shaw (as being the most notorious of the two) who was Born at Cotterstock, within a small Mile of Oundle in Northamptonshire, of very obscure Parents, who not willing, or at least not able to give their Daughter any manner of Education; she was left to shift for her self at the age of 14 years, at which time she got acquainted with a Partener in Wickedness, one Mary Phillips, Born at Oundle aforesaid, with whom she held a friendly correspondence for several Years together, and Work'd very hard in a seeming honest way for a livelihood; but when she arriv'd to the age of 21 she began to be a very wicked Person talk'd of not only in the Town of Cotterstock where she was Born, but at Oundle, Glapthorn, Benefield, Southwick, and several Parts adjacent, and that as well by Children of four or five Years of Age, as Persons of riper Years; so that by degrees her Name became so famous, or rather infamous, that she could hardly peep out of her Door, but the Children would point at her in a Scoffing manner, saying, There goes a Witch, there's Nell the Strumpet, &c. which repeated Disgrace, agravated her Passion to such a degree, that she Swore she would be revenged on her Enemies, tho she pawn'd her Soul for the Purchase. To Mary Phillips her Partener in Knitting, who was as bad as her self in the Vices aforesaid she then communicated her Thoughts, relating to a Contract with the Devil. . . . In fine, as these two agreed in their Wickedness, to go Hand in Hand to the Devil together for Company; but out of a kind of Civility, he sav'd them that Trouble for he immediately waited upon 'em to obtain his Booty, on Saturday the 12th of February 1704, about 12 a Clock at Night (according to their own Confessions) appearing in the shape of a black tall Man, at whose approach they were very much startled at first, but taking Ellinor Shaw by the Hand he spoke thus, says he, be not afraid for having power given me to bestow it on whom I please, I do assure you, that if you will pawn your Souls to me for only a Year and two Months, I will for all that time assist you in whatever you desire: Upon which he produced a little piece of Parchment, on which by their Consents (having prick't their Fingers ends) he wrote the Infernal Covenant in their own Blood, which they signed with their own Hands, after which he told them they were now as substantial Witches as were any in the World, and that they had power by the assistance of the Imps, that he would send them to do what Mischief they pleased.

The tract goes on to enumerate their crimes, and ends with their confessions – apparently extracted without any torture. Indeed 'as they liv'd the Devils true Factors, so they resolutely Dyed in his Service, to the Terror of all People who were eye Witnesses of their dreadful and amazing Exits'.

The three chief requirements of the novice were a free consent to the process of becoming a witch – sometimes subsequent to persuasive violence of the sort which was, no doubt, responsible for some free confessions later on. Then, denial of the new or Catholic faith, and, finally, a signing of the pact with the Devil. There followed attendance at the sabbat, and also initiatory practices which have their contemporary parallels in the Masonic and other Orders, and in the more backward English public schools or advanced American universities.

It is now time to discuss the pact with the Devil, and the witch mark. The pact might be either expressed or tacit, although the authorities disagree upon what they mean by these terms. The general sense seems, however, to have been, either that there was a direct vow to the Devil himself, in the person of the local master of the coven or his deputy – or a symbolic burning of the theological boats, as when a person 'useth the Words or Signs which Sorcerers use, knowing them to be such'. In other words, there was formal entry into the coven, or there was personal desertion of Christianity and adoption of magic ritual, which might have nothing to do with the organized cult at all. This private practitioner we can leave to her herbal magic, and the coming of the eighteenth century. The notice to the coven, however, had to undergo interesting processes, although these differed in various parts of Europe, as they differ in Africa today.

It appears that the witch had to be introduced formally before the coven, much as a member for Parliament is in the

House. This sponsoring, as well as being a precaution for securing secrecy and trustworthiness, may have been continued as a parody of the Christian practice of employing godparents. But security was the important reason for having an introducer, since people from witch families, more particularly men, were often admitted without this precaution.

First, the new witch denied the Christian faith and baptism, sometimes gratuitously emphasizing the sincerity of this by insulting the Virgin Mary (known as the Anomalous Woman), spitting on the Cross, and so on. This was followed by vows to the adopted god, the Devil. As time went on, he was the Christian Devil, but earlier he was more perceptibly the old fertility god, and the witches vowed themselves his not only soul, but body and soul. The process was pantomimed in the custom of the Scottish witches of putting one hand to the crown of the head, and the other on the sole of the foot, and dedicating to the service of the Master all that lay in between the two hands. Professor Murray quotes a case where a pregnant woman excepted the unborn child, and the Devil was very angry.

After this, there sometimes followed a ceremony of baptism, but this was in all probability a parody of the Christian rite – the mere giving of a name in Satan to counteract the possession of a name in Christ. At the same time, the possession of a secret name has always given a sense of power, as is recognized by small boys who call themselves Big Chief Laughing Fox or Scarface, and businessmen who join Elk societies and do almost the same. The Christian name itself was a secret one in the early days of the Church. Professor Murray has analysed the Christian names of witches and feels that the predominant ones, Joan, Isobel, and so on, are not those most common in general society at the period considered. This implies that witch societies probably avoided normally such very Christian names as Temperance, Faith, or Mary. At the same time, an additional Devil-name was clearly desirable. They were sometimes mere changes, as Margaret or Christine for Janet: sometimes the name was a nickname: 'weill dancing Janet', 'Able and Stout', 'Naip', 'Rob the Rowar' for one Robert Grierson who kept the rolls. In Scotland, the name was considered of the first importance, even where it was of a quite ridiculous sort – 'Pickle-nearest-the-Wind', 'Batter-them-down Maggy', or 'Blow-Kate'. Yet it never had the same significance in England, and in some instances several of the witches could not remember what names they had been given.

All this should be clearly distinguished from the fact that the ordinary surnames of the witches mentioned in the trials often sound ridiculous to the modern ear, which inclines us therefore to feel the whole evidence slightly grotesque. But it must be remembered that most late medieval names sound odd to us, even where the holders were dull dogs like John Jentleman, Ralph Jolebody, and John Stoutlock. Seventeenth-century names are even more curious.

The actual written covenant was another fairly late introduction, as clearly it can have formed no part of the earliest palaeolithic practice. At the same time, it is, equally, not a mere copy of Christian practice, since the signing of a Covenant does not appear there. Probably it was used to impress the solemnity of the occasion upon the half-literate. It certainly made it more solemn if the witch was caught, for a signed document appealed, as nothing else could, to the examiners. The contract was said to be signed in the novice's own blood, which is possible enough, for as Professor Murray says: 'It seems clear that part of the ceremony of initiation was the cutting of the skin of the candidate to the effusion of blood. This is the early rite, and it seems probable that when the written contract came into vogue the blood was found to be a convenient writing fluid, or was offered to the Devil in the form of a signature.' Blood has always been the most irrevocable medium, and there are many historic examples of its use. German university freshmen, as well as slitting each other's faces in the cause of culture, used also to sign leaves in each other's autograph albums with their own blood.

Most witches, of course, were unable to write, but they would then make their marks, as did the Somerset witches. Elizabeth Style explained, in 1664, how the Devil 'promised her Mony, and that she should live gallantly, and have the pleasure of the World for Twelve years, if she would with her Blood sign his Paper, which was to give her Soul to him'. Some few pacts with the Devil survive in museums in different parts of the world, and the theme is a favourite one in literature. The term of years which the contractor received before being carried off was not constant, and a fortunate Ann Arydon 'had a lease for fifty yeares of the divill, whereof (in 1673) ten ar expired' but the usual term was much shorter, and often seems to have been seven, with an option of renewal. As is indicated later, some of this may be post-rationalization after the Faustian myth had become known in Great Britain.

The ceremony sometimes proceeded with a sacrifice, usually black, and often a hen. The witch bound him or herself in vassalage to the Devil, and undertook to attend the appropriate meetings, make converts, and generally do as instructed. The name being entered in the Black Book or Roll, which was kept by the Master of the Coven or even by the Grand Master of the District, and obeisance having been paid, the witch received a Mark from the Devil.

This Mark which the Devil made upon the witch was regarded, when discovered by the examiners, as final and irrefutable evidence of guilt. The result was that there was a great tendency to find these marks when they clearly were not the true witch mark at all, but merely minor deformities or hardenings of the skin which were insensitive, or which did not bleed, when prodded with a pin. Initiates claim that most of us have insensitive spots, although finding them demands great skill. At all events, when a mark had been discovered, and had been pricked without bleeding or appearing to cause pain to the accused (who was blindfolded for this part of the investigation), conviction followed more or less automatically. The test for the mark was particularly regarded in the British Isles.

There were, of course, natural phenomena which were, especially by the time of the seventeenth century, mistaken for witch marks.

First were old scars which had hardened. Guazzo tells how 'At Brindisi in November 1590, when Claudia Bogarta was about to be tortured, she was closely shaved, as the custom is, and so a scar was exposed on the top of her bare brow. The Inquisitor then suspecting the truth, namely, that it was a mark made by the Devil's claw, which had before been hidden by her hair, ordered a pin to be thrust deep into it; and when this was done she neither felt any pain, nor did so much as a drop of blood come from the wound. Yet she persisted in denying the truth, saying that her insensitiveness was caused by an old blow from a stone.' Later, under torture, to Guazzo's pious gratification she broke down and confessed to 'abominable crimes'. But it may well have been that there was a hardening of the skin round an old scar; and pins were probably intruded longitudinally, not directly inwards.

Birthmarks, corns of various sorts, haemorrhoids, warts, and other protrusions and malformations, whether sensitive or not, could often be identified, by a malicious or credulous examiner, as either nipples for the feeding of familiars or as Devil marks.

Other criminal evidences would be supernumerary breasts: the 'little teat' of the witnesses. These occurred in various parts of the body, and were supposed to secrete milk and to give suck to familiars. The accused used on occasion to cut them off before being examined, in an attempt to elude conviction. Almost certainly they were the additional breasts (the condition of polymastia) or additional nipples (that of polythelia) fairly common in medical observation. The great anthropologist* Klaatsch, says, after pointing out that most mammals have a number of breasts, that 'there is still almost constantly at least one additional breast, above the real breast, even in the case of European women. It has no teat, and very rarely gives milk. It can almost always be seen on the breast of a well-formed woman; and classical statues like the Venus of Milo show it.' The mother of Alexander Severus was called Mammaea because of this phenomenon, and it is interesting to know that Anne Boleyn also had a supernumerary breast, although I have not discovered whether this was quoted as evidence against her when Henry VIII accused her of sorcery.

* One has to be reminded of his eminence, for, frankly, the phenomenon is hardly one of common remark.

At all events, the thing is still common enough, and Professor Murray quotes an experiment in which 315 people, taken indiscriminately and in succession, showed over seven per cent to have a supernumerary nipple.

One example of this sort of mark will be enough. Alice Gooderidge and her mother, Elizabeth Wright, came up for trial in 1597:

> The old woman they stript, and found behind her right sholder a thing much like the udder of an ewe that giveth sucke with two teates, like vnto two great wartes, the one behinde vnder her armehole, the other a hand off towardes the top of her sholder. Being demanded how long she had those teates, she answered she was borne so. Then did they search Alice Gooderidge, and found vpon her belly, a hole of the bignesse of two pence, fresh and bloudy, as though some great wart had beene cut off the place.

There is one other point about 'natural' marks. Witches were sometimes examined by a panel of matrons. In the coarser venom of the seventeenth century, however, they were examined in public, and it is possible that the psychological shock may have given temporary physical insensitivity. Here is an example from Newcastle-on-Tyne, in 1649:

> The said reputed witch-finder acquainted Lieutenant-Colonel Hobson that he knew women, whether they were witches or no by their looks, and when the said person was searching of a personable, and good like woman, the said Colonel replyed and said, surely this woman is none, and need not be tried, but the Scotch-man said she was, for the Town said she was, and therefore he would try her; and presently in sight of all the people, laid her body naked to the waste, with her cloaths over her head, by which fright and shame, all her blood contracted into one part of her body, and then he ran a pin into her thigh, and then suddenly let her coats fall, and then demanded whether she had nothing of his in her body but did not bleed, but she being amazed replied little, then he put his hand up her coats, and pulled out the pin and set her aside as a guilty person, and child of the Devil, and fell to try others, whom he made guilty.

Lieutenant-Colonel Hobson perceiving the alteration of the foresaid woman, by her blood settling in her right parts, caused that woman to be brought again, and her cloathes pulled up to her thigh, and required the Scot to run the pin into the same place, and then it gushed out of blood, and the said Scot cleared her, and said she was not a child of the Devil.

The pricker was ultimately exposed and hanged, after confessing that he had caused the death of 220 women, at 20*s*. a time.

These are examples from the days of hideous and professional witch-hunting, when the cult was very nearly over, and hatred, ignorance, and superstition prompted most of the trials. There remains, however, the Witch's Mark proper, which can certainly have been a genuine sign of the cult.

Primitive communities have from the earliest times practised tattooing: in light-coloured peoples by marking the skin through rubbing matter into holes pricked in the skin, in darker peoples by cicatrization – that is, inserting mud under the skin until a ridge is raised in the required pattern. Tattooing normally takes place as part of the initiation ceremonial. Procopius says that Christians had a cross, or monogram of Christ tattooed in this way on their wrists, and I have seen it in Iraq today.*

It seems possible that this common palaeolithic custom was continued as part of the witch ritual, and witches were scratched or bitten by the master devil of the coven, who would then rub the wound, inserting some colouring irritant which effected a more or less permanent mark. If cicatrization were practised as well, it might help to explain the alleged insensitivity, as a pin passed longitudinally into a mud-packed ridge of skin would be practically painless, and moreover would not draw blood.

At all events, a mark of some kind was definitely made. It was sometimes red, and sometimes blue (recalling the notorious woad of the early British). Occasionally the Devil is described as inflicting the wound with his teeth, and sometimes

* As an example, on Jesus, the barman at the Regent Hotel, in Baghdad. He introduced himself as 'me Jesus: inside Asia'. (*Inside Asia* was a book by an American journalist, Mr Gunther, in which he had been mentioned.) He explained that 2,000 years ago 'everyone in Baghdad Christian' – a nice prevision.

with his 'claws', and it gave considerable pain which might last for some time. Often it was a mark described as being like a flea-bite, small and circular, but sometimes, and particularly in eastern France, where the witches were normally marked on the left shoulder, it might be in the shape of a hare's footprint, or like a dog, a toad, a bat, a mouse, or some other creature. Elsewhere it might be concealed, and Delrio, writing in 1599, says 'In men it may often be seen under the eyelids, under the lips, under the armpits, on the shoulders, on the fundament; in women, moreover, on the breast or on the pudenda.' Professor Murray quotes several accounts, from the trials, of the infliction of the mark. Here are one or two: a witch of Yarmouth, in 1644, whom a tall black man told 'he must first see her Hand: and then taking out something like a Pen-knife, he gave it a little scratch, so that Blood followed, and the Mark remained to that time': Jonet ('bonny birde') Howat of Forfar, whom 'the devil kist and niped her vpon one of hir shoulders, so as shoe hade great paine for some tyme thereafter'. The Somerset witches, tried in 1664, were marked on the fingers, but John Reid of Renfrewshire in 1696 had 'a Bite or Nipp in his Loyn, which he found painfull for a Fortnight'.

It must be admitted that the hyperaesthesia of the spots inflicted has, in spite of various suggestions, never been satisfactorily explained. Another point which has not been stressed is that the witches were probably given some kind of drug at the time of their initiation. There are various accounts of people who enter the fairy kingdom and emerge after what appears to have been a short and paradisal period to find that a long time has in fact passed – the story of Thomas the Rhymer is an instance. There are numerous cases of the Devil giving money which, after he had gone, was shown to be mere rubbish or stones. There is ample evidence of excitement and hysteria. Now, ignoring for the moment possibilities of hypnotic or similar control, it is perfectly conceivable that a drug of some sort was administered. This is still done at the initiation ceremonies of West African secret societies, which in other respects closely parallel the recorded witch ritual. The West African has dreams of glory and happiness, loses all time sense, and returns to the tribe marked and devoted to the secret cult.

Before the days of the witch persecutions, thousands of men and women must have been initiated, year after year, with the full ceremonies of which these disjointed traces remain. Even the traces were enough, from the fourteenth century onwards, to damn their descendants, and the memory was enough to convict thousands of deformed innocents.

When the initiation was completed, a witch had been made.

# 8

## The Witch God

THEOLOGICALLY speaking, the Devil was first defined by the Council of Toledo in A.D. 447.

Nevertheless, the stock picture of the Devil has been recognizable throughout history, and still remains: a large black monstrous apparition with horns on his head, cloven hoofs – or one cloven hoof – ass's ears, hair, claws, fiery eyes, terrible teeth, an immense phallus, and a sulphurous smell. In this alarming disguise he appeared in the early Ethiopian *Book of Saints*, rashly revealed himself to a succession of pious ecclesiastics, delighted the audiences of the miracle plays and the masques, and proceeded, with the accretions dictated by the ingenuity of individual illustrators, into modern iconography. It is clearly the gothic embellishment of the combined idea of the classical satyr and the palaeolithic horned god. It was also, during the Middle Ages themselves, the literal description of the god of the witches, as he appeared to his worshippers at the sabbat.

It was shown earlier that the horned god of the primitive palaeolithic peoples, known in a number of different forms everywhere, took on an especial significance in Mesopotamia and Egypt, where he became associated with the whole ancient magical system. The same representation, with modifications, was revealed in Greece and in the later Mediterranean cultures. Finally most of the forms of the Old Religion resolved themselves again into a half-conscious alliance against Christianity. Christianity, as a matter of policy, included many old rites, festivals, and beliefs. But it relentlessly opposed magic and the fertility religions, since it was itself the product of an ascetic stage of culture. It fought the religion of the horned god. It still fights him when it combats the religions and the secret societies of Africa or of the African communities in the Americas. For, substantially, the ritual, and even the appearance of the god of the witches, was that of the high priest of African cults today. Their reindeer is a water buffalo perhaps, and their ritual does not consciously parody Christianity in the same way as did the cult in Europe. But the symbolism, the magical processes, and the diabolic appearance must be extremely similar.

As well as being the primitive horned god of the fertility cults, the god of the witches, already infected with dualistic ideas and those of a later symbolism, was also Dianus or Janus, the two-faced representative of the double side of the god-like nature – good and evil. He was memories of all the evil powers represented as black – Pluto, Set, the Northern Loki, Ahriman, the Jewish Satan, and aspects of Siva the Destroyer. He was associated with the local animal cults as well. He was a parody of the Christian representation of the Almighty. He was Pan. He was sometimes mixed with the Eastern conception of the djinn. He was a composite.

In the circumstances, it is surprising that a type devil emerges at all from the varying traditions and the theological morasses. When he does so it is as man, woman, or animal.

Throughout most primitive religions it has been customary for the god to be apparent to his followers at various supreme festivals. The king, witch-doctor, or priest, leader in the sacred dance, becomes for all practical purposes the godhead. In the most primitive totem tribes, all become the totem animal, but one, more closely identified with him than any other, is the leader, to whom the others become chorus. The process is discernible in the Christian Church. This leader assumed the disguise of the animal – horned or not – by the assumption of a mask, skins, claws, false hoof, shoes – even stilts – and whatever more was wanted to make him at once terrible in himself and recognizably the archetype of the totem animal. In this disguise he would come to the sacred festivals, appear suddenly and horribly when the proper setting had been created, and conduct the rites – no doubt much of the time in a possessed condition.

This chief priest of the cult, and high devil of the vicinity, might perhaps be someone remote from the ordinary life of the locality, or perhaps well known in it, much as a Master Free-mason today may be an undistinguished auctioneer, with high powers only revealed to the initiate at the appointed occasion, though he is equipped with means of making himself known to brethren at all times. The machinery of most secret societies – and witchcraft was a secret society – is alike, partly because they often derive from a common origin. Here is a description of such a leader:

He may be a well-known or little-known person in his district, living normally most of his days, and coming into ordinary daily contact with his officers and members, the majority not knowing, and others not telling, his society importance. During the few hours of the few days of each year when he assumes the livery of his office, his disguise will be as impenetrable as the closed armour of the knights of old.

This is the description of the Head Official of a West African secret society today.* It as aptly describes the position of the chief priest – who became on occasion the god – of the early witches.

The evidence collected by Professor Murray about the appearance of the Devil as a man is extensive: so much so that it seems impertinent to dip into it, and certainly wrong to copy it at length, whilst it is unnecessary to quote extensively other evidence of the same sort from the trials. This is the sort of entry: John Walsh of Dorsetshire, in 1566, saw the Devil 'sometymes like a man in all proportions, sauing that he had cloven feete'.

Margaret Johnson, of Lancashire, in 1633, as 'a spirit or divell in the similitude and proportion of a man, apparelled in a suite of black, tyed about with silke pointes'.

A witch of Yarmouth, in 1644, 'when she was in Bed, heard one knock at her Door, and rising to her Window, she saw, it being Moonlight, a tall black man there'.

Joan Wallis of Keiston, Huntingdon, in 1646, 'confessed the Devill came to her in the likenesse of a man in blackish cloathing, but had cloven feet'.

* Captain F. W. Butt-Thompson, *West African Secret Societies*.

Ann Armstrong of Northumberland, in 1673, 'she see the said Ann Forster (with twelve others and) a long black man rideing on a bay galloway, as she thought, which they call'd there protector'.

Bessie Dunlop of Ayrshire, who it will be remembered also met the matronly Queen of Elfhane, was particularly full in her description: 'ane honest wele elderlie man, gray bairdit, and had ane gray coitt with Lumbart slevis of the auld fassown: ane pair of gray brekis, and quhyte schankis, gartarit aboue the kne; ane blak bonet on his heid, cloise behind and plane befoir, with silkin laissis drawin throw the lippis thairof; and ane quhyte wand in his hand'.

Agnes Sampson of North Berwick is eloquently reported as stating, 'The deuell was cled in ane blak gown with ane blak hat vpon his head. . . . His faice was terrible, his noise lyk the bek of ane egle, gret bourning eyn; his handis and leggis wer herry, with clawes vpon his handis, and feit lyk the griffon.'

In France, Belgium, and even Salem in North America, the evidence is much the same: the sombre clothes, the hat, the garters, and the great burning eyes. Sometimes the Devil is described as an elderly man, and sometimes as a young and handsome one; very occasionally as a woman.

The evidence of the trials is, it must always be remembered, of a comparatively late period. But various things emerge from it quite clearly. The Devil – that is to say his personification – normally went about, and approached the members of the coven or those it was intended to recruit, in the normal dress of the period but with significant modifications. He was usually, one would expect, a mature person who had, no doubt, served a lengthy apprenticeship to the cult. On occasion, however, he might be young, and where there was more than one high official in any given locality, it would obviously be the young one who was used to approach those women whose distemper with orthodox religion was likely to be increased by the attraction of exaggerated diabolic masculinity.

The Queen of Elfhane, Maid Marian, Diana, the dedicated Virgin, and the wanton goddess of love and motherhood were also united in a representative high official. Today, in the secret societies of Africa, the supreme official is sometimes a woman. Although this form was perhaps an early one, the tradition would persist. It is even possible that officials would sometimes be sexual freaks – hermaphrodites and androgynae – always regarded with awe, and sometimes with reverence, in a phallic society. The wearing of the clothes appropriate to the opposite sex was always one of the rites of witchcraft, as it has been and is of primitive peoples, during their fertility festivals, throughout the history of the world.

The walking-out dress, so to speak, was normally of a sombre colour. It is usually given as black or grey, occasionally particoloured, and occasionally of the fairy colour green. Very rarely it is described as white. In the British Isles particular attention was paid by the witches, in their description, to the tall hat worn. This may, therefore, have been part of the recognized uniform – the hood already referred to in describing the place of Robin à Hood in the witch tradition, or a modification of this to come into line with seventeenth-century ideas of head-dressing.* The word hood may itself sometimes have meant a mask, however. The ceremony of hodening was carried on until within living memory in some country districts in England, when a dancer wore a white sheet and a horse's head. Miss Christina Hole writes, 'I have been told by many who saw him in their childhood that this man-horse, leaping and prancing and snapping the hinged jaws of the head was a truly alarming spectacle on a dark November night.'

Garters, too, are often mentioned in the evidence as a particular feature of the Devil's equipment. They were, for some reason, imbued with a special significance from the earliest times, and a stock picture of palaeolithic ritual shows long garters worn under the knees of the otherwise naked sorcerer. They are worn by conventionally dressed Morris dancers, even today. The garter, especially when red, has carried on its

---

* Compare *Hamlet* III: 4:

> What devil was't
> That thus hath cozened you at hoodman blind?

The game of Hoodman Blind, or Blind Man's Buff, was by origin religious.

mystical qualities in Brittany and Dorset, to give only two examples, and is still spoken of as a means to bewitching cattle or, by anti-magic, defending against a spell. It is a recurrent feature of legend and fairy story. In the Middle Ages, and even later, it was also used by the witch group as symbolic evidence of their responsibility for the murder of members who it was feared would confess, or whom it was for any other reason desirable to 'liquidate'. The body would be found strangled in prison, with a lace or garter tied loosely round the neck – a device which, in derivation, has proved a great boon to generations of detective-story writers.

As a pendant to this note of the emphasis on the garter – or 'pointes' – in the witch story, it should be added that Professor Murray traced the origin of the Order of the Garter, itself, to the witch-cult. The traditional story is of the Countess of Salisbury's garter falling down during a ball, to the dismay and embarrassment of all. Edward III, filled with virtue and a prophetic vision of the principles of Dr Arnold of Rugby, then picks up the garter, glowers round the room, pins it to his own leg, cries '*Honi soit qui mal y pense*', and founds a knightly order without a moment's hesitation. This moral little fable is ridiculous enough without remembering that, as Professor Murray points out, it took more than a slipped garter to flutter the modesty of a fourteenth-century court lady. It *is* interesting, however, if the garter was recognizably the sign of membership of the witch-cult, especially as the order which Edward founded was of twelve knights for himself and twelve for the Prince of Wales – two covens of thirteen. Moreover, the King's mantle, as Chief of the Order, was powdered over with 168 garters, which with that worn on his leg makes 169, or thirteen times thirteen, a high magical number. This ingenious implication is slightly invalidated by the fact that garters had been particularly in fashion for several years. However, Miss Murray's suggestion is attractive, and shoes with cleft toes, bitterly condemned by the Church, were, perhaps not entirely by coincidence, in vogue at much the same period.

The tall hat, the black clothes, the outstanding garters, and even the cloven shoes might be worn by the high priest, the Devil's human vehicle, for more or less conventional appearance to his flock. He might even assume a not too elaborate mask. But full-dress appearances would call for far more terrible mechanics.

The mask was, in early times, part of the head-dress of the leader of the totem dance. Sometimes even today a witch-doctor assumes the actual skeleton of an animal's head, with the horns attached. It is interesting to note the Irish folk memory of the witch-people – the Formorians – said to have come across the seas from Africa as monsters with the heads of horses or goats. From Tibet to South America the witch-doctor still wears a mask of elaborate frightfulness, as a symbol of his power and office. Even the Christian bishop's mitre has been apocryphally derived from the fish-head of the priests of Dagon. Frequently, today, the mask bears horns, and – as is significant when the dualistic idea mixed up with witch belief is remembered – it sometimes has two faces.

In the medieval cult, the evidence for the mask seems complete. First of all, by hypothesis, it is what one would expect of a religion with a strong palaeolithic ancestry. Then the practices of the classical world would confirm the custom, since the mask was freely employed in the Greek and Roman theatre, itself deriving from religious origin. It is sometimes said to have had a megaphonic effect which helped project the voice to the back of the huge open-air theatres. Next there is the evidence of the witches themselves. The Scottish witches said of the Devil that he spoke 'low but big'; that his voice 'was hough and goustie'; those of Alsace that 'their Demons spoke as if their mouths were in a jar or cracked pitcher' or else 'their voice is feeble and weak'. The same is true in the analogy of the witch-doctors of Africa, some of whose masks have definitely the effect of megaphones, whilst others merely obscure and distort the voice.* Finally, there is the Dorset Ooser, a painted wood mask with horns, which was worn over

* They also are said to possess various ventriloquial powers, and, in any case, the note of the voice changes in the true state of 'possession'. These circumstances may also have been true of the witch-god-priests.

the head, while the rest of the body was covered in skins. It was stolen within the last forty years, but it seems quite clear that there was a definite connexion between it and palaeolithic practice, carried on as part of a rustic ritual. It, too, had horns. The wearing of masks is described as normally taking place at the Feast of Fools, a fertility rite allowed to continue all over Europe until a very late period. At this 'priests and clerks may be seen wearing masks and monstrous visages at the hours of office. They dance in the choir dressed as women, or disreputable men, or minstrels. They sing wanton songs. They eat black puddings at the altar itself. . . .' The parallels are obvious.

For what it is worth, there is another interesting point. The word mascot, a good-luck sign, has almost certainly a common origin with mask and masque. But the staid *Encyclopaedia Britannica* hazards also that it derives from a Portuguese word, *mascotto*, meaning 'witchcraft'.

As well as the mask, which was so often in the form of an animal, the body was also covered with skins, hair, paint, charms, ointments, and the general make-up of the witch-doctor. After all, this was what the early Fathers had inveighed against. Frequently, too, the appearance would be shaped into a more exact representation of the two-faced Janus or Dianus. There are various pictures of this, and in many of them the second face is attached to the Devil's seat. It was this mask which the members of the coven kissed in the course of the ritual, when we read in the trials of witches 'kissing the Devil's fundament'. The implied idea of humility probably made the procedure of obeisance customary whether this mask was worn or not, and the salute has passed into gutter idiom. There seems little doubt that the Devil, when dressed and masked, did frequently wear such a face under his tail.

This mask, and the covering of hard leather in which the Devil was encased, helps to explain another common report of the Devil, as evidenced in the trials – his intense personal coldness. Margaret Murray gives numerous quotations evidencing this, as Agnes Sampson's story of how 'The deuell caused all the company to come and kiss his ers, quhilk they said was cauld like yce; his body was hard lyk yrn, as they thocht that handled him.' He was frequently described as being exceptionally and painfully cold in copulation, and probably, like the priests of various Oriental sects, used an artificial phallus, since he could obviously not serve all the female worshippers naturally. This would be the more necessary if, as was possible, he was a homosexual.

As well as in the form of a man the Devil also appeared as an animal. Having established that the Devil of the witches was normally the head of the local cult, either wearing a disguise or not, it is not necessary to set out at any great length exactly what animal forms these disguises took. In order to clarify, however, it may be noted that the animal manifestations in the history of witchcraft represent three different things – actual animals, reverenced as totems; members of the cult disguised as and simulating these animals; and, finally, domestic familiars – an entirely different phenomenon.

The second of these groups has been dealt with first, because the fact is not generally recognized that when a witch said that she saw a devil, all that she saw was the local leader of the cult, or one of his helpers. Most people still feel that an apparition with horns and a tail was either hallucination or fancy.

The third group, domestic familiars, more properly comes later.

There remain the totem animals.

When the origin of witchcraft is remembered, the identification of the master of the witches and the totem animal is not surprising. When Holy Church could solemnly try animals in court for causing breaches of the peace, and burn a cock for the biological extravagance and theological heresy of laying an egg, the Unholy Convocation of Satan could certainly worship a horse. It did, in fact, worship almost every kind of animal, although the horned types somewhat predominate. Naturally, those animals reasonably well known were more likely to survive as condensers of emotion than unknown ones, so that the Hebrides revered the seal as whole-heartedly as Ireland did the pig.

The bull's form is one of the most widespread in Europe. The tradition remained strong in the British Isles, and bull-baiting, carried on into the nineteenth century, certainly had a religious origin, presumably linking it with the bull-fighting of Spain and southern France. Where Spain and France, however, celebrate a late Mediterranean form of the bull symbol as exemplified in Mithraism, in the British Isles it carries on directly from the druidic oxen. It may not be too whimsical to reflect that the national identification with the bulldog, embodiment of invincible ugliness and illogical loyalties, itself derives from this source. It is unnecessary to show the link with the Egyptian and indeed the whole neolithic preoccupation with totems of horned cattle, either as oxen or in the sacred Isis cow.

There are a number of references in the trials to what in the Scottish instances are usually called 'beists'. A typical example is that in which at Aberdeen in 1597 Marion Grant confessed that 'the Devill apperit . . . sumtyme in the scheap of a beist, and sumtyme in the scheap of a man'. Sometimes he was only a sacred calf.

The goat is the classical form of the witch god, although this disguise does not appear at all in the British Isles. The symbol is, of course, the Mendes of the Egyptian decadence, a combination of faun, satyr, and the goat-god Pan. (The dionysiac frenzies of his worshippers, the proto-witches of the Mediterranean, give us the word 'panic', and a 'tragedy' was originally a goat-song.) The Devil often appeared in Lorraine as a goat, sometimes with a candle between his horns. Usually he was black.

Occasionally, and more especially in France, the Devil was a sheep. This may have been because sheep-skin was easier to come by, or in parody, possibly, of the Paschal lamb. It was, however, probably a variant of the goat form.

The form of a horse was fairly common in the British Isles, and the Devil rides on a Great Horse into much of the evidence. Seeing that he was probably of a better social status than the rest of the worshippers, this is not particularly remarkable. But the signs of horse worship all over the British Isles, from the dragon-horse of Uffington to the hobby-horse-dragon of Padstow in Cornwall makes the horse disguise one to be expected. The hobby-horse itself has a disreputable pedigree, and will be shown as one of the components of the broomstick.

The cat and the bear and the stag and the boar and the dog all have their place in the trials, and the wolf the special chapter of lycanthropy. But, although witches turned into hares* and some country people still hesitate to kill them for that reason, and although they were so sacred that Caesar tells us the Britons in his day never hunted them, yet the Devil, for some reason, is never chronicled as a hare.

The leaders of the dance who were the personification of the Devil, who identified themselves with these animals and wore their skins, who bayed or howled and muttered through masks, are not usually known. Some, perhaps, were caught and killed. Many probably escaped, literally to pass on their mantles to another prepared adept. Many no doubt died in their beds, unsuspected. A few were great lords or scholars, led – by reading the forbidden books, and the magic of the East, filtering back through the heresies of the intelligentsia or the credulity of the Crusaders – to direct the remains of the great pre-Christian folk religion they found still evidenced in peasant Europe. Very few indeed – de Rais, Bothwell, Rosimond, the Wise Man of Farnham, Hanchemond, or the Rev. George Burroughs of Salem, conceivably Joan of Arc – are actual names, even to scholars, today. Even Joan of Arc, if she really was a witch, as Professor Murray essays to demonstrate, must have been a symbol rather than an active practitioner. She may have heard voices and worn men's clothes – and transvestism was a sign of the cult. But it is wildly improbable that she ever wore a goat-skin.

In 1584, in a list of eighty-seven suspected persons, we read of 'Ould Birtles, the great devil'. But we know no more of him.

* In this connexion it is fascinating to remember the authenticated story of hares which, standing on their hind legs, dance in circles of several at a time, during certain seasons. I have met countrymen who have seen this.

This chapter has dealt with the historic devil as revealed in the witch trials. But the witches themselves sometimes, and their opponents almost always, mixed him with something else. It has been shown throughout that the mystical tradition of the Devil as the other nature of God, the dark force of evil, took on a name and a personality early in human thought. Wherever opposition to Christianity, or indeed to any orthodox religion, was found, therefore, the Devil was recognized. And so the Devil of the witches, the sulphurous masked human or nearly animal figure of hair, wax, and horn, was given the name of the theological concept. He became, familiarly, Old Nick. He became, more terrifically and powerfully, Lucifer, Beelzebub, Satan, Apollyon, Asmodeus, Abaddon, the Prince of Darkness, and the Foul Fiend himself.

He had been so from the earliest times, for we are told that, after the initiate to the Eleusinian mysteries had passed his various ordeals, had seen and touched the Holy Things, and was qualified, the final and awful secret was vouchsafed to him. At a flying pace a priest brushed by him, and breathed into his ear the ultimate mystery: 'Osiris is a Black God.'

This is the historical reconstruction of the nursery devil who has for centuries been employed to frighten children. So it was with sixteenth-century Reginald Scot, who complains, 'In our childhood our mother's maids have so terrified us with an ugly devil having horns on his head, fire in his mouth, a tail in his breech, eyes like a bison, fangs like a dog, a skin like a nigger, a voice roaring like a lion, whereby we start and are afraid when we hear one call "Boh".'

Now it was with the cry of 'Boh catch him' that my grandmother used to tease me as a child at the beginning of the twentieth century. Poor dear, she was very old, and worn out by begetting nineteen children, including one set of triplets and two of twins, but even when in her right mind she probably never knew that Boh was a name for the Devil. Yet it was.

# 9

## The Organization of the Cult

SEVERELY scientific writers and gravely theological ones agree in seeing the medieval witch-cult as at times reaching the dimensions of an organized counter-religion. This is natural. The severely scientific have been able to show that there was indeed a cult – a fact which had been popularly pooh-poohed – and are anxious to demonstrate that they know all about it. The gravely theological claim roundly that witch-craft was only extirpated by the Church after a tremendous struggle, and argue that it is certainly better to have over-thrown an organized Satan than one of only occasional and disconnected appearances. Montague Summers had no doubts that 'the witches were a vast political movement, an organized society, which was anti-social and anarchical, a world-wide plot against civilization'. To Professor Murray, witchcraft was an underground pre-Christian religion perhaps directed, at any given moment, by a supreme and recognized head. It is all very tidy.

Yet the evidence is always dubious. It has been emphasized that depositions at those trials of which we have record, and the opinions of even the earliest of professed demonologists, represent a late period, when the cult was already in decay. The witnesses were, as often as not, stupid, backward, or even deranged. The answers were made to leading questions. There had been overpowering moral suasion; often torture.

Only by relating the evidence of the trials to the known pro-cesses of pre-Christian myth and practice, and the activities of contemporary peoples in a comparable cultural state (if any contemporary state can be truly comparable) is it possible to obtain any real estimate of the witch tradition. When we do this, however, something of a picture does emerge.

Set out, it seems improbably formal, but it may perhaps be legitimately held that there is a parallel between the diabolic system and the feudal system – which was not invented, as the academic pleasantry points out, until the seventeenth century.

First, it is suggested that there was the supreme Devil of Europe: Satan's Vicar on earth. It is highly improbable that any such character ever existed, but it is just possible that, if there was a centre in the Hartz mountains to which representatives of the cult repaired from all directions for the supreme festivals, the officiating high-priest at such festivals had some senior authority. If the Templars really were riddled with Satanism, perhaps the Grand Master considered himself pre-eminently the vehicle of Satan in Europe. If a Gilles de Rais or a Joan of Arc felt themselves to be the appointed god-sacrifice of the witches, they may have felt that they were a sacrifice for members of the Old Religion everywhere.

It is all infinitely tentative and dependent on innumerable improbabilities. In any case, such significance would be well outside the knowledge or recognition of the ordinary practitioner of the cult.

Then there may have been the high devil or Grand Master of any given district. He might be attached to one coven or visit several. It is with him that the previous chapter largely concerned itself, and there is nothing to add except the guess, made by some writers, that this Grand Master was often a priest. He must at least have had the status of clerk, if he read the Black Book and the records.

It seems possible that the Officer, another title mentioned, was sometimes the Devil as well – that is to say, that he was an executive at ordinary meetings and personified the godhead on great occasions. There certainly was an Officer, and his duties included arranging meetings, seeing that the witches knew of the times and places of these, obtaining food for them, presenting new members, and keeping a record of all that was done. He also took part in the services, although it was the Grand Master devil who celebrated the actual mass. The North Berwick witches deposed, in 1590, that Johnne Fiene was their 'Regester', and he himself confessed that 'he was clarke to all those that were in subjection to the Divels service, bearing the name of witches; that always hee did take their oathes for their true service to the Divell still pleased to command him'. At Paisley, in 1678, Bessie Weir is described as 'Officer to their several meetings', and there are other references to this function. In the French trials the names are commoner.

If one of the above officials was not young and lithe enough, or if the dance had to be performed before him, a separate leader of the dance was appointed. Since dances were normally round-dances, leading would also involve catching up the rear, and the dancing-master would perhaps deputize for the devil in thwacking idle or slow dancers. This is supposed to be the origin of the phrase 'devil take the hindmost'. A Mr Gideon Penman, a renegade clergyman, was spoken of by the local Devil in 1678 as 'Mr Gideon, my chaplain', and it is said that 'ordinarily Mr Gideon was in the rear of all their dances, and beat up those that were slow'.

A Queen of the Sabbath is also sometimes mentioned. This official must have been the Queen of Elphane, although Professor Murray (who very carefully collected the references to all of them) pointed out that, in Scotland in the seventeenth century, there was a Maiden of the Coven who appears to have been distinct from the Queen of Faery. In France a Queen of the Sabbat, who sat at the Devil's right hand, was usual. Where the Robin Hood tradition remained, she would be called Maid Marian.

Ordinary members of the cult consisted of all those, however recruited, who normally attended the weekly esbat, and followed the witch practices. It is nonsense, from the evidence we possess, to try to give them individual functions, but clearly some were told off to play the pipes, hold the Devil's cloak, be summoner, keep watch, or whatever it might be. Meanwhile, the local peasantry might attend the festivals in greater or lesser numbers, and pay their traditional due to the Old Religion, much as, in another form, they paid it by dancing round the maypole or welcoming the Green Man into the village at springtime. They need not necessarily have been, so to speak, 'party members'.

However far the hierarchy was or was not standardized,

there seems no sort of doubt that the inner circle of practising witches was, at least until the seventeenth century, normally organized in covens. The word coven is a derivative of 'convene', and has various forms, which even extend to the sporting 'covey'. It also has associations with convent, which meant at one time both the place of a religious meeting and the meeting itself.

The number of those in the witch covens has been the subject of argument. On the balance it may be felt that there is a good case for this being thirteen – twelve men or women, and the god, who was almost always a man. Each group might meet for the weekly esbat, when they would report their activities since the last meeting, receive orders, derive instructions about poisons and processes, and effect magical ritual and physical group-release.

The argument about the numbers in the covens is interesting, as showing the sort of way it is possible to trace continuity in the cult.

Professor Murray devoted some industry to analysis of the various recorded trials, and has given examples of those in the British Isles in which thirteen – or a multiple of thirteen – appears either as the number of witches apprehended, or as the sum of those apprehended and those whose arrest was demanded: in France, one group, in Germany one, in Ireland one, in Scotland nine, in England five, and in North America one. These eighteen examples range from 1567 until 1673. 'The actual numbers can be obtained, as a rule,' says Professor Murray, 'only when the full record of the trial is available; for when several witches in one district are brought to trial at the same time they will always be found to be members of a Coven, and usually the other members of the Coven are implicated or at least mentioned.' The trouble about this is, that when the full record of the trial is indeed available, it sometimes reveals far more suspects, lurking in the wings, than are necessary to bring up the number to thirteen. There remain, however, definite statements. Isobel Gowdie of Auldcarne said in 1662, 'Jean Mairten is Maiden of owr Coeven. Johne Younge is Officer to owr Coeven – Ther ar threttein persons in ilk Coeven.' Ann Armstrong, at Newcastle-on-Tyne in 1673, spoke of 'five coveys consisting of thirteen persons in every covey', and of a large meeting where there were many witches, and 'every thirteen of them had a divell with them in sundry shapes'.

It is objected by the incredulous that judging by the rest of their evidence these women were crazy. Even so, the leading questions which they received had been given because there was a basis for the expectation of witches operating in cells of thirteen. Alternatively, the witnesses were repeating a number which from their childhood they had learned to associate with witch stories. Or, of course, the witches were not crazy, except that they believed and confessed to many fanciful pieces of symbolic nonsense to which we have lost the clue – as well as confessing certain truths.

Roman Catholic writers are naturally happy to accept the coven as being a body of thirteen, because they recognize the Devil merely as the Ape of God, and see thirteen, therefore, as a parody of the number of the Last Supper. This, too, no doubt, it was, which would lead careful inquisitors to press for such revelations.

There is a deeper reason why we might expect to find a symbolical importance in thirteen. This is, the mystic associations which that number has always had, since long before Christian times. Indeed, the Christian pattern of a messiah and twelve intimate followers may have been significant because the number already had a symbolism in the Mediterranean world. Thirteen follows the perfect cycle of twelve, and so represents death: it is the sun and moon and eleven stars of Joseph's dream: it represents Solomon and his twelve principal officers. In later myth, among other examples, it reappears with Romulus and his twelve lectors, Hrolf and his twelve berserks, King Arthur and his twelve knights, and Robin Hood with his twelve foresters. There are thirteen in a hand, at many card games. By the end of the Middle Ages, councils of twelve led by a thirteenth member, who was supreme, were becoming fairly common – King Charles IX of France and his council, the rising importance of the judge and small jury, or

The conventional witch
a. Fourteenth century, from Lyon Cathedral
b. Seventeenth century: Jennet Dibb and her cat
c. Nineteenth century: the crone on a broomstick
d. Twentieth century: the Walt Disney version

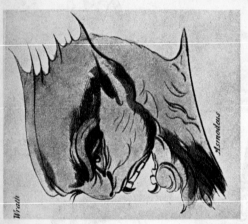

*Wrath*

*Asmodeus*

c

2. Types of the Devil
   a. Masked dancer of the Old Stone Age
   b. Asmodeus
   c. A devil from Notre Dame Cathedral

3. Goat worship
   a. From a fifteenth-century French miniature
   b. From a fresco by Goya in the Prado, Madrid

4. *The Sabbat* by Spranger

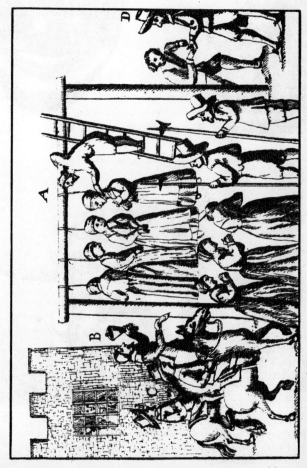

5. Execution of witches

6. Masks
   a. Egyptian jackal mask, *c.*600 B.C.
   b. North American Indian mask of the Seneca tribe
   c. The Dorset Ooser

*A Witch Preparing a Philtre* by an unknown master of the
Flemish School, mid fifteenth century

8. Back to back dancing, a detail from *The Entry of Isabel of Bavaria into Paris as Bride of Charles VI*

the Mayor and Corporation in England, are examples. On the Continent the belief in the number as being the appropriate quantity for the witches' coven became so clearly accepted that illustrated representations of sabbats usually followed it. It has never, I believe, been pointed out that the Hexenhams or House of the Witches, at Bamberg – a special prison, 'a marvel of human workmanship', built by a public-spirited George Fuchs the second of Dornheim, in 1627 – had separate cells for twenty-six witches, or two covens.

Before leaving the matter, here are several examples of groups of thirteen characters, from different historic periods. Each of these examples is one which can be readily explained by association with a witch-cult of the sort which I have indicated.

First, in the province of Granada, in southern Spain, has been discovered a neolithic sepulchral cave. This is known as the Cave of Bats. In it, when it was found, were twelve skeletons, sitting in a circle round a central skeleton which was dressed in a leather skin. The floor was covered with poppy heads.

In 1022, during the persecution of the Manichaeans, an inner circle of believers remained steadfast, in spite of all pleading and all torture, and were burned. The number of them was thirteen.

Thirdly, there remained in Gloucestershire, certainly until as late as 1841, when Hone published an account of it in his Every Day Book, a curious custom. This took place on 6 January. Twelve little fires were lighted, and one great one. The people assembled, from miles round, to 'burn the old witch' – to sing and drink and dance and celebrate.

As recently as in 1941, when one of the players described it in the Home Service programme of the B.B.C. – and perhaps today – an equally curious custom turns up in Lincolnshire. The date is again 6 January. Thirteen men assembled, as they had for hundreds of years, to take part in the Haxey Hood Game. 'The game,' said a player in the broadcast, after describing the peculiarly improbable legend of how it was started by a thirteenth-century Lady Mowbray, whose hat was chased by thirteen woodmen, 'is complicated. It is played with thirteen hoods, twelve sack hoods and the sway hood which is made of leather. Led by the lord, one by one the sack hoods are thrown up into the air and scrambled for by nearly everybody, and if it is touched by a boggen* it's boggened again, that is, returned to play. This goes on for roughly an hour. Then comes the great moment when the sway hood is thrown; this is the signal for the whole crowd to join in. A general cry of "sway" goes up and then the fun begins.'

Finally, in 1948, it was thirteen Nigerian Negroes who were condemned to death for ritual murders, committed in masks as 'leopard men'.

These are a few examples of what might be many. In all, the number thirteen is stressed. All have an obvious religious origin. It is, in no example, the religion of orthodox Christianity. In detail, each story has other circumstances attaching it to the practice of witchcraft, or of fairies, and one even has the hood theme as well.

There seems, then, a case for deciding that the group of thirteen celebrants did, in Western Europe at least, have a significance in pre-Christian ritual. This ritual has been continued in folk custom until today. One finds, therefore, every reason to suppose that the even stranger secret continuation of the Old Religion, called witchcraft, also used thirteen in its organization.

After a time, no doubt, even the witches themselves thought, if they thought about it at all, that the number was a parody of the number of Jesus and his apostles.

What happened at witch meetings must be the subject of a chapter to itself, because the meeting was the supreme realization of the cult. But here it should be noticed, as part of the organization, that meetings did periodically take place, and were of different sorts – large celebrations, including the sacrifice of the god after the full rites – and comparatively small

* There are eleven boggens, as well as the lord and the fool, who carries a wand of thirteen willows. In the north fairies – and so witches – were commonly called boggarts.

meetings of local covens. The two sorts of meetings are not always very easy to distinguish, although the smaller business meeting, the esbat, was probably a weekly one, and those which attracted attention were, normally, the more ambitious sabbats.

The word sabbat, or Sabbath, is tentatively derived, by Professor Murray, from *s'esbettre*, 'to frolic' – which she describes as 'a very suitable description of the joyous gaiety of the meetings'. Montague Summers prefers scholarly authorities who are 'agreed to derive it from the debased Bacchanalia', and relate the word to the Phrygian deity Sabazius, 'who', explains Summers with reverent repugnance, 'was generally regarded as the patron of licentiousness and worshipped with frantic debaucheries'. Sabazius was indeed, a Thracian beer god, who was worshipped in a nocturnal cult. Summers quotes the authority Littré, however, as one who 'entirely rejects any such facile etymology'. There have been other attempted explanations. But the etymologists agree, at all events, that sabbat has nothing whatever to do with the number seven, or the Jewish Sabbath.

The sites of the great meetings would naturally be in the traditional holy spots of the earliest religions, which had, in turn, inherited them from perhaps palaeolithic sources. When there were going to be many people, and there was going to be much noise, the spots selected would be, as far as possible, hidden ones. The sabbat was held near lakes or streams, in the heart of the forest; or held round the cromlechs and stones which, even today, keep such names as the Dancing Maidens or the Seven Sisters, and are spoken of as fairy mounds. Witches and fairies were said to dance at Avebury, and round the Rollright stones in Oxfordshire. It took place, where the new religion had usurped the structure of the old, in churchyards and charnel houses. Sometimes, where the original phallic symbol of the post, long used openly by all in the maypole on May Day, had remained, the tree would become a stone, and the dance take place about the market cross. Any crossroad, the sacred haunt of Diana, was possible. The crossroad was indeed sacred because, in the earliest days of few pathways, the spot where several paths joined would be the spot to which worshippers came for the great festivals. Caves, too, are traditionally associated with the cult – the bull-pot of the witches in the North Riding of Yorkshire, the witch of Wookey in Somerset, or the cave of the Lamb in the same county.

The smaller meetings would occur in the place most immediately convenient, so long as it remained secret. The great meetings would be, as far as possible, in the fixed, and hallowed, localities.

There are only three particular places which need mention: the Brocken, or Blocksburg, in the Hartz mountains, the Blocula in Sweden (presumably the names correspond in some way), and the summit of the Puy-de-Dôme, in Auvergne. The savage, wild, Black Forest centre on the Hartz mountains became the most famous of all. Even in the early eighteenth century, maps of Germany still peopled the air above it with property witches on broomsticks, whilst Goethe selected it as the site of the fantastically romantic Sabbath of his *Faust*. We shall now probably never know whether there was any reason, other than romance, for the tradition.

The Swedish Blocula was in a wide meadow. 'In a huge large Room of this House, they said, there stood a very long Table, at which the Witches did sit down: And that hard by this Room was another Chamber where there were very lovely and delicate Beds.' It is the description by a peasant woman of the unknown luxuries of a country house, perhaps that of a wealthy diabolist. At all events, she died for her vision of it. There probably were witches here indeed, for the district was known, as it happens, as Elfland.

As for the dates of the great assemblies, these seem to have been different in various parts of Europe. They do, however, follow some sort of pattern, and it has even been possible to suggest that they follow the May–November year and date from before agricultural practice, being mainly concerned with the appropriate ceremonies for the fertility of cattle. However this may be, they soon came to include later festivals, dating from agricultural practice, although they did not include such late Mithraic-Christian dates as 25 December.

The spring festival, on the eve of May Day, 30 April, was the first of the main dates. In England, this day was called Roodmas, but in Germany, from a popular Devonshire saint, St Walburga, who had gone to Germany, and died there, after a life of surpassing holiness, in A.D. 777, it was known as Walpurgis Nacht. The eve of the day of this gentle saint coincided with the greatest pagan festival of the West, and remains today, in the popular mind, pre-eminently the occasion of crones, cauldrons, and diabolical baby-basting.* Druids had long made mountain tops hideous with its celebrations in the British Isles, as had Finnish magicians their own hill tops.

May Day sports perpetuated the practices, including even transvestism, and it is reported that on this date, in Wales, there existed, into the nineteenth century, a peasant dance and march with a garland, led by a dancer, called the 'Cadi'. 'His countenance,' wrote an observer in 1825, still stirred with the memory fourteen days later, 'is also particularly distinguished by a hideous mask, or is blackened entirely over; and then the lips, cheeks, and orbits of the eyes are sometimes painted red. The number of the rest of the party, including the garland-bearer, is generally thirteen.' There was singing and the capering of round-dances – the legal vestigial remains of the old illegal witch ritual, which was for centuries carried out on that day or the night before. It is unnecessary to stress the point that May Day was also, traditionally, the day of Robin Hood festivals, and of hobby-horses, all over the country. The whole May Day custom of Europe, dating back to palaeolithic times, relates closely to the witch ceremony, and the tradition ascribed to the eve of that very day. It is now the festival of the official Labour movement.

The autumn festival on 31 October, Allhallow Eve, the second of the great occasions, was another Druidic festival. It was, as it even now is, particularly celebrated on the Celtic fringes of the British Isles. Traditionally, the occasion has always been particularly enlivened by games with apples and

---

* Perhaps, too, she inherited the symbolism attached to the name of the Earth Mother, Walburg.

nuts (witch hazel), and both of them are traditional forms of apparatus in the witch story.

These were the two greatest festivals, but there were others – Candlemas (2 February), the winter festival; Lammas (1 August), the summer festival; St Thomas Day (21 December), and the Eve of St John (23 June).

Boguet says that the witches kept all the great Christian festivals. So they did, but Christmas was at first rarely celebrated except in the New World (although the Christmas annual tradition makes witches, ghosts, Santa Claus, and the fairies all parade at cracker-time), for the great festivals were older than Christianity, and sacred long before it made them so.

The smaller esbat was probably held on whatever day of the week was most suitable, and this varied in different places. Such is the case in Haiti, today, where the meetings, with all the naked dancing and the rest of it, normally take place on a Saturday, going on until the bells are heard ringing for mass. Some European witches even spoke of convening twice a week. There would probably continue to be important meetings at the time of the full moon. As blackout experience has more recently taught us, it is, in a world deprived of artificial light, the only sensible time to undertake after-dark activities. Also, the full moon was the hunter's moon, as it became the bomber's moon, and the festivals of an early people, in the hunting stage of evolution, are naturally concerned with it.

The state of the moon, and the convenience of the society, also regulated the times of meetings. Traditionally, these lasted from midnight until cock-crow, and it is now time to describe as much as we can reconstruct of what happened there.

# 10

# The Sabbats

THERE is very little to be gained from demonstrating that the stock picture of a witches' sabbat has little historical basis. It derives from facetious or maudlin illustrators decorating the apparatus of the Romantic poets – ominous clouds, a thunderstorm, chain-rattling, and a Disney–Moussorgsky phantasmagoria of naked crones, ghouls, devils, and goats committing unnatural and orgiastic practices in a high wind. Details can be supplied from the phobias of individual child-hoods, but it remains largely a matter of the picture books.

Many of the stock properties, however, do have a basis in probability. This is shown in examining the first part of the ordinary tradition – the journey to the sabbat. The accepted conception here is of a young woman – less often in paintings an old one – taking off her clothes, rubbing herself, or being rubbed, with ointment, jumping on to a broomstick, skipping up the chimney or out of the window, and so flying malignant through the night to the place of assembly.

For most of this there is some sort of evidence or explana-tion in the trials, in the parallels of folk-lore, and in early magical practice. Like most traditions, it appears to be founded upon the truths of symbolism and belief, which were then quite as real as what we understand by rational fact. Here is some sort of explanation.

Primitive peoples, today, usually oil themselves before they dance. Indian tribes of North America are an example. Athletes do the same. The actual massage acts as a loosener of the limbs, and the oil also serves to keep out cold. Even the classical Greeks adhered to the conventional Eastern custom of oiling the body before sexual intercourse, as an incentive and a dedication. Our own kings are still crowned with sacred oil. In early times, the oil was probably grease, and coloured like war-paint.

It is, therefore, to be expected that witchcraft, itself at least in part the survival of an immensely old religion in which fertility practices and dances played a large share, should also use oil. Certainly the worshippers sometimes blacked their faces – a habit which survives in contemporary folk custom – they certainly wore masks, and when they stated that they rubbed their bodies with oil also, and volunteered details, there is very little reason to disbelieve the fact.

The composition of the ointment was various. It contained grease, a proportion of purely horrific ingredients – incorporated because they were related to the sex or excretory taboos, were customary, or were hard to acquire – and a quantity of drugs which certainly would have definite physiological consequences. Reginald Scot speaks, in 1584, of the ointment 'whereby they ride in the aire', as being compounded by obtaining 'the fat of yoong children, and seeth it with water in a brasen vessell, reseruing the thickest of that which remaineth boiled in the bottome, which they laie up and keepe, untill occasion serueth to use it. They put hereunto Eleoselinum, Aconitum, Frondes populeas, and Soote.' The directions he quotes (for another recipe) tell how, in its application, the witches 'stampe all these togither, and then they rubbe all parts of their bodys exceedinglie, till they looke red, and be verie hot, so as the pores may be opened, and their flesh soluble and loose. They ioine herewithall either fat, or oil in steed thereof, that the force of the ointment maie the rather pearse inwardly, and so be more effectuall.'

A. J. Clark, in an appendix to Professor Murray's *Witchcraft in Western Europe*, has analysed three of the recipes. Discounting the bat's blood and the baby's fat as picturesque accessories, oleaginous if otherwise ineffectual, he finds that the remaining ingredients do carry important toxic qualities. As he sums it up:

The first preparation, which contains hemlock and aconite would produce mental confusion, impaired movement, irregular action of the heart, dizziness and shortness of breath.

The belladonna in the second ointment would produce excitement which might pass to delirium.

The third ointment, containing both aconite and belladonna, would produce excitement and irregular action of the heart.

Therefore, although some contemporaries said that the ointments had no value, the evidence is that they did in fact have a chance of causing disturbing results. Taken internally, they would undoubtedly have done so. Even when rubbed into the skin, however, they would have an effect. The skin of a witch in the Middle Ages was not likely to be unbroken, and, in any case, the rubbing was largely concentrated on the legs and the vaginal membranes, which would more particularly convey the drugs into the bloodstream. Once there, they would cause hallucination and elevation of spirit. They might even cause the impression of flying, through their action in bringing about irregularity of the heart. The same effect in dreams – that of flying or being able to take seven-league steps – is still experienced by some people as the result of too much to eat or drink before going to bed. When actual poisons were at work, the impression would be immeasurably heightened. Persian dervishes and others have obtained the same sort of effect from hashish, passing from exaltation to complete hallucination. Under the influence of this drug, a little stone is said to appear as a huge block, a gutter as a wide stream, a path as a wide endless road. The addict fancies he has wings, and that he can rise from the ground. In degree, of course, ordinary drunkenness also distorts and minimizes the sense both of time and of distance.

Members of the witch society, then, did oil themselves with flying ointment, and it did, in all probability, have definite effects.

There are two possible explanations for the common belief that witches flew out of the window, or up the chimney, and not out of the door. The first is the very simple one that 'out of the chimney' or 'out of the window' meant going upwards. When it is remembered that the Celtiberian peoples were, usually, living under the level of the earth, it is obvious that to go upwards and out of an opening in the roof would be the only method of egress. The practice may have been remarked by peoples of a later culture, who came into touch with them and were already regarding them as witches and fairies. What makes this explanation attractive is that, until the late Middle Ages, no houses had chimneys, so that tradition must have referred to a hole in the roof.

The other, and equally strong, reason why a witch would not be expected to use a door, was because in a properly blessed and defended house she *could* not. The taboo of the threshold was almost universal, and many threshold superstitions still survive. The horseshoe was hung over the door, and the witch's magic – that of a pre-neolithic culture – was defeated by iron.

The ordinary method of going to the sabbat was certainly that of walking, or, where the witches were of a more prosperous class, going on horseback. The traditional story about flying is a mixture of a number of ideas.

As for its history, it is one of the earliest convictions, common to almost all peoples, that not only do supernatural beings, angels or devils, fly or float in the air at will, but so can those humans who invoke their assistance. Levitation among the saints was, and by the devout is, accepted as an objective fact. The most famous instance is that of St Joseph of Cupertino, whose ecstatic flights (and he perched in trees) caused embarrassment in the seventeenth century. Yet the appearance of flight, in celestial trance, has been claimed all through the history of the Church, and not only for such outstanding figures as St Francis, St Ignatius Loyola, or St Teresa. Gemma Galgani, of Lucca, appeared to be lifted up before a venerated crucifix, and to remain several minutes at a distance from the floor, on a September evening in 1901. Yogis and mystics, of all times, have frequently produced the same effect upon the faithful beholder, and secular practitioners, such as Home the medium, are famous. Friar Bacon's trick of seeming to walk between two spires, at Oxford, was no doubt an ingenious optical illusion* – but by whatever means achieved, physical or purely transmitted illusion, the feat of vectitation has always

* See *Letters on Natural Magic* by Sir David Brewster, 1842, an interesting contemporary reply to Sir Walter Scott's *Letters on Witchcraft*.

been known. In the Middle Ages it was regarded as a marvel, but a firmly established one. And tradition in the British Isles had always accepted that Druids could transport themselves through the air at will.

It is not, therefore, at all remarkable that witches were believed to fly. If anything, it is strange that during the period of the great persecutions so comparatively infrequent suggestion was made of the phenomenon. Of course, there was the Northern tradition of the Valkyries, and the classical witches had been accused of soaring as women or owls. Moreover, the Persian and Eastern devils, and the Peri (from whom the fairies partly took their name), all flew. Actual devils were in the air everywhere. But the Church expressly forbade, during the reign of Charlemagne, any belief that witches flew. This was condemned as a delusion, and, although it had been noted in the ninth and fourteenth centuries, the first instance that Professor Murray can record of the accusation is in the deposition about an Italian witch who, in 1526, was said to have flown with the help of a magic ointment. Reginald Scot says that, by oiling themselves with the brew mentioned, witches, 'in a moonlight night seem [*sic*] to be carried in the air'. But the witches themselves appear to have said little about it, nor does it seem to have been pressed by the Inquisitors. A few did, as notably the Devonshire witches tried in 1664, but the evidence is late, and perhaps merely shows that the witches were themselves caught up in the popular expectation of how they might be supposed to have behaved.

An explanation may be that the term 'flying' was merely used in a general sense for moving quickly over the ground – or through the air, in that the witches used poles to cross streams and obstacles by a 'boy-scout hop', at other times using poles as hobby-horses. Dame Alice Kyteler at her trial in 1324 was accused of having a staff 'on which she ambled through thick and thin, when and in what manner she listed, after having greased it with the ointment. . . '. There is, as Professor Murray shows, no suggestion of leaving the ground. It was probably a movement in imitation of horseback riding – the symbolized 'ride a cock horse'. Sometimes there may have been an attempt to bestride the appropriate cult animal, or take pick-a-back rides on other members of the coven, wearing the animal masks. The broomstick was a symbol of woman (as the pitchfork was of man), and was used, when placed outside the door of the house, to indicate the good-wife's absence from home. It also has affiliations with the magic wand, and would be supposed to be, normally, made of hazel. It does not, however, seem a basic ingredient of witchcraft, but rather an artistic device which served to condense the common belief.

We have, then, an accepted belief in flight as a supernatural practice. We have the possibility also of actual levitation in ecstatic states (which must be held unproven), and which might be an ingredient in the magical arcana of witchcraft. Obviously it could not be a means of locomotion for the ordinary visitor to the sabbat. We have (what I believe to be the explanation of the majority of instances) the belief of the witches, themselves, in their having flown – or in having been mysteriously transported over great areas – through hallucination under the action of drugs. This faith they retained, when returned to normality, through auto-suggestion, after the mind had been disturbed and conditioned by toxic action.

There appear to be authenticated instances of witches who fully believed themselves to have visited the sabbat, although there was ample evidence that they had not left their beds. One was so far gone in a trance, quotes Sprenger, in the *Malleus Maleficarum*, that she remained in it even when a lighted candle was applied to her foot by the officials who were watching her. When she came round, she insisted that she had been to the sabbat, and described what had taken place there. As Guazzo, that ardent enemy of witches, himself quotes in the *Compendium Maleficarum*: '. . . what is related in the life of St Germain is not impertinent in this connexion, to wit, when certain women declared that they had been present at a banquet, and all the time they slumbered and slept, as several persons attested'. He was not himself at all happy in accepting this, but it is obvious enough that it must often have happened.

It is easy to explain that it could be so. Even before reaching the sabbat the witch would no doubt have starved – as mystics always have before their transports, and so as part of the ritual. More immediately, too, she would have starved as a parody of the abstinence of the Christian before attending mass. Weakened by this, the witch would be the more susceptible to the ointments she rubbed into her body, and to any 'magic potion' she took as well, which contained the necessary disturbing properties.

This rubbing with ointment must have dated from the earliest ritual. For witches, it was standard practice, and the great illustrators of the cult – Hans Baldung, Frans Francken, and Quervido – all painted pictures of athletic models having oil rubbed on to well-developed posteriors which would certainly seem to need a great deal of it, if they were to go up any chimneys. A number of formulas for these ointments are in existence.

Whilst, therefore, Boguet (and the orthodox Montague Summers) feel that the ointments can have had no effect (other no doubt than to keep out the cold), scientific evidence is very much more confident that they may have done so.

Add this to extreme suggestibility and a genuine belief in the sabbat (which might have been visited in the flesh on a previous occasion) and it is not hard to see how many subjects may genuinely have believed themselves to have flown to the Devil's feast, and to have enjoyed its orgies. This, without the accessory stimulus of a relentless inquisitor and his questions, ruthless, thrusting, informed, and backed by the rack and the thumbscrews.

Those who also took potions internally, either before going to the sabbat, or when they were there, would be even more likely to believe anything which ritual approved and opinion expected. For the effects would almost certainly be to create a predisposition to auditory and visual hallucination of exactly the quality which outside suggestion demanded and the capacity of the individual permitted – in the intellectual, of the most recondite and extravagant fantasies; and, in the peasant, of the observed and reported luxuries, parodied, swelled, and inverted, of the court, the castle, and the more sybaritic refectory. If stones became gold under the hypnosis of initiation, might not dreams seem real indeed, in the delusion of the completed act? For drugs have always been called upon to heighten the mystic perception – or if you prefer, to drown the earthbound attachments – of mankind. Individuals, like Coleridge and De Quincey, have used them to produce mighty poetry and sonorous prose in our own tongue, and, to obtain the same elevation of spirit, coca has been employed in South America, or ololiqui and psyotl in Mexico. These affect the nervous system, and give hypnotic sleep with hallucinations, leading to enphoric bliss. In the East soma is used for the same purpose by the practising Yogis, to release the subconscious and to give cessation of the physical and intellectual functions through control of the nervous system. If the individual receives only local comfort and temporary elevation, which may end in death and despair, to some it has illumined incredible yet, for a besotted period, attainable heights of beauty. Certainly cocaine produces slight visions, while hashish, opium, and alcohol produce magnificent, brilliant illusions, psychologically comforting if physiologically suspect. The exhalations of the caverns of Delphi and Eleusis, toxic or not, still provide inexhaustible theses for the ingenuity of scholars.

Witches, if they were rich enough, rode to the sabbat, in a state of ecstasy or not, and their less sophisticated colleagues doubtless thought that they rode thither with the Devil, although they were also observed going to the meeting-place in groups, 'cheerily conversing' as they walked.

What happened when they had arrived depended upon the occasion of the feast, the standards of whoever was the leading spirit, the numbers, the likelihood of interruption, and so on. It was a religious feast – the meeting of a secret society, an institute picnic, a drunken orgy, and a carnival – all combined with the overriding sense of conscious rebellion against God and orthodox society, and with the threat of probable death, if there was discovery. There would be variation according to country, and to local conditions. Also, according to period, alterations, as the early conglomeration of avid worshippers, led by a powerful intelligence, shrank to a pitiful handful of evil eccentrics. But for generations they did meet, and usually the ceremonies began at midnight, so far as the worshippers could establish it – 'the witching hour of night'.

The smaller meeting, the esbat, was a more or less formal occasion, conducted by the local officer. The individual members of the coven no doubt reported the success, or otherwise, of tasks they had been given on the previous occasion, and joint plans of action for the future would be arranged. Clay figures might be contrived for the purposes of harming selected victims by sympathetic magic, spells might be cast, graves opened to obtain dead men's bones. There might be a cauldron. There would probably be some sort of food. There would be a spree, and perhaps dancing. It would all appear mysterious, and forbidding enough, to the homing drunkard or to the benighted traveller who happened on the scene; but it was not a diabolical celebration on any scale.

Whoever stumbled on the occasion of a real sabbat must have seen something very terrible. One can understand the consternation of those eye-witnesses who do, from time to time, crop up in the evidence, even if they do obviously enhance the numbers of those they saw. Perhaps, too, they substitute the romantic expectation for the grim enough reality in some details of what they observed. For their experiences must have been similar to those of the shocked Europeans who, for the first time, witnessed the dances of the Obeyah in the New World, the ceremonies of the inner Brazilian tribes, or the devil dances of West Africa. Moreover, the witnesses were not sophisticated travellers, but men who saw what they could only feel to be unhallowed and demoniac exhibitions by people whom they recognized, in everyday life, as ordinary citizens of their locality. They saw processions of rich and poor persons, perhaps naked, perhaps masked, bearing torches glowing (because of the ingredients) with sulphurous flames. They saw, it might be, the Hand of Glory itself – the human hand with the fingers ignited as candles. They saw even a devil god, monstrously masked, with a candle spluttering between its horns. They were seeing a degenerate form of the saturnalia of the classical world – a barbaric release into an even earlier worship.

But, as on those distant evenings the returning revellers picked out the lights, heard the gabble and the inhuman music, smelt the sulphur and the reek of incense and debauchery, they must have been frightened men. They were involuntary witnesses of the oldest and most barbaric rites – rites half the proud worship of a disintegrating culture, half the conscious abandon of self-devoted blasphemers. It is not surprising that they lost little time in informing the nearest bishop, and so initiating another holocaust of those who followed the Old Ways.

When the company had assembled, the first process was often a roll-call. Neophytes would be introduced, if this had not been previously done privately. In any case, there would be vows of fidelity and obedience, and a report on previous commissions, as 'the Devil commands' we are informed 'that each tell what wickedness he hath committed'. There would be adoration of the Grand Master, in his guise of the evening, with genuflections and a copy, or parody, of the Christian obeisance. The Grand Devil might ask the initiates to kiss his person, and, if he did so, it might well be with the Kiss of Shame – which has so inflamed the chroniclers, and inspired the perpetrators of those rather clumsy woodcuts which adorn most demonographical works. As Guazzo says, 'as a sign of homage witches kiss the Devil's fundament'. Or, as the garrulous Agnes Sampson – she was one of the North Berwick witches who conspired against James I – put it, the Devil, because they were some of them late in arriving, 'at their comming enjoyned them all to a pennance, which was, that they should kisse his buttocks, in sign of duety to him, which being put over the pulpit bare (for it was in Church) every one did as he had enjoyned them'. This is dismissed as adolescent nastiness (which it may sometimes have been) only by those writers who do not realize that frequently the Devil wore that other face – the dualistic Other Side of Janus – under his tail. The witches themselves, who admitted most things readily enough, almost always claimed this, and historically it seems likely enough. The *osculum infame* is claimed against both the Waldenses and the Templars. Shameful, shameless, it was supreme homage.

After this, no doubt, the dancing began. The importance of the dance, as the origin of almost all expression – religious, dramatic, poetic, mimetic, or to invoke superhuman aid by pantomime – has been stressed already. Moreover, the parallel of any savage tribal festival, today, is sufficiently obvious, without reference to all classical ceremony and folk tradition through the ages. Even the dance of the Seven Veils, whose vulgarized editions proved so unedifying a spectacle to the British and American soldiers recently in the Middle East, was religious – the dance of Ishtar on her way to the innermost sanctuary, with one veil off to tempt each successive janitor. But it should perhaps be pointed out that dancing was employed, much as it was by the witches, even by the Catholic Church itself. Until the seventeenth century, there was ceremonial dancing in churches, especially in Spain. It still exists in the Church of Abyssinia – that pithecoid sport of the Christian religion – today. We learn that in France, in the Middle Ages, young people were permitted to ride in church upon wooden horses, and to dance, masked and disguised, through the churchyard on the eve of dedication day. Yet, in spite of the obviously reverent and legitimate use of the dance as a means of orthodox religious expression, the more severe of the Fathers frowned upon it, seeing it as an obvious excitant, with unhealthy tendencies. St Augustine was opposed to dancing, and the author of the *Speculum Morale* thought that dances ought to be avoided, for many reasons, saying that they were 'an invention of the Devil, the occasion of frequent sin, an insult to God, and a matter of foolish joy'. They were, certainly, sins against the ascetic hatred of expressive animal beauty, and as such the more detested by the Puritans, in their generation.

To the new witch, therefore, the dance, as a religious expression, would not be unusual. But in the witch tradition it was the necessary preliminary to the climax of the sabbat. It might be a parody of the Christians, but it was also the expression of the whole fertility theme – the dance of the animals, for fecundity in beasts, humans, or of the god himself.

The dancing was of different kinds. It might be an ordinary

folk dance, performed in clothes. It might be a wilder disport, in the clothes of the other sex. Or it might be, and, apart from the masks worn, no doubt often was, naked.

Mr L'Estrange Ewen, who has done much research into the witch trials in the British Isles, but who, in presenting it adds his own observations in a tone of sturdy and sometimes facetious scepticism, feels it 'incredible that people, however devil-ridden, would turn out of bed, winter and summer, regardless of weather, and proceed naked at dead of night to some desolate rendezvous. . . '. Probability is very much against him. Apodysia is common in the ritual dances of all primitive races, at all times. It was practised by the ancients and the Red Indians. The Adamites, in temperate climates, managed without clothes, and so do those equally eccentric devotees, the nudists, today. But it is, perhaps, only necessary to remember that, even in the seventeenth century, we find a traveller in Ireland describing the colleens, whom he found spinning stark naked, without any benefit of witchcraft at all: or that Adam and Eve before the Fall were, as a matter of course, represented in Biblical nakedness, in the Coventry Mystery Plays. The witches, moreover, were coated with oil, heated with drink and drugs, and animated by religious fervour.

The dances were performed to music. This is variously described, and obviously was played on the instruments common in the locality, and to the principal members. Whilst the passionate opponents of the sect write of unspeakable discords and disharmonious cat-calls, the witches themselves spoke of 'the sound of many pleasant instruments'. These would be the tambourine, violin, or pipes, and, in Scotland, there is mention of a Jews' harp. The tunes for merry-making and gambolling would be the ordinary ones of the time, with a tendency towards the contemporary equivalent of our vulgarer catches – what Milton frowned upon as 'lean and flashy songs'. The saying that 'the Devil has the best tunes', proves he must have had excellent ones – since the phrase was coined in an age far more musical than our own. The music for the specifically sacred dances was no doubt very old indeed, and it would be surprising if it was not accompanied by clapping and percussion.

There were, naturally enough, different dances for different purposes. There were ring dances round a central object – which might be the Devil himself, a stone, or a pillar, no doubt of phallic significance. It was this common form of dance (which would indeed mark the ground considerably) which gave a perfectly sensible origin to the idea of fairy* rings – although the term has for hundreds of years been applied to a natural phenomenon. In the ring dances, couples were often back to back, as is seen in peasant dances in parts of Europe today. The method is occasionally exploited for palais-de-danse tastes – as in the behind-bumping vogue of the 1930s for such dances as 'Hands, knees, and bumps-a-daisy'.

There was also a follow-my-leader dance. It was, no doubt, performed like the procession of the Conga – a dance of similar origins outcropping in the twentieth century. An official with a whip brought up the tail, to stimulate laggards, as in the Scottish trials it was Gideon Penman who 'was in the rear at all their dances and beat up all those that were slow'. There were dances performed sitting on branches – used as hobby-horses – or upon broomsticks. There was *La Volta*, a leaping measure brought out of Italy into France. No doubt there were numerous others, whose descendants we have today, for the round dances were usually perfomed widdershins – against the sun – and so we still proceed in our ball-rooms. It may explain part of the bitter opposition there was to the waltz, when this was introduced: to shock, among others, Byron, who wrote:

> Wide and more wide thy witching circle spreads
> And turns – if nothing else – at least our *heads*.

*La Volta*, and the leaping steps, were considered incredible by onlookers, and by this stage the worshippers must indeed

---

* In spite of all the other derivations of 'fairy' it is hard not to believe that it also has connexions with 'ferae', and a fairy dance be a dance of animal-masked witches. Compare, for instance, the Furry Dance in Cornwall.

have been in the same ecstatic condition as those in the tri-pudium of the ancients – when the dancers exhibited unsus-pected and incredible powers of acrobatic agility. Professor Murray quotes a contemporary description of a French witch dance, which 'is strange, and wonderful, as well as diabolical, for turning themselves back to back, they take one another by the arms and raise each other from the ground, then shake their heads to and fro like Anticks, and turn themselves as if they were mad'. This is an exact description of the Negro jive, as now practised – not only on the stage – but also as per-formed, for untold generations, in the forests of Africa, before being taken to North America by Negro slaves. It is interesting that tests of jive addicts show them to be definitely abnormal by the end of a 'session',* and it is only a number of steps, from this, to the ecstatic state of the whirling dervish. The Middle Ages themselves had their outbreaks of dancing mania – notably after the horrors of the Black Death – with convulsions and every evidence of epileptic abandon. At the sabbat, the masks would no doubt help, just as (Klaatsch states) the masks worn at their dances by Australian aborigines certainly exert a hypnotic effect.

At some point, and probably before the final paroxysms, there would be food, preceded by a grace which was a parody of Christian practice. It might be just such picnic fare as the peasants had brought with them, or it might be a more lavish spread, given by a wealthy member – the Grand Master him-self, perhaps. Thus the Lancashire witches of 1613 ate 'beefe, bacon and roasted mutton', and the Pendle witches, tried in 1638, described 'flesh-smoking, butter in lumps, and milk' – that is to say, the food of the common people, since the rich only used butter for cooking. Other descriptions, however, speak of exotic food and wines, as in the description of the witches at Aix, in 1610, who drank malmsey 'to excite them to venery'. In parts of Europe, salt and bread were said never to be served – as Sir Walter Scott says that fairies never eat salt. This might show that the rites originated with a pastoral people, since salt is normally used by settled peoples. But,

* A curious misnomer of the dance-band world.

everywhere, there are romantic descriptions of gluttony, cramming, drunkenness, and so on, and no doubt the half-crazed creatures did enjoy a considerable orgy, even before the more ceremonial eating. At all events, the wine, on top of the witch ointment, the whirling dances, the tension, and the hypnotic influence of the masks certainly explain the effects described – as by Joanna Michaelis of Château-Salins, in 1590, who observed that the eyes of those at the Assemblies 'are not sure and clear of sight, but that all is confused and disturbed and appears vague to them, like those who are blended by drunkenness'. All would be in wild and abandoned excitement.

The Grand Master, or Devil, if it were a great occasion, would not take on the attributes of the god, and might well be in a state of possession. This condition has been exhaustively studied by lay psychologists, by theologians, by pathologists, and by sceptics. It can be quite involuntary, as will be mentioned in assessing the powers of the witches over their victims. Alternatively, it can be voluntary, and combined with the conscious effects described, according to taste, as shameless trickery or pious fraud. The shaman of Asia or America is a typical example of this. His performance has been described as 'a combination of expert showmanship and management and of auto-hypnosis'. His voice changes, he takes on the appearance and character of the spirit who possesses him, and combines conjuring tricks with phenomena which really do appear supernatural. He can provoke 'Arctic hysteria', when his audience becomes incapable of doing anything but mimic his actions and repeat his words.

Even in our own time, and in Europe and America, the phenomena are much the same. A person possessed acquires an altogether new physiognomy, the transformation sometimes being bewilderingly speedy. The voice alters. A female voice can become a deep bass one. The subject entranced gives off a foetid unpleasant smell – as the Devil was described as doing. But these are individual maladies. In the witch-master, in Africa today – and as certainly in the medieval witch-cult – there is induced possession, in early days no doubt possession by the cult animal. The dancer *becomes* the animal, and plays out a ritual which led originally to the animal's death in his own: the sacrifice of the god.

For this must, in the early times, have been the culmination of the witch sabbat – the eating of the god. Yet, as has been said, the tradition was a muddied one by the time of the recorded trials, when a palimpsest of early rituals was overlaid by the desire to parody the Christian mass. As the cult declined, any sort of common practice must have been lost, until, by the nineteenth century, the indoor practitioners of self-conscious diabolism merely conducted the Black Mass of inverted Catholicism.

At the time of the trials there clearly was some sort of formal 'service' quite apart from the crescendo of the fertility dance. It would, in a Catholic age, be very like the known pageantry of the Church's own celebrations, with candles, vestments, and a parody of the Sacrament. It might moreover be conducted, and we have evidence that it frequently was, by an unfrocked priest. For its purpose, either hosts were made for the occasion with the Devil's name stamped on them instead of that of Jesus – as were found in the possession of Lady Alice Kyteler, at the time of her arrest in 1324 – or, if they could be smuggled out, hosts already consecrated in Church, and retained in the mouth for the purpose. There would be an elevation – in one instance of a black piece of sliced turnip – the defiling of a crucifix, and such dirty, unpleasant, and rather childish blasphemies as ingenuity prompted, to insult Christians and so please the Devil. The Devil himself received praise and renewed homage, and the Lord's Prayer was repeated backwards. A liturgy of evil would be repeated. There might be a mock sermon, and there would be an absolution – made with the left hand and an inverted Cross. '*Hoc est Corpus*' became hocus-pocus.

Constant charges were made against witches of cannibalism, and the eating of unbaptized children. It is just possible that there was a basis for this. Ritual cannibalism, combined with eating the god, is common in primitive religion, and would have magical properties. On a sophisticated level, it was practised by the Abbé Guiberg, who conducted Black Masses for

Madame de Montespan. Often, however, it was no doubt a tale of horror merely added to embellish the pictures of depravity – just as the same charges were currently made (and repeated in Hitler's Germany) against the Jewish community. In this connexion it is interesting that the witches were accused of eating 'Red Bread'. The main authorities seem to find this obscure. I suggest that the explanation is the same as that of the ritual-murder story circulated against the Jews, and quoted by Louis Golding.* He writes, 'It was in 1215 that the Fourth Lateran Council recognized officially the doctrine of Transubstantiation – that is, that in the ceremony of the Holy Communion, the consecrated elements become the actual Body and Blood of Jesus Christ. Now, it so happens that a microscopical scarlet (known as the *micrococcus prodigiosus*), having an appearance not unlike that of blood, may sometimes form on stale food kept in a dry place. This similarity to blood led in the Middle Ages to the assumption that it was blood, and was regarded as proof of maltreatment.' The Jews were supposed to have reduced the Host to this condition by torturing it with pincers. It was a common accusation, and was obviously extended to the witches.

Finally there would sometimes be the sacrifice of an animal, if not of the god himself, voluntarily immolated, and his ashes reverently preserved and distributed among the believers as a great magic.

And at the end, or before it, would be full abandon to the fertility tradition – the phallic release which sent the pens of horrified inquisitors scratching so industriously, shocked the orthodox, and which so disgusted and alarmed those nineteenth- and twentieth-century observers who have come on its parallels among primitive peoples. The Devil himself – the priest of the coven – would be expected to copulate with all the women. There is the evidence, already quoted, that connexion with him was painful, and that his semen was thought unnatural. He may have used an artificial phallus. The theory is borne out by the fact that pregnancy by the Devil was by arrangement, not involuntary. Where it was required it often

* *The Jewish Problem* by Louis Golding (Penguin Special), 1938.

occurred, and the Devil would, of course, have the privilege of his choice, which would be welcomed as ritual distinction by the woman concerned. After all the *jus primae noctis*, in its origins, had a religious significance and was accepted by the entire community.

But the whole group would take part in indiscriminate and promiscuous 'wantoning', and no doubt the results were as in the seventeenth-century wedding revels, in Tom Durfey's poem:

> Sukey that danced with the cushion
> An hour from the room had been gone
> And Barnaby knew by her blushing
> That some other dance had been done!
> And thus, of fifty fair maids
> That came to the wedding with men
> Scarce five of the fifty was left ye
> That so did return again!

I drag this in because in fact the parallel is a genuine one. The wedding revels (the cushion dance was regarded as very provocative) or the dance round the phallic maypole, the green man, the hobby-horses – all these were seen by the Puritans as the signs of the Devil. As carried out in many of the country districts, it may have been literally enough true.

At cock-crow, a people without watches knew that dawn was coming. The haggard dancers would take their several paths home, exhausted, the fumes in their heads, the wild cries behind them, the masks put away, and only sometimes bearing with them the post about which they had danced, and would dance again, calling it a maypole.* Some were perhaps dissipated perverts, and had shame or guilty pride. Some were just members of a primitive stock, already disappearing, but following the ways of their fathers, knowing that the Church disapproved, yet finding physical and psychological satisfaction. Some were ecstatics. 'The Sabbath,' said one of these, 'is the true Paradise.'

* The Puritan Stubbes saw and with fury described it like this: 'And then they fall to banquet and feast, daunce and leap about it, as the heathen people did at the dedication of their idolles, whereof this is a perfect pattern, or the thing itself.'

# 11

## The Powers and Practices

THE sabbat and the other meetings were always noted by those studying the witch-cult. Because the evidence appeared unintelligible to the early sceptics, it was thus discounted. Now, however, we accept the existence of these meetings, because parallels today, and the whole thesis of the anthropological pattern of witchcraft, predisposes us to do so. Yet other manifestations ranked quite as importantly to contemporaries. The witch mark, flying-ointment, and some of the popular associations have been noted, but it is time here to look at the remaining powers of the witch, as accepted and feared at least until the eighteenth century. For, whilst defiance of the Church and organized worship of the Devil were the offence against society, it was individual acts of malevolence which led to the majority of the accusations. These acts and practices went on long after the organized cult had decayed.

The darker and more sophisticated activities of the adepts – thaumaturgic and goetic magic – were the pursuits of the intellectual. Rites of criminal curiosity, rationalized perversion, mathematical magic, the evocation of evil spirits, talismans, and aspects of astrology derived from the Egyptian mysteries, the Kabbalah, Pythagoras, and the aristocratic stream of diabolism. They were not refinements argued, except by implication, against the ordinary witch – the member of the decaying group enemy of Christianity. Against the witch, or those mistaken as witches, the accusations were mainly of natural magic, venefic magic, spell-casting, fire or storm raising, lycanthropy, and the keeping of familiars.

In looking at the deeds claimed against the witches as being effected by natural and venefic magic, it is important to remember that mere faith-healing and the peddling of unusual herbal remedies was not witchcraft. Or it was white; theologically reprehensible but probably merely a department of 'country medicine'. Witchcraft proper exists only where the powers called upon are consciously felt to be evil ones, and those concerned in the operation are seeking aid from some force exterior to accepted institutions and beliefs. The whole of early medicine was saddled with a rag-bag of preconceptions which we now regard as 'unscientific', although, as medical fashions change, and the interaction of mind and body are more closely studied, our appraisement grows less complaisant. Astrology, for instance, was not witchcraft (although the astrologer, a sturdy stem from the more sophisticated tree of mystical practice, was always suspect), and astrologers were attached to most great households of the sixteenth and seventeenth centuries.

The distinction between medicine and magic can be reviewed later, when underlining how the rise of new medical methods did so much to help in discrediting the witch. Here it is only necessary to note that the medicine of the witches was the oldest medicine, the magic of the dawn, common to all mankind. It acted through a combination of faith on the part of the victim and the application of actual physical contributions by the practitioner. Only when the faith was consciously felt to be an evil faith – that is, opposed to the forces of orthodox belief – was it witchcraft. This does not mean that the witches did not have certain beneficent powers. The Red Book of Appin – a manuscript which Professor Murray says was last heard of in the possession of the now extinct Stewarts of Invernahyle – was reputed to possess charms for curing diseases of cattle, promoting fertility, and so on. But a depressed minority naturally and necessarily turned to destruction, not to preservation and begetting. Only the black deeds, obviously, came up in the trials. And how far a good deed done for evil ends is a permissible one is a question for the theologians – who deliberate it at great length.

The physical resources of the witch were those of the prehistoric peoples – who, after all, practised a clumsy form of trepanning, which their children forgot for human beings (even if they remembered into the nineteenth century how to apply it to sheep). They had scraps of herbal memory already half-way to being forgotten, and, in dealing with animals, the stored dexterity of generations. Gipsies, as those who deal in horses will explain in interminable anecdote, have it today.

As with gipsies, and with contemporary African witch-doctors, we do not know what the secrets are. But they were no doubt useful ones, and with faith in the cult and the almost personal identification with animal life which it presupposes, no doubt witches could wonderfully affect cattle and horses. They knew what was good (they became white witches) and they knew what was bad. They could cause lameness, abortion, and many evils by physical means. Even when the magic had rusted and the tradition failed, little ingenuity was needed to throw a handful of poison into a pig-trough, or to abort a sheep. For many witches, particularly in the later days, seem to have been midwives. They were the survivors of a cattle people. Should they not use their knowledge to injure their enemies?

They also used their physical knowledge to do evil to humans, for they were notoriously poisoners, and the Italian name for a witch (as the biblical one) is that of poisoner. One hundred and seventy Roman women were condemned for poisoning under the pretence of incantation, incurring the *Lex Cordelia* against sorcery – *veneficus* – and peasant peoples of less sophistication carried it on, as witches or not, all through history – to be called in by their betters as circumstances dictated. By the Middle Ages, they were naturally accused of poisoning wells and Holy Water stoups, infecting barbers' flour, smearing corrosives on door handles, and making a malicious distribution of toadstools. Also with creating sexual strangulation in men – as perhaps *can* be done by physical means. They spread the plague, and provided phials of murderous acids as readily as they provided aphrodisiacs. Lady Alice Kyteler is accused of 'the making of potions and lotions from obscene and foul recipes' (the hot-house prose is that of Dr Summers), 'the slaying of enemies by lingering disease, and many black secrets beside'. The full tally of the employment of witches as poisoners, by politicians and wealthy women, would be tedious.

The witch-doctors of Africa today, or of the Nevaho

Indians, do the same. And so, from mother to daughter, for generations, the properties of plants or animal products, and the spells that went with them, must have been handed down. Often instruction in these arts would be at home, but sometimes in the sabbat itself. Sometimes, even without suggestion, the drugs must have worked. Much additional and childish fire-raising and 'devilishness', in a schoolboy sense, may have been prompted by the general anarchism of the cult, but it is hardly activity needing profound investigation or explanation.

The effects caused by actual suggestion – auto-suggestion and hetero-suggestion – are far more interesting. It is these which account for the great majority of 'spells', of sexual inhibition, of casting of the evil eye, of wasting deaths caused through sympathetic magic, and of actual possession, of which there are so many examples throughout the evidence of the witch trials. The witches believed that they had these powers, the people believed that they had them, and they worked. Exactly the same evidence is found in the miracles of all Churches: the orthodox use of the power the witches used for unorthodox ends.

The most obvious form of causing ill (or occasionally good) through this means is by sympathetic magic – the Law of Similarity. What is done to the symbol happens to the reality, and a red-hot pin through the vitals of the waxen image of a man will cause his actual stomach to contract and wither. The evidence of primitive peoples, all over the world, shows how effective this can be if the victim knows what is being done. The only problem is, how far the faith of the witch and her employer can produce the necessary results *without* the victim's actual knowledge that the operation is taking place. It is a matter upon which much research is still being done, but it is perhaps best merely to say that the evidence, at the moment, seems to be that (where the unknowing victim himself accepts the convention) long-range destruction by sympathetic magic does seem a possibility. It is hard to believe that, in fact, the palaeolithic cave-dwellers actually persuaded bison to offer themselves the more readily for killing because a clay model had been symbolically speared in a cave. But an African native whose hair or nails have been incorporated in a wax model, then slowly destroyed, does in fact seem to wither away, without visible reason. Is poison administered as well? I do not think that at the moment it is possible always to assume it.

Sympathetic magic is claimed against the witches in a large number of the recorded trials. Perhaps a very few examples are all that is necessary here, since the practice is world-wide even today. The Anglo-Saxons and Normans legislated against a crime already condemned in the Roman world, but the first record, in the English courts, is in 1324. In that year Robert le Mareschal, of Leicester, accused a witch of Coventry of performing magic, and named twenty-seven of the witch's clients. The witch (a man) was to receive twenty pounds, and Robert fifteen pounds, to kill the King, the Prior of Coventry, and others. They made seven figures of wax and canvas, representing their enemies, and also one Richard de Sowe, who was to be what we should now call a control. A lead pin was stuck into the head of the image of Richard de Sowe, who obediently went out of his mind. He died three days after the pin had subsequently been thrust into the heart of his effigy. Robert at this point turned king's evidence, the customers escaped, and the witch died in jail.

Six years before, in France, the Bishop of Troyes had undergone a long trial for the murder of Queen Jeanne, the wife of Philip IV. After various indignities to her wax image had failed to produce any effect, the bishop had lost his temper, it was alleged. He tore the image to bits, trampling on them, and throwing the pieces into the fire. Whereupon the queen died. But James I did not die, although he was severely frightened, when Bothwell and the Scottish witches tried to dispose of him in a similar way, and Mr Peter Fleming has fortunately survived successfully that silly prank of 1928. But we undergraduates did not, after all, take that episode seriously, and probably enough, in sophisticated circles, simple sympathetic magic soon lost its power. Yet the use of puppets, in a more credulous society, was always part of the stock in trade – whether it was John Walsh of Dorset, in 1566, or Elizabeth

Device, of the Lancashire witches, who crumbled away marl
puppets of her enemies at the beginning of the next century.
There used to be hearts stuck with pins in the Ruskin museum
at Oxford,* and every now and again one reads, even today,
of devoted maidens of the eastern counties who attempt by
sympathetic magic to influence the hearts of village policemen.
In Italy, the practice is fairly widespread among the peasants,
and in really primitive communities it is, with Contagious
Magic, everyday activity. We still burn an unpopular figure
in effigy on 5 November.

The evil eye was merely the physical signal of bewitchment
– the sense which the eye can give of being personally and
intimately compromised. The hypnotist uses the power of the
eye, and it is, obviously enough, a means of communicating
personal force – vindictive, as in witches, or favourable, as in
lovers. The phallic sign, the thumb between the fingers, is
still involved in Italy to destroy its power, and amulets of the
phallic sign are still sold in the coptic shops in Cairo, and for
all I know elsewhere. The squint was abnormal, and evil –
although a large number of beautiful women have always
squinted slightly. The evil eye is a transmitter of power and of
ill-intent.

Spells were innumerable: spells of the eye, of the knot, of
the configuration in wood or sand. Every evil wish could be
projected by symbolic magic, given predisposition in the subject. Once ill-wished, the victim was bewitched, or, still worse,
possessed.

The literature of possession is vast. It veers from the convo-
lutions of theological mysticism to the case histories of native
mumbo-jumbo enthusiasts, by way of demented servant girls
of the nineteenth century. It is riddled with improbabilities
and authenticated by prigs. But nothing can do away with the
recognition, common to biblical enthusiasts and anyone who
has dealt with 'backward' peoples or psychopathic cases, that
the phenomenon exists. The vomiting of pins may be a local
and unusual manifestation, but the simple fact that people

* Another turned up in a Dorset chimney in 1950, walled in with a
broomstick.

do appear to be inhabited by forces alien to their normal selves, with violent and demarcated characteristics, is merely a matter of observation. It is abundantly clear that suggestion may have an influence over physical phenomena, quite apart from its psychical effects – especially when the 'victim' or 'patient' has confidence in the person exerting the suggestion. As Arturo Castiglioni* writes:

> The effect of psychic factors on the development of physical phenomena, such as changes of temperature, the stopping of menstruation, brought about by suggestion, the appearance of bleeding stigmata, a phenomenon that has been repeated in many cases as an experiment, and other reliable demonstrations, is well known. Such are the so-called miraculous healings, the successes achieved by Coué's method and other similar systems, of which that of Christian Scientists is the best known. Real cures, whose asserted miraculous origins magnify the importance and effects, determining illusions and even hallucinations of well-being, are well known to all physicians who have had occasion to study similar cases . . . a fortune-teller or a soothsayer who claims to have supernatural visions or an old peasant who enjoys the reputation of a wizard is able to obtain results that would be impossible for the most famous physician possessing perfect scientific equipment.

Just as local anaesthesia can be brought about, so can local damage, or in extreme cases, death itself. This is called 'thanatomania', and the death impulse can only be remedied by the counteracting influence of another wizard. For it is now a commonplace that primitive peoples can die if they realize that they have broken the taboo, and that the curse is upon them. I have, on a different level, met old men in Dorset who claim to have been immobilized by the evil eye. Certainly, such highly sensitive processes as sexual intercourse can be affected by mental factors, of which psychic control is one. The Church claimed that spells could inhibit sexual competence, because connexion was in any case the Devil's work. But whether it is the Devil's work or whether the witches also used drugs, there is every reason that, purely psychologically, external influences should create the sexual repugnance in an individual which

* Arturo Castiglioni, *Adventures of the Mind*, London, 1947.

Summers translated from Sprenger, for some reason, as 'hebe-
tation'. Impotence is largely of the mind. So, sometimes, is
abortion, although this is better achieved by the physical
means that the witches also possessed.

Schizophrenia and hysteria, individual or in the mass, is
only just becoming a study with a wide literature that the lay-
man can master and the film distort. Obviously a vast number
of mental disturbances which today we still do not understand
were, previously, attributed to witches, when such appropriate
victims were available.* Moreover, an age with so ready an
explanation, and no reason for scepticism, accepted as genuine
manifestations that were, particularly where children were
concerned, merely malicious manipulation. The vomiting of
pins is a late trick, peculiarly found in the British Isles and New
England, and in spite of the good name and obvious sincerity
of those who sometimes report the instances, it is hard not to
believe that their piety overcame their critical powers of observation. It is now far too late to examine the evidence of
past trials to find out the truth. Perhaps a large majority of
major cases of 'possession' by devils are nothing whatever to
do with exterior influence. Yet local physical incapacity,
derived from fear of witchcraft, seems possible enough. Where
extreme suggestibility and auto-suggestibility were present, as
in primitive peoples today, they might even help in bringing
out symptoms for which we should diagnose a purely physical
cause.

* The witch, black or white, was called in to deal with the phenomena,
as well as being supposed to have caused them, often to his or her own dis-
advantage. Failure properly to effect exorcism could usually be explained
by the Church, but was dangerous for the individual practitioner. Here is a
cutting from the *Egyptian Gazette* for 11 November 1944, to give an
up-to-date example:
'BEAT PATIENT TO DEATH. Hussein Ayad, a Cairo "jinn doctor"
charged with manslaughter, admitted at the Assizes that he had beaten his
patient to death. "I refused to treat him," he said, "but his family insisted,
in fact, threatened me. When I saw the sick man I discovered that he was
obsessed by a jinn." The Judge asked if the prisoner had beaten his victim.
"I had to scare the jinn out of the man," he replied. "And in doing so you
killed your patient," commented the Bench, condemning Ayad to five
years' hard labour.'

The whole question of familiars, whilst not (as is sometimes said) exclusive to the British Isles, is very specially developed there. It illustrates, particularly well, the way in which a ritual and metaphysical concept became degraded and mixed with lower and material things. It might at first be supposed, having regard to the connexion with animal cults which is a basic strand of the whole witch theme, that this was another appearance of the totem animal, in a personal attachment. This does not seem to be so. If a particular 'devil' associated with any individual woman, outside the formal ceremonies, he might no doubt be considered an incubus, or in some terminology a familiar. This may account for a few of the stories which crop up of human familiars, as for instance in the Trial of Abre Grinset, the Suffolk witch tried in 1667, and her 'Pretty handsome Young Man'. But the essence of the belief seems very different, and goats, bulls, and the larger mammals are hardly ever mentioned. It is true that large birds and animals are sometimes spoken of as being used as auguries, just as fortune-tellers sometimes have small birds or animals today, as part of their stock in trade. There is here probably a confusion with the lover or devil of the sabbat, in his cult accoutrement. At all events, the Devil who was claimed variously to have appeared to Margaret Nin-Gilbert of Thurso, in 1719, as a great black horse, a man riding upon a great black horse, a black cloud, or a black hen, must have been the invention of a very confused mind.

The metaphysical concept of a personal spirit, an evil attachment permanently in waiting, is very old indeed – older than Plato's hypothesis of aerial daemons. Pythagoras was supposed to have conversed with an eagle, and the whole idea was adopted by the earliest Christians, so that we find the Ethiopian Book of Saints setting out the belief in personal devils. In the same way we find already, at that time, the belief in the personal agent of good – the Guardian Angel later invoked, by our own mothers, in childhood. It is, of course, a personification of the whole dualist idea: the two sides of the human-deistic character, striving in every individual to achieve mastery. The thread goes through all mystical writing, and the Strange Satellite, the Astral Mentor, the grey eminence of the soul, pops up everywhere in the esoteric legend. As ritual became complicated by a deeper knowledge of the Kabbalistic writings, so it was felt that an individual could, by conjuration, summon up spirits of a chosen cast, to carry out his particular demands. This idea found a new impetus in the enormous popularity of the Faust books and the whole Faustian legend. Later it became a literary device and a pedant's paradise. In spite of the complexities and, often, fatuities of the ritual, the basic idea was the earlier one, inherent in all dualistic teaching.

This idea of a personal devil – a servant in human, heraldic, or animal form – obeying the conjurer (who in the later versions had sold his soul to the Devil for the privilege) was common everywhere, and especially so in Germany, in the sixteenth century. What appears most in the accounts of trials in Great Britain is the domestic familiar in animal form – more especially in the eastern counties, during the time of the worst witch persecution there.

The domestic familiar of the trials had a variety of names: an angel, a little master, imp, fury, maumet, nigget, or one of various terms of endearment, equally used for perfectly innocent households pets. These covered most of the normal and some of the less known domestic animals and fowls, with a sprinkling of ferrets, rats, and even butterflies or wasps. Toads were particularly often mentioned – no doubt because of the horror notoriously associated with their believed capacity for spitting poison. There was naturally a high percentage of cats and gods, and sometimes miscellaneous but ill-described small mammals. They were called Suckin, or Titty, or something equally suggestive, or just one of the odd, understandable names – Hiff Hiff, or Puppet – which an old woman might bestow on something of which she was fond. They were (it was held) adopted, inherited, or bestowed by the Devil, and they went about to do the witch's evil work, returning to be fed on blood, or suckled by the witch herself at supernumerary nipples created for the purpose.

A combination of circumstances may account for these beliefs. First, there may at some time have been a remnant of custom by which members of the coven were given animal tokens – although the evidence for this appears very slight. Secondly, when the continental idea of a personal devil reached England (with much else of the whole rigmarole of debased ritual which flooded the Continent after the popularization of the Faust story and the adoption of witch-hunting by the Calvinists), it may have been argued that witches *ipso facto* must own devils. If this were so, as I believe, then much of the whole ghastly preconception can be laid down to Matthew Hopkins and whatever inspired him. For the search for supernumerary nipples was particularly his preoccupation, and the nipples were related essentially to the belief in the domestic familiar. When there were nipples – and (in spite of all that has been said in Chapter 7) these certainly were often the most ordinary blemishes – they must, it was held, have suckled something. It was easy to induce tortured and frightened people, bemused and inarticulate at best, to condemn, with themselves, the pets who lived near to them. Conversely, as the idea spread, any remaining individuals of the old belief who had actually become convinced that they had sold themselves to the Devil, might well feel that a familiar was a necessary part of the deed, and acquire one or more.

Finally, eccentric people, and more particularly elderly ones living alone, do have the most extraordinary pet animals. The toad, for instance, is sometimes domesticated even today (it likes bread and milk), and, even in the eighteenth century, Gilbert White in the *Natural History of Selborne* mentioned a toad 'of monstrous size' kept as a pet – apparently without any charge of occult significance. Even the suckling and blood-sucking is by no means impossible, and any psychopathist can give evidence of much more complicated forms of bestiality and diseased practices with animals.

In spite of the mystical and literary origins of the familiar, and the divination through animals which may have lingered as a decaying practice, the vast majority of domestic familiars, as described in the trials, were probably either the hallucinations of the demented, or the dirty and devoted pets of lonely, unsympathetic, old women. If the cat has predominated in folk memory, it is more probably because old women do keep cats than because a very different sort of cat was once worshipped in Egypt, or because cat familiars are known in India. Through the freakishness of folk-etymology the old word 'cat', meaning a stick, may have become confused with the animal: the familiar with the broomstick. The trials are gloomy reading enough all through, and the passages about domestic familiars some of the most pathetic and horrifying.

Orthodox diabolists and theologians naturally accept familiars at their face value, as positive materializations of the Evil One. They are equally prepared to accept, with shudders and prophylactic prayer, the associated idea of lycanthropy. Yet a historical and unsatanic explanation of this complicated if early conception is available.

Lycanthropy is not quite the same thing as metamorphosis, so common in the literature of the ancients. In this, a human being is transformed into an animal, usually involuntarily, and stays in the animal shape until the spell is removed and the story ends. Its use is mainly symbolic. Lycanthropy, in its two simplest forms, is either the belief that a witch or devil-ridden person temporarily assumes an animal form, to ravage or destroy; or, that they create an animal 'double' in which leaving the lifeless human body at home, he or she can wander terrorize, and batten on mankind.

Pathology knows a morbid condition known as lycorexia which involves a wolfish hunger and a fixation in the patient that he actually is a wolf or some other animal. He howls or makes whatever is the appropriate sound: he lusts for raw flesh: he mimics the movements of the animal. For practical purposes, he *is* the animal. There is glandular disturbance and on the mental side, all those symptoms which are sometimes diagnosed as possession. This very horrible disorder, backed by the literary example of King Nebuchadnezzar, defied in early times any explanation other than that the deranged person concerned, who no doubt was dangerous enough, had in fact been diabolically transformed, probably by personal volition.

This uncommon, but observed and notorious aberration

endorsed belief in the absolute fact of that human identification with animals which, as has been shown, was already part of cult belief and practice. It is a belief which still exists in many parts of the world, and there are tribes where the initiation ceremonies at adolescence involve the entwining of the novitiate's life with that of an animal. In some places the identification is held to be so close that the man or the animal dies when the other partner does so. This is the individual application of what, in a group, is identification with the totem animal. Group lycanthropy has been described already: the frenzied worshippers, covered in the skins of the cult animal, mimicking its actions in the dance or the ritual activities. Probably Herodotus was writing of something like this when he tells of a tribe called the Neuri, in eastern Europe, who for a few days every year were transformed into wolves. The latest popularized example is that of the leopard men of West Africa, a number of whom were recently sentenced to death for ritual murder, committed in leopard fashion, with leopard claws attached to the hands, whilst the body was covered with leopard-skin. They no doubt felt that they had actually become leopards, and it is likely that they had drugged themselves as well. It is quite possible that, as group activities diminished, and the cult declined, occasional individuals did separately dress up in skins to harm their neighbours. If so, the circumstance, added to examples of the pathological condition described, would be quite enough to fix lycanthropy in the popular mind. Strength would no doubt be given to it by the freak creatures who from time to time turn up even today, having been reared by animals. We can discount Romulus and Remus, but Mowgli is hardly fiction in India. Odd things happen all the time in Africa, and an 'antelope boy', wild, speechless, bounding, and photogenic, emerged into the news from Syria in 1947 – although his subsequent history has been tactfully suppressed.

Everyone knows the stock story of the werewolf – the *loup-garou* – even if only in the tidied version we see at Christmas, in Little Red Riding Hood. It is popular in romantic fiction, and the principal variant on the chopping off of a limb from the marauding beast – only to find that a wicked old woman in the village has lost a similar limb at that precise moment – is the hag being shot with a silver bullet. It is unnecessary to give a full example: the ingredients are a terrified peasantry, a huge ravaging wolf, avid for blood, a moonlight hunt through the forest, the shot that wounds the beast, the trail of blood that accompanies its slot in the midnight pursuit, leading to a cottage. There lies the witch, sorely wounded, usually to be dispatched with an axe.

A variant, quoted because there is every reason to believe the outcome authentic, is the story of a sensational case reported in the sixteenth century, from a village in the mountains of Auvergne. Here the gentleman hunting (as usual) was suddenly set upon by a wolf of monstrous size which his bullets could not harm. However, in the struggle he lopped off one of its fore-paws. This he placed in his pocket and set off terrified for home. On the way he showed the trophy to a friend, only to discover, not the bleeding paw he had put in his pocket, but a woman's hand, upon which was a wedding ring. The friend recognized the ring as that of his wife. He went in search of her, and found her sitting by the fire in the kitchen, her arm hidden beneath her apron. When he seized her by the arm his suspicions were verified, for there was the ghastly stump, fresh from the wound. She was arrested, and subsequently burnt in Riom, in the presence of thousands of spectators.

This is the European form, commonest in our own writers. It is only necessary to say that the legend is world-wide, and normally attached to the largest and fiercest of the wild beasts operating in the locality. Whilst the wolf was commonest in central Europe, the bear is the most usual form in the North (hence the expression 'berserk'), with hyenas in Abyssinia and the Sudan, boars in Greece, leopards or lions in Africa, jaguars in the New World, and tigers in the East. The last wolf in England was killed in the early sixteenth century, and in Scotland in the middle of the eighteenth century. Witches were therefore supposed to take on the form of cats – perhaps the indigenous wild cat – or of the hare, doubtless because of the sacred associations the hare had in England in pre-Roman times – as Caesar noted, and thousands of little boys have laboriously translated from the first book of the Gallic Wars. The evidence in this country is strained, and usually little more than the unfortunate coincidence that someone who injured an animal found that the injury synchronized with a similar one to an unpopular and feared old woman in the same locality. The one or two witches who claimed to have been able to turn themselves into toads or bats seem to have been hysterical or merely trying to please their tormentors.

Lycanthropy, then, had a historical origin, but in Europe it was folk legend, and no real activity, that for hundreds of years made it another charge against witches. An exception is sixteenth-century France, where there does seem to have been an outbreak of murder and cannibalism consciously associated with werewolfism. Among primitive peoples the phenomenon still exists: sometimes in inexplicable forms.

As the witches were the Devil's agents, so they were accused of causing not only pestilence and every physical or mental ailment, but also of control of destructive natural phenomena. We have, therefore, detailed accounts of their powers in bringing about storms at sea, or precipitations of hail and rain. The most famous case is that of the witches of North Berwick, with whom Bothwell's name is closely associated. At the trial of Major Weir, in Edinburgh in 1670, it was claimed and admitted by some of the accused, that they had used incantations to produce a storm to wreck the vessel carrying King James to bring his bride-to-be to Scotland. The evidence was obtained after torture, and the means the somewhat improbable one of casting a cat into the sea. Yet a great storm did, in fact, occur. It nearly wrecked the ship, and it was only after this that the confederation (whose political associations were clearly defined) resorted to poison. Storm-raising had a long history, illustrated in the *Malleus Maleficarum* from biblical authority, although it is not there stressed that the procedure largely coincided with that employed for the same end by the prophet Samuel.

If the witches did regard themselves as storm-raisers, it may have been from the tradition of the old goddesses of the North, who controlled the winds. But more certainly it must have been from the early property of being rain-makers, which is still the principal function of many African witch-doctors.

Witches cast spells; they raised havoc; they poisoned; they aborted cattle and inhibited human beings; they served the Devil, parodied Christian practices, allied themselves with the king's enemies; they copulated with other witches in male or female form, whom they took to be incubi or succubi; they committed abuses with domestic animals. More, they did these things consciously, in the belief that they served a diabolic master and challenged Heaven. Their motives were confused, their impulses bemused, and their proceedings more and more remote from any common original practice. Yet they did them, and the reasons for what they did lie in the earliest religions and beliefs.

Besides these witches, thousands of technically innocent people died, as a result of mass hysteria and pious fear. The symptoms caused death, long after the disease had virtually expired.

*Part Three*

# THE DECLINE IN EUROPE

## 12

## *Prosecution and Persecution*

ALTHOUGH witchcraft still exists beneath the surface wherever there is strong and primitive religious belief, it is now virtually extinct in Europe and America. This is therefore the place to examine the reasons for the decline of the cult. They are the physical and moral opposition of Christianity, together with economic, social, and intellectual developments. All these causes interrelate, but in this chapter I propose to examine briefly the positive measures of the Churches and States, which did in fact decimate the practitioners of the cult – as well as thousands of other people – through measures which constitute the first really large-scale and ruthless purge since classical times.

The punishment of those successfully accused of witchcraft operated in three ways: through ecclesiastical law, civil law, and lynch law. It is, roughly, true to say that ecclesiastical law was primarily the effective prosecutor for the longest period, and was succeeded by civil law, with lynch law alone operating, illegally, during the final period. Yet there are many local exceptions to this.

It is interesting to notice that there were also three peaks in the persecution of witchcraft. Each of them was at a period when new ideas were threatening the authoritarian framework of the Church, and there had been latitude of faith with the threat of disintegration. The first peak was after the original wave of the Crusades had expended itself. The Norman expansion into the Near East had blocked the Seljuk incursion from the East, and Europe seemed saved from direct Mohammedan invasion. Unfortunately, there appeared to be undue fraternization at the front, and dualistic ideas from the East reinforced latent heresies at home, where anyhow there was dangerous modernism. The Church countered. With the external enemy held, it could consolidate. The witches suffered at the hand of the new instrument that it founded, the Inquisition. This was in the thirteenth century. A second wave of persecution broke out with the beginning of the fifteenth century – after the Black Death, the long-drawn Hundred Years War, and the development of nationalism had brought another period of disillusion and questioning. The great trials of this time started a further increase of witch-hunting which went on until it accentuated into a third climax in the sixteenth and seventeenth centuries, when the Renaissance and the Reformation had finally disrupted the fabric of Catholic Europe. Then, the Counter-Reformation and the protesting Churches alike, in their fury of religious intolerance, purged and cauterized their own forces by burning and hanging the heretic and the witch, to purify themselves for the struggle with the new orthodox enemy. Neither side could afford what would today be called backward deviationists. It should be stressed that each of these major attempts to stamp out witchcraft, although largely successful, made its task more difficult for a time by, no doubt, recruiting to the cause of magic and the forbidden arts all manner of religious and social irreconcilables. Antibodies, in fact, were set up.

The place of witchcraft and the magicians in the ancient world has been noticed. It has been stressed that legislation was against the criminal offence of bewitching, rather than against any insult to the gods. The condition of hyperaesthesia was accepted, spells were everyday occurrences, and it was only when these were directed for gain, and more especially, supposed to be so directed against the person of the emperor, that action was taken. Individual magicians were suppressed, and those who sought supernatural powers exterior to the orthodox pantheon were feared. Yet there were many gods, and many strange things, in a philosophy which made obedience to the deity of the emperor the only real test of conformity to spiritual convention. Barbarian peoples had weird and terrifying ways, and slaves and captives had strange practices. There was no persecution of such a witch-cult as was known to the Middle Ages.

There was legislation in Rome in the time of the Republic,

and the Decemviral code demanded the extreme penalty for conjuration, and 'whoever shall have bewitched the fruits of the earth'. A hundred and fifty years later, the *Lex Cordelia* laid down penalties which may have been directed against sorcery, but were more obviously against 'substantial poisoning', for which the 170 Roman matrons, as already stated, were convicted, with evidences of incantation, at the time. Senatorial and imperial anathemas continued, but poisoners, mathematicians, and astrologers who foresaw anything but immortality for the heads of state, were the main ones to suffer. Constantine, in adopting Christianity, limited the legitimate use of magic, and ordered the severe punishment of those 'charming the minds of modest persons to the practice of debauchery'. He had no objection, however, to the prevention by magic of premature rains, or to white magic generally, and made careful distinction between theurgic and goetic practices – as the later Church did not. Julian 'the Apostate' was accused by clerical historians of being a necromancer, and certainly did extend toleration and interest to all kinds of arts. He was a scholar of the old tradition. It was his Christian successors, Valentinian and Valens, who started, in A.D. 373, a persecution of appalling ferocity which extended throughout both the Eastern and Western Empires. The charges were of treason, poisoning, and adultery in palace circles, mainly by conjuration, and the results were horrible enough. To quote Gibbon:

From the extremity of Italy and Asia the young and the aged were dragged in chains to the tribunals of Rome and Antioch. Senators, matrons, and philosophers expired in ignominious and cruel tortures. The soldiers who were appointed to guard the prisons declared, with a murmur of pity and indignation, that their numbers were insufficient to oppose the flight or resistance of the multitude of captives. The wealthiest families were ruined by fines and confiscation; the most innocent citizens trembled for their safety: and we may form some notion of the magnitude of the evil from the extravagant assertion of an ancient writer, that in the obnoxious provinces the prisoners, the exiles, and the fugitives formed the greatest part of the inhabitants.

Yet, although magic was claimed, the grave offence was still clearly that of political conspiracy. Magicians, astrologers, and mathematicians were individually feared and proscribed, and their books burned. The sophisticated, gnostic side of the ritual was relentlessly if intermittently opposed: but a cult of Devil worshippers was still undetected – if only because the Devil himself was as yet so ill-defined.

Gradually the Roman peace gave way to local anarchy and to a universal lowering of material standards of living. Christian redemptionism and the old religions struggled on, at a low spiritual level, while traces of the classical order of life in Europe continued in the ecclesiastical establishments – themselves, often enough, ignorant, fearful, and bigoted. Out of this night of disintegration shine little oases of security, lit by orderly legislation. The Church defended the Roman tradition as it best could, and formulated its own system. It can be said to have been doing so until the middle of the eleventh century. Meanwhile, the error of witchcraft was dealt with by local legislation, rather than universal decree.

In fact, much of the old tolerance still persisted. Where Christianity was new, obviously the earlier beliefs could not be too quickly transmuted or exterminated, and seers remained, outside everyday worship. In the north were scalds, druids, Lapland wizards, and runic charms. The whole mythology of sorceric magic and the hexe went on in Germany, with the prophetess as revered as she had been in the time of Tacitus. The Mediterranean world merged on the east into an Asia where divining and necromantic faculties were regarded as honourable – venerated and feared, not execrated and feared. South lay Africa and the remains, stronger then even than now, of the earliest group releases and the most primitive and powerful formulas. The Church could only consolidate, not attack.

Whilst consolidating, its approach to witchcraft was extremely tentative, and the punishments were comparatively tame. Some idea of a pact with the Devil was formulated in A.D. 306, and the Council of Ancyra, in A.D. 314, forbade witchcraft as a branch of pharmacy, demanding a few years' penance from any found guilty of it. St Basil, more stern, recommended an atonement of thirty years. Anglo-Saxon law exacted three years' penance if the magic failed, seven if it succeeded and the victim died – three years of these on bread and water unless the victim died out of his mind, when the magician must spend *five* years on bread and water. By the time of Canute, the law had hardened, and punishment was banishment, or death if unrepentant. Charlemagne had severely condemned both witchcraft and the belief in some forms of its manifestation.

There was, then, no general law; nor could there be, in a Europe without a general rule, which was assimilating successive invaders, marrying diverse cultures, speaking innumerable and half-formed languages, and still largely swamp and forest. There was a steady decline in humanity which was not arrested until the thirteenth century – with the exception of the period of the Carolingian renaissance, during which, incidentally, torture was for the time being abolished. Yet whilst popes and emperors disputed authority in the decaying cities of Rome and Germany, and peasants everywhere obeyed the whim of a local overlord and the Sunday rule of a foreign priest, the fathers of the Church gradually forged their faith, determined doctrine, and defined the Evil One. With the decline of humanity and the humanities, toleration also faded. There were contradictions and anomalies, but throughout all this period, the laws against heresy and witchcraft grew gradually more severe, ready for the period of the first great attack – during the aggressive and reconstructive period from 1050 until 1300 or so.

By this time, the first ardour of the Crusades was exhausted. The economic adventure of the fourth crusade had ended quite simply in the plunder of Constantinople, and the expeditions (with the exception of a few personal acts of fanaticism) had become a penitential duty or a politico-economic exercise. As an organized eastward thrust of the Christian world (in so far as they were ever this), they had served their purpose. The medieval system was emerging. Nationalism was not yet a grave danger: the Magyars and Slavs were being absorbed:

localism could be attacked everywhere: Europe could become Christendom. The triple conception of Universality, Authority, and the Horizontal Division of Society could perhaps be put into practice.

Yet, if all this potential existed, the spiritual situation was anything but comforting to the statesmen of the Vatican. Travel and the ideas of the east, the old dualism and residuary paganism combined to create disillusion, hysteria, or indifference. They also infiltrated as heresy. What had been pagan survival was, now, seen as conscious antagonism inspired only by the Devil. The south was full of the Catharist, Waldensian, and Bulgarian heresies, and individual practitioners (Friar Bacon was an example) were experimenting dangerously. Infallibility was challenged. Volumes of Arabic philosophy has been introduced in the twelfth century, and people were, in places, questioning the basic mysteries of the Faith. There was proto-protestantism, and the Albigenses had the earliest translations of the Bible into vernacular French. While scholasticism defined, and re-defined, the way of the Church, dangerous free-thinkers revived the orphic and gnostic mysteries. Even where the people were faithful, it was with extravagance – the most fantastic of the Children's Crusades* took place in 1212, only just before the fourth Lateran Council and the death of Innocent III. His analysis of the whole position, and initiation of a positive campaign against heresy, formed a climax to the period. Significantly, surgery became a crime at the same time.

The campaign opened on several fronts. In the north, the Prussians were brought to a more stable conversion by the Bishop of Albrecht (although as late as the twentieth century they were reverting to their war gods). In the south, the heavy cavalry of the Norman French plundered and devastated the Languedoc. The Inquisition was set up as a travelling panel of investigators, charged to discover, report, and advise the local episcopal courts on the crushing of heresy in any form.

* Although it is possible to see this as a cynical expedient for coping with the problem of dispossessed children who roamed the south after the Albigensian persecutions had purged their parents.

Heresy implied an intellectual process of guilty defiance of the Almighty and His Vicar on earth, and witchcraft became at last identified with heresy. As witchcraft – the evidence of the old pre-Christian faith and the practice of its rites – was rampant in the peasant classes, it soon became one of the easiest forms of heresy to discover and to punish. Local bishops, who had observed tolerantly, through apathy or condescension, the immemorial customs of their flocks, found themselves forced by visiting spiritual commissars to take savage notice of these customs, as crimes against God and society.

As a result, the trials and the purges increased in tempo and ferocity, and thousands were handed over for execution to the secular arm after torture, evidence from the most disreputable informers, and a court system which, until recently, only professional historians could believe to be exercised by men most of them intellectually honest enough. This system we will look at again, when it had become finally codified in the fifteenth century. The dead were tried as well as the living, and no doubt a hysterical situation was created in which many became witches, if they could, simply because they imagined themselves branded by one of the symptoms of the cult – or from a mere belief, through whatever spiritual doubts or peccadillos, in their eternal damnation. If heresy was death anyhow, as well be hung for a goat as a misinterpretation of the Paschal Lamb. St Dominic, a devoted ascetic who whipped himself three times daily, may not necessarily have been the begetter of the Inquisition which procured the torture of thousands of others. But the friars in general (though the Franciscans were more tolerant), and the Dominicans who so particularly operated the Holy Office, spread in their travels the news of the conspiracy against Christ, and condensed and fired the evil they sought to destroy – and, by opposing lynch law, to contain.

This process continued sporadically, and with, if anything, growing intensity, for the next two hundred years, when it again mounted into a mania of witch-hunting. But whilst the Old Religion and customs were now heresy, and were suppressed among the peasant communities which still observed them, an early manifestation of the new zeal was great state trials of people in high places – only comparable (and very comparable indeed) to the state trials of authoritarian systems today.

An early body to be attacked was that of the Knights Templars, whose original deeds for the Cross had by this time receded in the common mind before the evidence of their enormous temporal wealth, arrogance, and independence. They constituted a body within the fabric of the Church which in fact, had its own independent officers and policy: an imperium within an imperium which Rome could hardly regard with equanimity. To the lay ruler, they were a privileged class owning huge powers and owing small allegiance. On both counts, they were a body to destroy, and the charge put against them was one of heresy. In 1307 they were accused, by Philip IV of France, of crimes which involved selling their souls to the Devil, and every sort of bestiality at their secret meetings – including the throwing about of babies to be sacrificed – and burning the bodies of dead members of the Order, afterwards ceremonially drinking the ashes. They were also accused of worshipping idols, and of gnosticism. Whatever their lapses, the story of their overthrow is a distasteful one. Whilst, to begin with, Philip merely confiscated their goods and property, justification had to be found, and the members of the Order were racked unsparingly until confessions admitting every kind of enormity had been wrung from them. The confessions they then often denied, and were retortured, the more rigorously in that they had relapsed. By 1312, the Order was broken and disbanded, most of its 9,000 manorial estates confiscated, with many of its 1,500 members destroyed – fifty-four of them together in a slow fire outside Paris, to the end claiming their innocence. The Grand Master, Jacques de Moley, after appalling sufferings, was roasted to death in 1314, on the island of the Seine, and 'in the light of the setting sun'.

How far the Templars were technically guilty is a ground for rare dispute between Roman Catholic and Protestant rationalist historians. Many Templars were, no doubt, innocent of all the charges of conscious heresy, and obeyed the rules of the Order without examining the symbolism. Most had probably condoned pacts with the Turks, and had adopted luxurious

Oriental ideas and Mohammedan latitude. Theirs was, moreover, the sort of institution in which homosexuality was likely to be endemic. A few of the inner circle probably did adopt the gnostic views which lay beneath the surface of Mediterranean society, and practised the ritual of the higher magic. Their dualism may have led to a denial of Christ. But no confessions appear to have been given freely. We cannot tell. It is clear, however, that the Roman Church (the Pope himself was at this time a puppet at Avignon), perhaps short-sightedly, perhaps ignorantly, accepted, because of the prevailing witch mania and the political pressure exerted, the pleas of a powerful temporal power against one of its own great institutions.

The pattern of accusation showed that the Inquisition, inspired or not by the avarice of Philip, did consider that the heresy of the Templars represented one facet of what was now seen as a general plague of witchcraft. Fear unslaked, the trials were hurried on, with a quickening of suspicion and an increased use of torture to obtain confession.

Ten years after the death of the Grand Master of the Templars, there took place in Ireland the famous case of Lady Alice Kyteler of Kilkenny. In the same year, 1324, there occurred in England the affair of John de Nottinghame. Witchcraft in high places was by no means a new accusation in the British Isles. Hubert de Burgh had been accused of charming his way into the favours of King John* in 1232. This, however, was the first case in Ireland, and the last for a considerable time. It has already been quoted, but it may be worth setting out briefly, since it illustrates the whole field of accusation now in vogue.

It is the vogue that is important, for the case was not of local initiation, and Lady Alice might have continued her career of high-born and ceremonial poisoning had not the Bishop of Ossery, acting in the light of the new bulls against sorcery just promulgated by Pope John XXII, investigated

---

* It was in John's reign that we find the first formal judicial trial for witchcraft in England, when 'Agnes, the wife of Odo the Merchant, accused Gideon of sorcery; and he was acquitted by the judgement of iron'.

charges brought against her by her third husband – that he
was being bewitched. The Bishop was an Englishman, clearly
no favourite with the local nobility, and the secular authorities
refused to help. Lady Alice, a person of position, was let off
with little more than a warning. She relapsed, however, and
was then accused with the full blast of charges by this time
common on the Continent. Many of them may well have been
accurate. They were, briefly, accusations of a denial of Christ,
the Hecatian practice of sacrificing living creatures at cross-
roads, the casting of lots, the ceremonial cursing of Lady Alice's
husband in a ritual centring on the burning of diabolical
candles, and the concocting of hell-brews from a pharmacopoeia including the intestines of cocks, herbs, hairs, unbaptized babes, and other messes, all boiled in the skull of a lately
beheaded robber. Further, she had co-habited with the mysterious Robin Artisson (who disappears from the scene) and
was discovered to be in possession of the Holy Wafer with the
Devil's name substituted for that of Jesus, and the 'pipe of
ointment' by means of which she 'galloped through thick
and thin'.

All this was after she herself had escaped, eventually reaching England, through the assistance of her powerful friends.
These either did not believe the charges; were themselves of
the movement; merely thought the case to have been brought
through jealousy of the wealth she was acquiring for a favourite son by her first husband; or because they were broad-
minded in these matters. Some others of the accused also
escaped. Lady Alice's chief attendant, Petronilla de Meath,
confirmed the charges, but not until she had been flogged six
times, at the Bishop's orders. When what was left of her was
brought up for the seventh flogging, she confirmed everything.
She was carried out into the city and publicly burned, spurning
the clergy and scorning and reviling her executioners.

Two others were publicly burned, some flogged in the
market place or through the city, one or two banished: and
witchcraft in Ireland resubmerged, for a century or so, below
the surface of recorded history.

All through the fourteenth century the trials went on, in a

Europe racked by the Babylonish Captivity, the Great Schism, the long-drawn exhaustion of the Hundred Years War. Intellectually and culturally new ideas were being thrown up, usually to be greeted by the Church, at least in their early forms, as heretical. The Papacy fought against the new nationalism, and the new municipalities, with only partial success – and against the Old Religion with an abandon comparable to the last anti-Jewish furies of the retracting Reich in 1945. Hearts must be pure, that right might conquer against the new economics, the new loyalties, and the challenge of the barbarian from the East, renewed by the threat of Tamburlaine. Heretics must die, witches must burn. Socially, too, there was chaos. In 1345 the Black Death, spreading the virus of Asia, finally hit western Europe, and was one of the causes of the great peasant upheavals: the Jacquerie in France and the Peasants' Revolt in England. Sporadically there were extremist outbreaks of hysteria: the dancing mania or that of the flagellants. A great fear was upon Europe. Wycliffe in England and John Huss in Czechoslovakia – burnt in Agincourt year, 1415 – heretically denied authority and introduced forms of personal religion and theological democracy.

As a result, the Church increased the tempo of its fight against Jews and against witches, whom it saw as the agents of the Devil responsible for all these manifestations of evil. Thousands were tried and burnt, and although, as late as 1340, there had been no precedent in Italy for the activities of the Inquisition, by the end of the century proceedings were more or less standardized throughout the Continent. Judges shuddered at the streams of evidence, and among the people there was violent curiosity, blended with fear and a sadistic joy at vengeance. Three great trials of this period are worth mention, although I do not propose to set out the evidence of these – or any – trials at length.

The first is the trial of Jeanne d'Arc, the Pucelle d'Orleans, in 1430. The orthodox textbook story has been conditioned by the circumstance that the Roman Catholic Church, some five hundred years after her death, canonized the young woman it had burnt; by admiration for nascent nationalism; and by the romantic glow of admiration which the English have always cultivated towards a selected number of their enemies, from Saladin to Rommel. It is the story of the peasant girl of noble enthusiasm and heroic bravery who leads her country to victory over its invaders, and dies at the stake, after betrayal, not without an English soldier to hand her a cross as she expires in the flames. It is a moral tale, and a stick to beat the Inquisition. It is still widely received outside the ranks of historians, in spite of the excellent corrective supplied by Bernard Shaw in the introduction to his *St Joan*.

In actual fact, the rehabilitation was a far less satisfactory and honest affair than the conviction, and although one can have every confidence that Jeanne was a person of high convictions, courage, and enterprise, there seems equal reason to agree with the findings of the court which sentenced her – if one accepts the premises of the time. Sentimental regard for her was not indeed a particularly early phenomenon, and Shakespeare, for instance, does not question her guilt. He represents this opponent of his adventurous Englishman as bewailing that

> My ancient incantations are too weak
> And Hell too strong for me to buckle with.

Whilst Roman Catholics must of course accept St Joan's sanctity, some other historians now incline to favour her technical guilt, and at least there was a strong case against her, which seems to have been pressed without torture. It is one of which we possess full records.

It may not be necessary to follow Professor Murray all the way and regard Jeanne as the accepted head of the Dianic cult, the 'God Incarnate' of the old faith, recognized and followed by the common soldiery where the crown had failed.* But

---

* The case is briefly but strongly presented in an appendix to Professor Murray's *Witch-Cult in Western Europe*. Her further suggestion that William Rufus and Thomas à Becket were similar sacrifices (hidden leaders of the Old Religion, and accepted as such by the common people) is closely argued by Hugh Ross Williamson in *The Arrow and the Sword* (Faber & Faber, 1947). The special pleading extending from this does read rather like Baconian theory.

threading through the extensive literature on the subject there are a number of circumstances which do show a close identification with known witch parallels, and not all of them were even denied. Jeanne d'Arc refused at her trial to say the Paternoster – or only if in the protection of the Confessional – and notoriously witches were 'unable' to do so. She did not use the name of Christ, but steadfastly used the rather unnecessary form 'my Lord', which Professor Murray interprets as being the head of the cult. She spoke of the people of 'our party', and described her 'Voices' as being frequently seen in human form walking about 'amongst the Christians'. The voices themselves she admitted hearing amongst the woods of her native Domrémy, where the peasants danced round a sacred tree in a fairy wood. She practised transvestism, wearing short hair and men's clothes by preference. She refused to say whether the 'St Michael' who visited her appeared naked or not, which may have led her accusers to believe him to have been an incubus. Above all, she heretically claimed personal revelation. When she had been burned her ashes were cast into the river at Rouen, as had been those of human sacrifices there for centuries.

Gilles de Rais, Marshal of France, who had been the Maid's comrade in arms, and no doubt on the military side had played a large part in her victories, followed her ten years later. He has his paragraph in the textbooks, and there are a string of padded-out curiosa about him – tiresome pamphlets with 'Bluebeard' and 'nameless orgies' all over the cover. His story is indeed tragic and disgusting enough, and it is probably true, although the number of boys he procured and sacrificed (they change sex in the drawing-room Bluebeard version)* seems excessive. There is too much blood altogether. But undoubtedly de Rais, power-mad and perverted, did more than dabble in magic, urged on by the desire for money to repair his huge but ravaged fortune, by a ranging and distorted spirit of speculation, and more especially by the rather mysterious adept

---

* De Rais had pinned on to him a bluebeard legend which first appears in Breton folklore of the sixth century, and subsequently was discovered in the Polynesian islands – by way of a Frenchman from Nantes.

Francesco Prelati, a diabolist with psychic powers. Under the threat, but not the application of torture, de Rais confessed to a loathsome and monotonous string of murders and abnormalities, exercised to obtain superhuman powers. In spite of his position, he was condemned and executed, with two of his nearest assistants, on 28 October 1440. It is only speculation, I feel, that he was another leader of the Dianic cult, and the next sacrifice after Jeanne d'Arc. But he was suspiciously connected with her, and certainly he practised the arts of the adepts of the higher mysteries, if not that of the peasant followers of the Old Religion.

The third major trial of this period differed from the others by being urban. Normally, the greater sophistication of towns meant that, whilst passionately enough believing in witchcraft, they were remote from the old ways and religions. The adepts and higher practitioners might thrive in towns, but the cult was a thing of the country. However, a resounding trial took place in Arras in 1459 of a large number of people of every social degree living in the city. They were perhaps Waldenses, and whilst, to Montague Summers, for instance, 'wretches whose heresies and sorceries were the scandal of the province' and 'had long been grievously suspected of robbing the tabernacles and using the Hosts to mingle with their broths and hellish unguents', they were to a typical nineteenth-century Protestant writer 'a devoted congregation . . . who used to repair at night to worship God in their own manner in solitary places'. The evidence seems to have been less convincing than usual, and obtained by torture. While the original witches 'examined' may have had cult connexions, the field of people incriminated by tortured confessions was, no doubt, that wished by the Inquisitors: dictated in this instance by motives of private vengeance and self-interest, as much as fear of heresy. So much so that the parliament of Paris declared the sentences illegal – but thirty-two years too late to help anybody. If any considerable witch group did exist in Arras, its activities followed the usual pattern – the ointment, the assembly, the Devil in the form of a man (with his face masked), the kiss, the instruction, the sexual dance, and so on.

But, as might be expected in a wealthy community, they were regaled with 'great plenty of meats and wines'. At all events, during two years Arras was distracted with fear, as confessions and accusations multiplied. Many of the rich bought their freedom, but most of the poorer of the accused were burned, to the wonder of thousands of spectators from all the country-side round – five of the first accused with paper mitres on their heads, on which were painted representations of the Devil as he was described as having appeared to them.

There were other trials of the prominent and influential. There were many more of humbler people, singly or collectively, who obscurely suffered as terrible, or more terrible, deaths. In the higher and more esoteric ranks, the teaching became more secret, and the torch was handed on carefully to picked adepts, with the rites corporately observed rarely, and with elaborate precautions. The philosophical stream of the old magic was largely divorced from the primitive peasant stream, and its practitioners were suspected, but rarely brought to trial. But ordinary people, of the old stocks, suffered under a campaign of rising fury. There was suspicion, accusation, and dread, everywhere. Courts worked overtime, and pyres burnt furiously and more often, as the Renaissance and then the Reformation brought on the third and last climax of extermination. The Renaissance itself meant an increasing latitude of mind, and a spirit of speculation which challenged orthodox dogma, and invited reinvestigation of older beliefs. One outcome of this was the Reformation. But this was not yet tolerance, and the Reformers were even more bitter opponents of witchcraft than the Catholics. With every other point of belief in dispute, all were as convinced of the danger of witchcraft as of scriptural authenticity or the existence of the Deity. Indeed, the reliance of the reformed churches upon Holy Writ ('Thou shalt not suffer a witch to live'), made them the more violent. 'I would have no compassion on the witches,' cried Luther. 'I would burn them all.'

Calvin, when remodelling the laws of Geneva, preserved and fieceley prosecuted those against witches. The mad fury spread across Europe, and when the authorities were not thought sufficiently diligent, the terrified populace took things into their own hands and lynched anyone whom malice or fear suggested. Florimond, the author of a work *On Antichrist*, as reported by the Jesuit Delrio, is always quoted at this point. He wrote:

All those who have afforded us some signs of the approach of Antichrist agree that the increase of sorcery and witchcraft is to distinguish the melancholy period of his advent: and was ever an age so afflicted as ours? The seats destined for criminals in our courts of justice are blackened with persons accused of this guilt. There are not judges enough to try them. Our dungeons are gorged with them. No day passes that we do not render our tribunals bloody by the dooms which we pronounce, or in which we do not return to our homes discountenanced and terrified at the horrible confessions which we have heard. And The Devil is accounted so good a master, that we cannot commit so great a number of his slaves to the flames but what there shall arise from their ashes a sufficient number to supply their place.

It did not seem hyperbole.

Impetus to this holocaust had been given by the famous Bull of 1484. *Summis desiderantes affectibus.* Giovanni Battista Cibo was in that year elected to the Tiara, and issued this manifesto against sorcerers, magicians, and witches. It was only one in the series of such pronouncements, but it was a particularly fierce broadside against heresy generally – nascent Protestantism on one hand, and on the other the old enemy dualism, in all its clandestine organizations. To make the Bull effective it was followed by the appointment of judges with powers of jurisdiction for various areas.

Two of these officials were Father James Sprenger, of Bâle, and Father Henry Krämer – both Dominicans – associated together as Chief Inquisitors for Germany. Together they produced, in 1490, the textbook of procedure in the conduct of their duties – the *Malleus Maleficarum*: the codification of the whole campaign, and an examination of the behaviour of witches, with the rules for their extermination.

To us, the basis of the whole work is mad and cruel. To them, it was necessary and cruel, and our views would have seemed mad ones. For we live in a time of religious tolerance, which to them would have seemed the abandoning of God. They would, however, have approved and understood the convictions (if they did not share the premises) procured by the servants of authoritarian states, whose idea of preserving society by eliminating the heretic, by any and every means, is identical with what was that of the authoritarian Church. Where you fought ultimate and positive evil it was better that the innocent should suffer than that the guilty, anywhere, should prosper. And the guilty were felt to be everywhere. Sprenger and Krämer, and their contemporaries, believed that malevolence existed, and must be defeated. It was a dogma of their faith. The authority of the papacy and the sympathy of the populace supported them. They had no doubts in their grisly work. They were subtle men, but they would simply not have understood any charge of dishonesty. Malice was in the world, and had to be defeated, for the survival of Christ and His religion. They must attack, not defend. They were high-principled men, not self-indulgent sadists, any more than have normally been the judges of Communist or Nazi courts, equally confronted with heresy against the political creeds of our own time. Their sin was greater than themselves: it was that of absolute faith, absolute conviction. Even a great rationalist like Lecky could write:

The judges had no motive whatever to desire the condemnation of the accused; and, as conviction would be followed by a fearful death they had the strongest motives to exercise their power with caution and deliberation. . . . The evidence [of witchcraft] is essentially cumulative. Some cases may be explained by monomania, others by imposture, others by chance coincidences, and others by optical delusions: but, when we consider the multitude of strange statements that were sworn and registered in legal documents, it is very difficult to frame a general rationalistic explanation which will not involve an extreme improbability. In our own day, it may be said with confidence, that it would be altogether impossible for such an amount of evidence to accumulate round a conception which had no substantial basis in fact. . . . If we considered witchcraft probable, a hundredth part of the evidence we possess would have placed it beyond the region of doubt. If it were a natural but improbable fact, our reluctance to believe it would have been completely stifled by the multiplicity of the proofs.

The Inquisitors did believe. The bloodstained proofs were there. In charity they condemned.

All this is merely to say that the men of the Middle Ages and the Renaissance did not, if they were orthodox, think as we do. By every standard to which we normally subscribe, the *Malleus Maleficarum* is a most hideous document. It defied all that we mean by the laws of evidence. It presumed guilt and it advocated torture. It allowed virtually no defence, yet it made suggestions for ways to confuse and betray the prisoner. It advocated as punishment cruel and protracted death. It used devilish ingenuity to trap a devil who can rarely have been present. It provided a weapon to send to a writhing death thousands of misguided, superstitious, and ignorant souls, of whom only a few were perhaps actuated consciously by the motives and beliefs it sought to destroy.

To begin with, common defamation was enough to merit arrest. St Bernard had ruled that 'an evident fact' was sufficient in charges of heresy, so that public ill-fame* was all that was necessary to justify the calling in for questioning of all but the very wealthy or powerful. A good life was not enough, for it has already been shown that the ascetic behaviour of the Albigenses was enough to make them liable to suspicion. Indeed, the more obviously devout the accused, the more likely that they were the subtle agents of the Enemy. The ordinary medieval test for allegations against the character – the trial by ordeal – was not permitted, as witches might charm themselves to immunity from the effects of heat.† 'Weighing against the Bible' could be damning, but, if successful for the accused, was merely negative evidence.

* As in racial charges in South Africa in our own time.

† The real witches no doubt could, just as could those favoured by the priests in a civil ordeal, for the use of an asbestos fluid was known very early – quite apart from any hyperaesthetic powers the adept might possess.

Although a general defamation was enough, witnesses were an asset. For so grave a crime, they need not be people of good repute, and ordinary practice was discarded, in that even criminals and excommunicates could give evidence against the prisoner. Children were encouraged to betray their parents. The only people who could not give evidence were blood enemies, activated by malice. Since a witch who knew the witness could always claim such enmity, therefore, the witness's name could be withheld, or the defendant could be misled as to who had said what. And the defendant was likely enough to be the only person to try to establish such malice, since any advocate for the defence was a very formal and unreal figure indeed. It was argued that heresy was in its essence indefensible, and, as in political trials in many countries today, any lawyer undertaking the defence was himself likely to be a suspect. If he spoke at all, he could make no counter-charges, nor take advantage of technical slips by the prosecution. To be accused was, therefore, almost inevitably to come to trial, and to come to trial was almost inevitably to be condemned. Bodin, the great authority of the seventeenth century, wrote, 'The trial of this offence must not be conducted like other crimes. Whoever adheres to the ordinary course of justice prevents the spirit of the law, both divine and human. He who is accused of sorcery should never be acquitted. . . .' He rarely was.

With relentless logic it was argued, however, that justice might miscarry if the prisoner did not himself or herself make 'voluntary' confession. Torture was therefore employed – the whip, the fires, the rack, the thumbscrew, a horrible studded chair slowly heated from below, or whatever inhuman ingenuity could contrive. The witch had already been shaved all over in the search for the witch-mark. Torture might not be repeated, but it could be 'continued'. We have seen too much in our own age not to know that there is a point beyond which practically no human being can endure indefinite mental and physical torture, and confessions, and the required denunciations of others, were rarely withheld. One horrible and pathetic instance of someone – not a witch – caught in this machine, is enough. It is translated from the shaky hand of Burgomaster Junius to his daughter, and dated 24 July 1628. He writes:

Many hundred thousand good-nights, dearly beloved daughter Veronica. Innocent have I come to prison, innocent have I been tortured, innocent must I die. For whoever comes into the witch prison [at Bamberg] must become a witch or be tortured until he invents something out of his head – God pity him, bethinks him of something. I will tell you how it has gone with me. . . . And then came – God in highest Heaven have mercy – the executioner, and put the thumbscrews on me, so that the blood ran out at the nails and everywhere, so that for four weeks I could not use my hands as you can see from the writing. . . . Thereafter they first stripped me, bound my hands behind me, and drew me up in the torture. (By means of a rope attached to the hands tied behind the back, and carried over a pulley on the ceiling.) Then I thought Heaven and Earth were at an end; eight times did they draw me up and let me fall again, so that I suffered terrible agony. The executioner said, 'Sir, I beg you for God's sake confess something, whether it be true or not, for you cannot endure the torture which you will be put to, and even if you bear it all, yet you will not escape. . . .'

He begged a day to think, invented a story of a witch meeting, and under threat of further torture named various people as being present, and confessed to various crimes.

Now, dear child, here you have all my confession, for which I must die. And they are sheer lies and made-up things, so help me God. For all this I was forced to say through fear of the torture which was threatened beyond what I had already endured. For they never leave off with the torture till one confesses something; be he never so good, he must be a witch. Nobody escapes, though he were an earl. . . .

Dear child, keep this letter secret so that people do not find it, else I shall be tortured most piteously, and the jailers will be beheaded. So strictly is it forbidden. . . . Dear Child, pay this man a dollar. . . . I have taken several days to write this; my hands are both lame. I am in a sad plight. Good night, for your father Johannes Junius will never see you more. July 24th. 1628.

[On the margin]. Dear child, six have confessed against me at once: the Chancellor, his son . . . all false, through compulsion, as they have told me, and begged my forgiveness in God's name before they were executed.*

If all else failed, it was permissible for the judge to promise mercy – with the mental reservation that he meant mercy to the community, not to the prisoner. Or of course he could, if pricked by conscience, promise mercy and turn over the act of sentence to someone else. Escape was a very rare occurrence indeed. The forms differed as between those who had confessed but were not penitent, who were penitent, who had relapsed 'albeit now penitent', who had relapsed but remained impenitent, who still denied everything, and so on. When the appropriate sentence had been passed by the ecclesiastical authorities, what was left was handed over to the civil powers. Laconically it was recorded: '*convicta et combusta*'.

The *Bull* and the *Malleus* were text-books especially employed in Germany, France, and the disintegrating Empire, but observed by Catholic communities generally, as James the First's *Daemonologie* later became the official guide in Protestant Britain. The figures of victims mounted. In almost every province of Germany the persecution raged with increasing intensity. Six hundred were said to have been burned by a single bishop in Bamberg, where the special witch jail was kept fully packed. Nine hundred were destroyed in a single year in the bishopric of Würzburg, and in Nuremberg and the other great cities, there were one or two hundred burnings a year. So there were in France and in Switzerland. A thousand people were put to death in one year in the district of Como. Remigius, one of the Inquisitors, who was author of *Daemonolatvia*, and a judge at Nancy boasted of having personally caused the burning of nine hundred persons in the course of fifteen years. Delrio says that five hundred were executed in Geneva in three terrified months in 1515. The Inquisition at Toulouse destroyed four hundred persons in a single execution, and there were fifty at Douai in a single year. In Paris,

* *The Witch Persecutions*, ed. by G. L. Burt in 'Translations and Reprints' (University of Pennsylvania) and quoted by C. L'Estrange Ewen in *Witchcraft and Demonianism*, London, 1933. Quoted here by kind permission of Mr Burt and of the University of Pennsylvania.

executions were continuous. In the Pyrenees, a wolf country, the popular form was that of the *loup-garou*, and De L'Ancre at Labout burned two hundred. If the Devil could enter into swine, it was felt, so he could into wolves. And no doubt there were wolf-maddened individuals, with or without cult connexions, like that Gilles Garnier who in 1573 was accused of devastating the countryside and ravaging children. He admitted to killing a little girl of twelve, tearing her in pieces with his teeth and his wolf claws, and eating of her what he did not providently take home to his wife. He killed another girl and tore limb from limb a boy of thirteen. There were fifty witnesses and a rack. The sentence concluded: 'the said Gilles to be this day taken in a cart from this spot to the place of execution, accompanied by the executioner, where he, by the said executioner, shall be tied to a stake and burned alive, and that his ashes be then scattered to the winds. The court further condemns him, the said Gilles, to the costs of this prosecution.' It was typical enough. The terror spread, only dying down when general influences had conditioned rulers to some sort of scepticism. Important among these were the Duke of Brunswick, and the Elector of Metz, half-way through the seventeenth century, who forbade torture and spoke of the 'delusion' of witchcraft; and Louis XIV, a little later, who, in 1670, commuted to banishment for life a sentence condemning to death a number of old women from Normandy, charged with riding on broomsticks. In the Hartz mountains and the great forests, in Brittany and Provence, where society was still very primitive, the old beliefs went on. Dualism, inside or outside the Church, had infiltrated. Everywhere individual magicians or societies, studying the higher mysteries, continued. But the terror had burnt itself out, burning with it thousands upon thousands of ignorant and innocent people. Perhaps typically, it was only the Germans who, in the midst of the waves of horror, found the torture amusing, and made songs about the contortions of those who went quick to their deaths.

Apart from the pattern which the evidence builds up, description of the trials and sentences in different countries can only appeal to the sadist. Human terror and the abuse of the limbs, the racking, beating, and squeezing, the suspension from beams, the thumbscrewing and the hot-iron plates recur too obviously. They are live terrors, and we live too near them for the moralization in which the secure Victorian historians could indulge. For again we live in the age of faith and so of fear – although now it is political.

England was outside the general orbit of orthodoxy, and always had been. Hysteria, like armies and the Colorado beetle, found it hard to cross the Channel. And so, in England, there was rarely the universal fear and the instantaneous suspicion which existed on the Continent. There was, indeed, no legal torture, and no witch in England was ever, except perhaps by mob violence, burned alive.* Yet, in torture there are only degrees, and old women kept from sleep, tied up in unnatural positions, nagged, cuffed, bullied, and 'watched', must have suffered inexpressibly, even when there was not unofficial use of 'great heat applied to the feet', or beating.

It was not until a comparatively late period that the hunting out and destroying of witches became in England anything that could be called a campaign. One or two of the 'noble' trials have been quoted, and on different levels there must have been a number of cases of sympathetic magic, the Evil Eye, the bewitching of cattle, poisoning, and so on. Witches certainly existed, and the old beliefs existed, sometimes very widely held. But they were mainly countered by the local remedies of drawing witches' blood (as still happens today in unsophisticated backwaters) or lynching. There were few formal laws against sorcery, as such, until 1542 and the influence of the Reformation – earlier laws having been against homicide by witchcraft, heresy, poisoning, swindling, or sexual depravity, with varying degrees of punishment. Indeed, when in the mid fifteenth century a Henry Hoigges of Bodmin had

---

*That is to say, no one was legally burnt for being a witch. Numbers were no doubt burnt, and others boiled to death, because their case was defined as husband-murder, poisoning, or treason. But there is no case of a witch being sent to the stake or the pot in the records of the Home Circuit.

'brake his legge and foule was hert' by, he believed, the 'sotill craftys of enchauntement wyccecraft & sorcerye' of Sir John Harry (who boasted of it and said that he would next break the complainant's neck in the same way), Hoigges found that he had no remedy at common law. There was much legal uncertainty.

When the influence of the Reformation really made its impact, much of its ferocity was contributed by the Marian exiles who returned to England on the accession of Elizabeth. These men were largely responsible for the first great scare, from 1588 until 1620 or so. For many of them had been to Geneva and had become impregnated with the morbid witch-mania of the Calvinists – a tenet derived from their doctrine of the total depravity of mankind, their belief in the verbal inspiration of the Scriptures, and from their situation in an area notoriously addicted to witchcraft and heresy. It may also be true that to an extent there was, at the same time, and also due to continental influence, an increase in England, in actual practice, of the more cerebral sorts of witchcraft, which the exiles' experience enabled them to detect. These fanatics happened largely to settle in the eastern counties, where local cult practices probably did go on, on a low level, among the primitive peoples segregated behind the undredged fen country round about the Wash. They lost no time in clamouring for blood.

The law of Henry VIII against witch practices had been repealed in the following reign. Elizabeth, however, passed a new law, in 1563, encouraged by John Jewel, Bishop of Salisbury, and Edmund Grindal, Bishop of London. Both were newly returned from abroad, and were scandalized at the already observed number of 'fantasticall and devilishe persons' openly in practice. Jewel, preaching before the queen, feeling that the laws needed amending, prayed 'May it please Your Grace to understand that witches and sorcerers within these few years are marvellously increased within Your Grace's realm. Your Grace's subjects pine away even unto the death; their colour fadeth, their flesh rotteth, their speech is benumbed, their senses are bereft. . . . I pray God they never practise

further than upon the *subject*.' The implication was obvious
enough, and endorsed by Grindal's plea – that the temporal
law was incapable of coping with the menace, whilst the ecclesiastical law imposed too slender punishments – the Bill went
through. Yet, even so, it was far milder than anything on the
Continent, and unless evil spirits had been invoked, or death
caused by supernatural means, witches were only punished in
the first instance by imprisonment or the pillory. Those condemned to death were punished by hanging, and not at the
stake. Moreover, torture was still not legally employed –
although on occasion called in to help with a difficult confession. Yet, even during the worst period, from 1598 to 1607,
when the much stricter law of James I had supplemented that
of Elizabeth, only forty per cent of those indicted on the
Home Circuit went to the gallows.

The fear of witchcraft was greatly spread by the famous
Warboys case. At this small village near Huntingdon, an old
woman, Mother Samuel, confessed in 1590 to the astute Lady
Cromwell, second wife of the Protector's grandfather, that she
was responsible for the fits besetting the five little girls of a
neighbour. After a trial she, her daughter, and her husband
were all found guilty and hanged, and their naked bodies –
the perquisite of the jailor – displayed afterwards for the edification of the curious beholders. Sir Henry Cromwell, who was
Lord of the Manor, came into the property of the Samuels, and
of it gave 'goods to forty pounds' value to provide for a sermon to be preached yearly, upon Lady Day, by a Doctor or
Bachelor of Divinity, at Queens' College, Cambridge, in which
he should preach and inveigh against 'the detestable practice
sin and offence of witchcraft, enchantment, charm and sorcery'. So that, quite apart from the notoriety of the case, and
the high position of those involved, a centre for the propaga-
tion of the campaign against the crime was set up for per-
petuity – and indeed the sermon was preached as late as 1718.

Further stimulus came in 1603 with the accession of James I
to the throne. He brought with him a horde of Scots, imbued
with their own dogmatic and cruel variant of the continental
hysteria, some personal experience of the activities of witches,

and his authority as the compiler of *Daemonologie*, which he had published six years previously. In the first Bill of his first Parliament, he introduced legislation far more severe than that of Elizabeth, for the first time making witchcraft, as such, punishable by death on first conviction. Prosecutions mounted, fanned by a wave of pamphlet literature, which repeated the current versions of the Faustian pact theme – now popular on the Continent – and also scarifying accounts of the Warboys (and other) trials in James's new realm. The emphasis upon the pact is important, as this soon became the real test of witchcraft, distinguishing it from sorcery, enchantment, and magic generally.

Many pamphlets were circulated about the famous case of the Lancashire witches, romantically interpreted in the nineteenth century by Harrison Ainsworth. This had two phases. The first was in 1613, when nineteen prisoners were charged, including the 'Mother Demdike' made famous in the drama of a poet laureate. The second phase was in 1634, when a boy (of extremely doubtful integrity) renewed the charges, more particularly against an old woman called Mother Dickenson. Some forty persons were altogether charged, although a number escaped – through a change in the temper of the authorities which was highly repugnant to Puritan London and to Parliamentary opinion.

For, by this time, opposite opinions were operating in Court circles. In an extremely interesting work, *Four Centuries of Witch Beliefs*,* Mr Trevor Davies has stressed the manner in which that shrewd monarch, James I, largely recanted his views about witchcraft, and how his Stuart successors exercised a growing scepticism, which, when adopted by most of the members of the Royal Society, was to spread throughout intelligent circles. Mr Davies suggests that this belief or disbelief in witchcraft became an issue in the Civil Wars. It is, at all events, true enough that the Long Parliament evidenced a ferocious preoccupation with searching out witches. Moreover, the second most virulent wave of trials was during the period from 1642 to 1649, when the Parliamentary armies were

* London, 1947.

spreading throughout what had previously been territories loyal to the king. The Solemn League and Covenant reinforced the Scottish influence.

It was during this second and worse wave that the notorious Matthew Hopkins operated, under the self-adopted title of Witchfinder-General. It was, significantly enough, in the eastern counties, where he had operated at Ipswich as a 'lawyer but of little note'. He had evidently read James's *Daemonologie* and the more obvious continental authorities. He moved to Manningtree in Essex some time before 1644, when he became suspicious of seven or eight witches who, he claimed, held a sabbat near his house every sixth Friday. He was a quite blatant liar, and whether he ever came across genuine witches it is impossible to say. He became an adept at extracting confessions, however, by pricking and 'watching', and had twenty-nine condemned at Chelmsford, to start with. He and Sterne, his chief assistant then, at a cost of 20s. a visit and 20s. a head for each conviction, in turn visited Suffolk, Norfolk, Cambridgeshire, Huntingdonshire, Bedfordshire, and elsewhere. We have records that some two hundred people, mainly women, were killed as a result of his campaign, and there were perhaps hundreds of others. The Puritan authorities supported him, until his avarice turned even them against him, and he was forced to retire in 1646. The old story that he was himself put to his own test and burned as a witch' appears quite untrue.

Hopkins used 'pricking' as a test, as earlier described, and the discovery of any small malformation was identified as a Devil's teat. He would also place the suspected witch in the middle of a room, cross-legged or otherwise painfully bound. She was then 'watched' by relays of observers, and kept without food or sleep for twenty-four hours, or more. Any animal or insect appearing in the room was seen as her imp, come to suckle from her. Or, of course, she might confess from the pain and exhaustion. Or, as in the case of a former vicar of Brandeston, John Lowes, the suspect could be kept awake several nights, by watchers who 'ran him backwards and forwards about the room till he was out of breath. They then rested him a little and ran him again: and this they did till he was weary of life and scarce sensible of what he did or said.'

Hopkins also believed in the water test, strongly advocated by James I. This was the old ordeal by water dating from pre-Christian times, the idea being that water, a sacred substance, would reject suspects if they were guilty, and they would only sink if innocent. The idea was later connected with that of baptism, and continued in common use in England, with strict regulations and appropriate prayer and ceremonial, until abolished by Henry III in 1219. It continued, however – though not in common law – to be employed for witches, perhaps with some muddled idea that those of the Old Belief should be tested by the old pre-Christian methods. Some of the accused asked for it. Ordeal was, as has been said, specifically discountenanced by the *Malleus*, but it was very popular in Scotland and England. Here the later form has been described for us. It appears to have involved the suspect being hustled to the waterside, naked or in a shirt, and thrown in with the hands and feet bound crosswise, the left foot to the right hand and vice versa. A rope round the waist was supposed to secure rescue if she sank, but it very often did not do so. If the witch floated – and many people would do so, in spite of the ministrations of sympathetic bystanders with poles to push them in – she was guilty. If she did not float, the experiment could be, and often was, repeated. Ultimately the original symbolism was forgotten, and ducking merely became a cruel form of punishment, rather than a test.

Other seventeenth-century tests included weighing against the great metal-bound church Bible, blood-letting, ability correctly to repeat the Lord's Prayer, and boiling the suspect's blood or urine to see if a familiar – any live creature would do – came into the room.

The tradition went on for a long time in Puritan districts, reinforced later by the witch-belief of the Methodists, and the whole business remained, with outcroppings which sometimes reached the courts, in folk-lore. Yet scepticism, and the evidently arbitrary nature of the accusations, with the tragic inadequacy of the evidence in the majority of the cases brought for trial, meant that educated opinion was, by the middle of the eighteenth century, on the whole opposed to witch prosecution. The numbers of those brought to trial declined rapidly after 1665, and the last recorded executions on the Home Circuit were in 1657. One Mary Baguely went to the gallows, at Chester, in 1675. Hangings went on in the west (where the records are incomplete) and elsewhere, and Alice Molland was executed, at Exeter, in 1684. In 1712, a wise woman of Walkern in Hertfordshire, suspected by many people locally, including two clergymen, was sentenced to death but reprieved, and, in spite of a pamphlet war against her, lived on another twenty years. Occasional lynchings occurred, notably at Long Marston, near Tring, in 1751, when an angry mob burst into the workhouse and dragged an old couple of over seventy years each, John and Ruth Osborne, two miles to the local pond, where they were stripped, tied, and thrown in. Both died as a result of the treatment, and a chimney-sweep who had distinguished himself by outstanding brutality in the episode was hanged as a murderer. There were, in differing degrees, much later cases than this.

In 1736, however, the Act of George II had swept away the penal laws. From now onwards there were penalties against the misdemeanour of pretending 'to exercise or use any kind of Witchcraft, Sorcery, Inchantment, or Conjuration, or undertake to tell Fortunes, or pretend, from his or her Skill or Knowledge in any occult or crafty Science, to discover where or in what manner any Goods or Chattels, supposed to have been stolen or lost. . . '. But the penalties against those included – gipsies, white witches, wisewomen, and market-place charlatans – were light. The fury was spent.

In Scotland, trials went on later, and the procedure had from the beginning been far more virulent. Charles Mackay, who as a Scotsman should have known, writing in 1841 on the Witch Mania, explains this by saying that

we naturally expect that the Scotch (as it was still possible to describe my sensitive kinsmen) – a people renowned from the earliest times for their powers of imagination – should be more deeply imbued with this gloomy superstition than their neighbours of the south. The nature of their soil and climate tended to encourage the dreams of early ignorance. Ghosts, goblins, wraiths, kelpies and a whole host of spiritual beings, were familiar to the dwellers by the misty glens of the Highlands, and the romantic streams of the Lowlands.

Accepting any truth there may be in this conventional definition of the genius of the Scots, there were two good reasons for the epidemic outbreak of fear in Scotland. The first was that undoubtedly there did exist in the north, until a very late period, and in individuals to some extent today, something of that quality of hyperaesthesia and prevision which it is suggested did belong to the oldest peoples. There were almost certainly cult practices as well, and plenty of malevolence and knowledge of poisons. On the esoteric side, there had been, earlier, such legendary figures as Michael Scott, who had studied at Toledo – a great centre of magic – and practised divination at the Court of the heretical Frederick II. Or there had been William, Lord Soulis, who sold himself to the Devil and could not be injured by rope or steel, so that when his enemies caught him he had to be rolled up in sheets of lead, and boiled to death.

Secondly, the connexion with Calvinist Europe was closer even than in the eastern counties of England, and the traditional relations with France, too, meant that continental methods were more understood. The ninth Parliament of Queen Mary passed, in 1563, an Act which decreed death to all witches and those who consulted with them, and the terror quickly spread. Witches were discovered in all classes, but it is impossible to assess the numbers destroyed, since most were sent to the stake by the local magistrates. Tradition makes them thousands, and the whole procedure, which involved regular torture and burning at the stake, was far more comparable to what was going on in Europe than to what happened in England.

The witches were particularly employed by the political opposition, and the famous trial of 1591 against Gellie Duncan, Dr Fiene, and some sixty-odd others, has already been quoted. It was a genuine conspiracy to overthrow James in the interests of Francis, afterwards Earl of Bothwell, who was notoriously addicted to black arts, and who had claims to be heir to the throne. Whilst all the ordinary paraphernalia of sympathetic magic, storm-raising, and so on was brought into play, the intention was also to use poison and corrosive ointments. Gellie Duncan, under torture, named the leaders of the conspiracy – most of them respected people of Edinburgh and the district round about – and under the duress of the pillie-winks (which were a sort of thumbscrews) and the rack, Agnes Sampson and the others told identical stories of the great meeting at North Berwick, and the full ritual practised there. Bothwell's secretary, himself a student of magic and an expert in poisons, was one Cunningham, known as Dr John Fiene. He was racked and then put to the torture of the 'boots'; after which, whilst still little more than semi-conscious, he signed a full confession. He then escaped from jail, probably with the connivance of a sympathizer, and returned to his own home, where he tamely waited for recapture. It was James's belief that in the meantime he met the Devil – that is Bothwell. If so, his faith was restored, for on being returned to jail he refused utterly to agree to his former confession, in spite of ghastly attempts to break down his 'stubborn wilfulness'. His finger-nails were pulled out with pincers, and needles thrust up to the eye into the quick. He was again put into the 'boots', in which he was kept so long 'and abode so many blows in them, that his legs were crushed and beaten together as small as might be, and the bones and flesh so bruised that the blood and marrow spouted forth in great abundance, whereby they were made unserviceable for ever'. 'For ever' was not long, and he was executed on Castle Hill. He may have managed to get some sort of anaesthetic during the period of his escape. It is as likely that he died steadfastly, and by ordinary fortitude, a martyr to his belief.

The number of executions mounted, and it is estimated, for what it is worth, that from the passing of the Act of Queen Mary until the accession of James to the throne of England, the number of executions in Scotland was some 7,000, or two hundred a year. Many of the trials have already been quoted, where relevant, and the grisly stories of horror, blood, and torture are easily available to those with a taste for them. The last execution seems to have been in 1722, when an old woman, having sat patiently warming her hands at the flames that were waiting to consume her (for it was a raw morning) was burnt to death for a witch at Dornoch. There were no doubt many lynchings later, and there are still reputed witches enough in the Highlands – eccentric or malevolent creatures whose powers are firmly believed in, and so no doubt to some degree valid.

The story of the persecutions in the British Isles has been set out at some length, and it is not necessary to tell the details of the campaigns in all the countries of Europe. In Scandinavia, there was the 'Blocula' case in 1669, when seventy people were condemned to death – including fifteen children; in Italy there was a special emphasis upon the national aptitude for poisoning; in Spain the theatrical horrors of the *autos-da-fé*. Everywhere, and in some countries down into the late eighteenth century, the trials continued. It is worth recording, however, a singular offshoot from the Old World which occurred in America. When the largely Puritan immigrants settled on the eastern coasts of the new continent, they took with them the general habits and beliefs of the society which they were relinquishing. They took the language, and today speak something more nearly resembling it than can be found in most of Great Britain. They took a majority of the laws – as for instance the provision that marriages can be performed by a Justice of the Peace, which was for a time current under the Commonwealth, but now somewhat bewilders the less sophisticated English addicts of American films. They took their Puritan prejudices against 'immorality', and created laws, against the individual, as harsh as those laws against the conscience which had constrained them to leave. They took a firm faith in witchcraft, and perhaps a few witches. The colonists were of exactly the sort, and from exactly the districts – Lancashire and the eastern counties – most possessed with the witch fever. As Montague Summers describes them, with somewhat gratuitous disfavour, there were many 'discontented Genevans whose brabbles had made England too hot to hold them'. The manifestations in New England, revealed with sanctimonious piety by the various members of the Cotton family, themselves somewhat disreputable characters, were those of the last and worst phase of the English persecutions: epileptic possession, the action of poltergeists, the inventions of imaginative and highly strung children, and simple persecution of disagreeable old women. There was some perception that the practices of witches, as remembered from England, tied up with the practices of Red Indians. But the settlers were Presbyterian theologians, not anthropologists. A number of old women died, some men, a child or so. Numbers more people were persecuted. However, the interest was quickly distracted into different fields, and no place has been more ready to accept freak religions, and mystical curiosa, than the energetic – if theologically somewhat naïve – North American continent.

Witchcraft in the world went on: in some places the established religion – in some, a folk memory beneath the surface. In others, it was an esoteric belief of various sophisticated initiates. But in Europe the centuries of conscious opposition and hostility meant that thousands of the old stock had been wiped out, as well as many credulous old folks, unpopular scapegoats, perfectly innocent people, and self-destroying monomaniacs.

The number who died as witches is purely problematical. Someone has suggested nine millions. It may be many more.

# 13

## Economic, Social, and Intellectual
## Causes of Decline

THE effect of the opposition of the Churches to the Old Religion, the old beliefs, and anything which could be identified with them by panic or anxious logic, is obvious enough. Other and even more important causes were at work to undermine the remaining pockets of the cult in Europe in the seventeenth century. The pockets were absorbed by a Christianity whose own fervour was entering an eclipse.

The absorption into the new pattern of life of those remaining districts populated by the oldest stocks occurred at different times. Because of the preoccupation of early conventional historians with princes, rather than peoples, and 'national' affairs rather than local and social urgencies, it is now difficult to unearth. In England and the British Isles, it is, however, easy to recognize certain districts where primitive peoples were, at this period, forced by economic circumstances to lay aside their old ideas, and to merge gradually into the orthodoxy of the Church and State. The full effect of these influences became active in the eighteenth century, with the Industrial Revolution and its disintegration of the earliest habits of life, and with the increase in the volume and ease of travel. But, by early in the seventeenth century, economic forces were at work which broke down much of the isolation of the primitive peoples. The woollen and cotton industries had developed, and that of wool, in particular, meant a new habit of behaviour. As Lecky wrote, 'It is impossible to lay down a railway without creating an intellectual influence,' and it must be agreed that the rise of the wool industry did much to alter the faith of the mainly agricultural and cattle-grazing peoples of an earlier civilization. In eastern England, moreover, there was the

196

draining of the Fens, which had an effect upon the Civil Wars which has still to be fully described by historians. It has a relevance to witchcraft, in that the considerable local opposition which it encountered had something to do with the emigration of many families (who firmly accepted witchcraft) to America. It also revealed, to those who remained, a community which had only accepted Christianity as a necessary accessory to ideas older and more revered. Roots, grasses, and drainage improved conditions in the eastern counties, and elsewhere. As Professor Murray quotes: 'the sheep ate up the fairies' – a cattle people became a shepherd people, and ideas changed. There is as yet, I believe, no full work specifically dealing with this economic change, but it is to be hoped that there will be one. Meanwhile Cornwall was becoming part of England, and losing its language, Wales was becoming bilingual, and the Highlands were looking south, in spite of old women and a few others who still preserved the art of looking forward by 'supernatural' means. The Age of Reason was on the threshold.

When the Age of Reason arrived, it represented a great many ideas, of which a scepticism about witchcraft was merely a symptom. To analyse the ideas of the eighteenth century would be too long a study for the special purposes of this essay. Very broadly, it can be said that the secondary results of the Renaissance, with its fresh assessment of ideas, and the Reformation, with its fresh assessment of the individual, overthrew the rule of spiritual orthodoxy. Authority was shaken, and tolerance became a virtue. Material inventions helped the revolution of ideas, and, as John Aubrey wrote, 'the divine art of Printing and Gunpowder have frightened away Robin Goodfellow and the Fayries'. The leaders of opinion examined the premises of the Ages of Faith, and found them wanting. With the decline of belief in God and His Church, came decline in belief in the Devil and his servants. Fear became ridicule. The hysterical outcries of the seventeenth century, and its predecessors, faded – at least among intellectuals – behind the polite titters of the eighteenth-century salons. Protestant countries, at first as bitter in their intolerance and hatred of witches as Catholic ones, now identified witch-craft with the Old Religion, and saw both witches and fairies as popish superstitions.* The poem *Farewell to the Fairies* had shown the tendency quite early:

> Witness those rings and roundelays
>    Of their's, which yet remain
> Were footed in Queen Mary's days
>    On many a grassy plain;
> But since of late Elizabeth
>    And later, James came in
> They never danced on any heath
>    As when the time hath been.

> By which we note the fairies
>    Were of the old profession,
> Their songs were Ave-Maries
>    Their dances were procession.
> But now, alas! they all are dead,
>    Or gone beyond the seas;
> Or further for religion fled,
>    Or else they take their ease.

Soon the fairies were to sprout gauzy wings, and be relegated to nursemaids and local superstition.

Naturally, the new conceptions did not gently succeed the old without a conflict. That great, beloved, and universally pillaged anthologist, Robert Burton, writing in 1621, listed the protagonists, and some of the arguments, in writing of the green circle of the fairies or witches 'which we commonly find in plain fields, and which others hold to proceed from a meteor falling'. 'Many,' he wrote, 'deny witches at all, or if there be any that they can do no harm . . . but on the contrary are most lawyers, divines, physicians, philosophers. . . .' This was early, but already nearly a hundred years before, Jean Wier, physician to the Duke of Clèves, had attacked the

---

* This in itself was of course a change from the earlier period when, as described, it was the Royalist and not the Protestant intellectuals who were on the whole comparatively sceptical about witchcraft – although other Royalists were prepared to accept the legend of Cromwell's pact with the Devil.

orthodox position – whilst accepting the existence of witches – in his *De Praestigiis Daemonum*. In 1584, twenty years later, Dr Reginald Scot, of Kent, had published his famous *Discoverie of Witchcraft*. He set out the view that the common opinions about witches' activities were 'but imaginary, erroneous conceptions and novelties', in a work 'wherein also the lewd, unchristian practices of witchmongers upon aged, melancholy, ignorant, and superstitious people, in extorting confessions by inhuman terrors and tortures, is notably detected'. Scot accepted ghosts, but his attack meant that all available copies of his work were burnt by the order of James I, when that king arrived fresh from his witch experiences in Scotland. Other early writers against the reality of witchcraft were Balthasar Bekker, Frederick Spee, and Jean Uvier.

In the early stages of this revolution of ideas, however, the best minds were probably those of the defenders of authority and belief: Erasmus, Nider, Bodin, Delrio, James I himself, and above all, Joseph Glanvil – a brilliant man, born at Plymouth in 1636, and who was 'a zealous Person for the Commonwealth. After His Majesty's Restoration', however, 'by duly weighing Matters, he became convinced of his mistaken Notions, wrote an elaborate Treatise, called "The Vanity of Dogmatizm", for which he was made a Fellow of the Royal Society [and] entered into Holy Orders'. Yet he was by no means merely a Vicar of Bray, and his *Sadducismus Triumphatus* has been described as perhaps the ablest book published which defends, after analysis and with detailed evidence (so far as that lay open to him), the belief in witches.

Glanvil was a Chaplain in Ordinary to Charles II, as well as a member of the Royal Society. The approach of the Society was what we now call 'objective'; the critical examination of phenomena without recourse to dogma. John Aubrey found membership quite compatible with his profound belief in astrology and marvels, and Glanvil's arguments, even if today we cannot always accept the premises on which they were based, were for his age 'scientific'. We should not be misled into despising these men because other forces, and an increased knowledge of natural sciences, made their particular interpretations of the phenomena they observed unfashionable to later centuries. In fact, it was the other development of the work of the Society – the medical reassessment and the reaction from Faith into a definite refusal to accept supernatural (i.e. not material) phenomena on any account – which prevailed. That it did so was largely due to the profound influence of Thomas Hobbes, himself developing some of the ideas of Francis Bacon.

Yet great men, compassionate and honest, accepted the witch conceptions of the seventeenth century almost entire, and Sir Matthew Hale, the jurist, was one of them. He lived in an age of transition, and in one trial discharged an old woman, brought before him as a witch, for insufficient evidence, further observing that when she left the precincts whether she returned home on her feet or rode through the air was immaterial to the court. However, in 1664, he condemned to death two old women of Edmundsbury, upon the evidence of children and an epileptic, with no compunction, and with the aid – as witness for the prosecution and as medical authority – of Sir Thomas Browne. Yet, if intelligent men could still accept the reality of an underground force antithetical to Christian society, men of 'common-sense' and 'sound bottom', brave in their generation, protested. Well they might, when Sir John Holt discovered that the written charm for the possession of which an old woman had been brought before him, for condemnation, was the very piece of parchment on which in an Oxford prank of his youth he had paid off a landlady, with a few scribbled words of Latin, to cure her sick daughter.*

* Another and earlier story is that quoted in an important work, *A Candle in the Dark*, by the sceptical Thomas Ady, in 1656. The anecdote runs:

'A Butcher in *Essex* having lost Cattel, hee resolved hee would go to a Cunning man, to know what was become of his Cattel, and so went to a notable cousening Knave, that was (as common people say) skilful in the Black Art, and this deceiving Witch, seeing his opportunity of gaining a Fee, for the purpose in hand, used his Conjuration in a room contrived for his usual impostures, and presently came in a Confederate of his covered over with a Bull's Hide, and a pair of horns on his head, the poor Butcher

This case, and others on the threshold of the eighteenth century, convinced the law and most of the well-read classes (a tiny minority, but of greater influence than the educated possess today). Meanwhile the mob remained true to their fears, their scratchings, and the ducking-stool. Dr Samuel Johnson was of the people, and part of the difficulty of interpreting his front of full-barrelled orthodoxy and his interior hauntings of doubt and insecurity may lie in this inability to marry the tradition of a Lichfield youth with the spiritual hardware of Grub Street. At all events, he was interested in the Cock Lane Ghost, and when he visited Skye, accepted the second-sight of the Highlands. Addison, who was what would now be called a middle-brow essayist, hedged. 'I believe in general there is,' he wrote in 1711, 'and has been such a thing as Witch-craft; but at the same time can give no Credit to any particular Instance of it.' Fifty years later, he need hardly have been so careful, and most of the literary and cultivated by then saw witchcraft, on the popular level, as a literary device, a historical anachronism, a rural diversion, or a Popish pretence. If anything, they erred towards the credulity of unbelief – Bacon's 'Superstition in avoiding superstition'. Natural events had natural causes, and so, they felt, had unnatural ones.

---

sitting and looking in a Glass made for that purpose, in which he was to behold the Object more terrible, and not so easily discovered as if he had looked right upon it, for he was charged by the Conjurer not to look behind him, for if he did, the Devil would be outrageous; this Confederate, or counterfeit Devil, after the Conjurer's many exorcising Charms, or Conjurations, willed the Butcher to look East and West, North and South to find his Cattel; the Butcher sought much to finde his Cattel according to the Devil's counsel, but yet perceiving after much seeking and not finding, that it was a mean piece of Knavery, returned to the Conjurer again, and desired him to call up the Devil once again, which he did as formerly, but the Butcher had appointed his Boy to stand near hand without the house with a Mastiff Dogge, and at the Butcher's whistle, the Boy as he was appointed, let go the Dogge, which came in presently to his Master, and seized upon the Knave in the Bull's hide; the Conjurer cried out, as likewise the Devil, *For the love of God take off your Dogge, Nay,* said the Butcher, *fight Dogge, fight Devil, if you will venture your Devil, I will venture my Dogge*; but yet after much intreaty he called off his Dogge, but wittily discovered the cheating craft of Conjuring.'

It has been sufficiently underlined that one of the gifts of the witches, both white and black, was a knowledge of herbal and other natural magic, dating from the earliest times, and intensified by faith and fear. The witches had, as well as certain hyperaesthetic or even hypnotic powers, herbal and animal wisdom older than Christianity. They were therefore suspect. Jews were branded as usurers because no one but a Jew was permitted to lend money under the medieval system, and they were allowed few other professions. In the same way, witches had largely a monopoly of the powers of healing – the dual powers of healing and harming – because of the medieval injunction against medicine. The curiosity of the Renaissance meant an end of this monopoly, and as soon as good citizens might legitimately effect cures as competently as could witches, the witches' powers fell into decline. The rise of a better system of diagnosis, moreover, meant that fewer ills could be held to be caused by magic at all. How far the critical intellectual approach preceded the observed material comparison of phenomena, it is difficult to say: certainly the rise of medicine accelerated decay in faith and in that medical ignorance which had accepted the world of devils, miracles, and spells.

It would, of course, be grossly untrue to pretend that there were no legitimate arts of healing in the Middle Ages. Memorries and distortions of classical medical knowledge did remain. The general decline was held up, if little new added, by the Salerno School, at the time of the thirteenth-century renaissance. At the same time there was an advanced medical system, with free treatment for the poor, in the Sicily of free-thinking Frederick II, who was advised by Michael Scott the 'Wizard'. Nursing was carried out by the Benedictines and in other monasteries. Arabic and Byzantine methods crept in from the south and east. There were the ministrations of barbers, and rough attempts, on many levels, at alleviation of human suffering – and indeed that of animals, since, typically enough, horses were doctored with consecrated water. It was on the whole true, however, that asceticism, prudery, and preoccupation with the next world rejected any interference with the traditional procedure, and it was felt that men vowed to religion should not tamper with 'those things which cannot honourably be mentioned in speech'. One Francis of Abingdon was refused a bishopric because he had been a physician. The feeling accounts partly for the repugnance at midwives and for their identification with the witches. Clericism officially frowned at interference with the will of the Almighty as evidenced by disease, and attributed epidemics to sin or to the Jews; with most individual illness to the intervention of devils – either direct or through the agency of the witch. All otherwise inexplicable physical occurrences were the work of supernatural agencies – if pleasant, of saints – if unpleasant, of devils or their votaries. There were few such borderline cases as that in which a woman, given blessed water to drink by St Finnen of Fore, brought forth, prodigiously, a trout, a lamb, and a child. A few hundred years later, St Finnen would have been burnt rather than canonized. Often the physical treatment did not differ between faiths, and only the psychological sanctions were not the same. For instance, osteo-arthritis was cured by the application of oil, warmth, and the solaces, either of the Church, or of the pagans: among the bewildered, perhaps, of both.

A remarkable change came with the Renaissance, although the Catholic Church remained aloof or actively perturbed by it. (It has in more recent times opposed, after all, the use of chloroform and any appeasement of the pains of childbirth.) The revival of classical learning meant that there were, at last, approximately correct editions of the codes of Hippocrates and Galen, which had previously been known only in Latin versions of Arabic translations of indifferent Greek. Moreover, anatomy was once again practised – thanks to the work of Rabelais, Versalius of Padua, and others. Thus, medicine and surgery were again separately defined, although this had first happened as early as the Council of Tours of 1163, which prohibited ecclesiastics from shedding blood in conducting any operation. (The same laws applied to Jews, which the glossing scholars may care to relate to the *Merchant of Venice*.) At all events, after the Renaissance, precedent and authority were overthrown, and a spirit of inquiry and experiment blew away the mystical, sin-burdened approach to physical pain. There was still a realization of the inter-relation of mental and physical processes, and their adjustment to the world as a whole. This involved much that the more pragmatic nineteenth century took as mumbo-jumbo, but which we may see, more sympathetically, as the sense of the coordination of all phenomena.

This idea, developed by Agrippa of Nettesheim, was applied in a new way by the prodigious 'Paracelsus' – Philippus Aureolus Theophrastus Bombastus von Hohenheim, born in Switzerland in 1493. He was a rebel against authority and dogmatism, a romantic, an empirical physician of great skill, and a student of magic – both the inner magic of the secret initiates and the herbal lore of the peasants. He is one of the most direct reasons why alchemy became chemistry. He anticipated homoeopathy, and was a pioneer of magnetic healing. It is ironical that recognition of the values lying in the hidden tradition of the adepts – the esoteric magicians who derived from Egypt and even earlier – on the intellectual level, should, on the folk level, be responsible for helping to destroy the remaining pockets of the witch-cult. For, if the sheep ate up the fairies, the advance of medicine poisoned the witches.

New drugs were used: some to combat new diseases imported from the Americas, and for which tradition had no advice. New experiments meant new developments, ranging from Harvey's discovery of the circulation of the blood, first announced to the College of Physicians in London in 1616, down to Jenner and vaccination in 1768. Possession, among the new and increasingly sceptical physicians, was regarded as a disease, though not yet as evidencing a divided personality. The Church might still practise exorcism (often successfully) and many manifestations might occur which natural science was at a loss to explain. But the pendulum was swinging from the fixed credulity of faith, towards that fixed incredulity of materialism which represented medical orthodoxy by the time of the nineteenth century.

Meanwhile, the new practices and prescriptions did not penetrate rapidly into backward areas. Those in touch with

medical discoveries, and predisposed by the intellectual temper of the age, might welcome them. The countryside remained,
on the whole, true to 'country medicine' – the white witch,
and drawing the blood of the black one, above the brow, to
counteract the evil eye. Everyone knows the sort of thing
meant by country medicine – for earache: the froth from a
pricked snail dropped into the orifice. For fits: a small portion
of human skull, grated like ginger, mixed with the food. (Even
a great and fashionable physician like Robert Boyle advocated
this.) Gout: a spider, with its legs pulled off, wrapped to the
foot with deerskin; for dropsy: several large toads, reduced to
ashes, put in a wide-mouthed jar, corked closely, and kept in a
dry place, to be taken one teaspoonful at a time in milk, at the
growing of the moon for nine mornings; whooping-cough:
fried mice.

These are some of the more nasty and inadvisable examples,
but many others contain elements which may have had some
kind of useful effect. Faith did the rest. Faith must have done
everything in Royal Touching for scrofula – which, although
the later Stuarts disliked the practice, went on until the time
of William III, who rebuffed a sufferer who wanted to be
touched with the recommendation 'God give you better health
and more sense'. But faith was no longer the prerogative solely
of the Church, of the witches, or of immemorial practice.
Gradually there grew faith, for his skill alone, in the physician.*

In the new welter of ideas, there was every opportunity for
the charlatan to practise, so that the eighteenth century was the
hey-day of the experimental quack, the mountebank, the
market-place conjurer, and the dangerous if expensive vision-
ary. These people mainly derived their ideas from the half-
digested dregs of gnosticism, and from the various channels
(and infrequent publications) into which the Secret Doctrine
of the Adepts had leaked. The activity of these exhibitionists is

---

* Although the law has only just been repealed which technically required all surgeons or physicians operating within seven miles of the centre
of the City of London to be approved by the Bishop of London. The
Church retained what sanctions it could.

fascinating – especially when, like Cagliostro, they were clearly not concerned with obvious gain. I have been writing, however, of witchcraft, and not of the intricacies into which the mystic and intellectual stream of the old religion deviated. I will not, therefore, take a perfunctory dip at this point into so important a question. Too many writers on witchcraft pad out the end of their approaches to a profound subject with unrelated chapters on talismans, astrology, table-turning, cheiromancy, rhabdomancy, metoposcopy, or animal magic. It will be possible to look at what had happened to the truer hierarchal tradition in the final chapter. Here it is enough to repeat that much discovery in medicine was the direct result not perhaps of alchemy, which was philosophical, but of the degenerate alchemists, the Puffers, who, for instance, accidentally effected the isolation of phosphorus. Others – some of them renegades from the Rosicrucians or the Illuminati, some Cabbalists – were feeling towards magnetic medicine, or practising auto- and hetero-suggestive feats which were to lead to the somewhat more vulgar system sensationally demonstrated by Mesmer.

There is one more influence, however, which should be noticed in recording the overthrow, in the West, of the popular system of witchcraft. This is the writing of the dramatists, and particularly of Shakespeare. It is true that Shakespeare was not accepted to be a genius so immediately as later writers about English Literature are liable to assume. But he was a portent, and a force. Also, he illustrated what the decorative fringe of contemporary thought felt to be the appropriate approaches to any given subject; and this for occasions designed to flatter the great and sophisticated but at the same time to appeal to the common experience of the groundlings. It has been mentioned that, in the old mystery plays, Adam and Eve had been played naked, and the Devil in full accoutrements – goat's horns, asses' ears, cloven hoofs, and an exaggerated phallus. This tradition went on until the time of the Elizabethan dramatists – and later. There were, moreover, pot-boilers, sometimes able enough, about particular witch trials – the witch of Edmonton, Mother Shepley, or the Lancashire witches. These legendary hags flew across the stages of even the eighteenth-century theatres, with mechanical accuracy and a great deal of wild music. On the other side, Marlowe, himself deeply interested in mystical matters, made great drama of the Faustian legend, as did others. Shakespeare dealt with the philosophical side of magic in the *Tempest* and elsewhere, and with the contemporary and the northern legend in *Macbeth*. All this history can be found, in great detail and the usual over-heightened vocabulary, in Chapter 7 of Montague Summers's *History of Witchcraft and Demonology*. What he fails to point out, however, is that Shakespeare, whilst adopting such admirable dramatic devices, shows little belief in their historical validity. His Joan of Arc is a witch, but his crones in *Macbeth* are stage parodies, and his fairies are not witches at all. He, indeed, perhaps from Italian sources, introduced the idea of the Little People as Lilliputian people. Fairies are figures of mischievous fun, not synonyms for the strange forces of evil enchantment. Shakespeare's writing shows little deep sense of religion, and equally little of its necessary counterpart, diabolism.

Witches suffered persecution at the hands of both the Church and the State. Where they remained as pockets of an older, pre-Christian faith, they were destroyed (in Europe) by economic development. They were regarded as improbable myths by those who already mistrusted the faith of the Christianity they parodied. They were turned by popular entertainers into stock themes for romance. And, by the end of the eighteenth century, most of them themselves, as active practitioners of a common cult, were dead.

# 14

## The Contemporary Situation

THE story, then, of the witch-cult in Europe is that of the peasant belief in a decadent form of the first philosophical and magical considerations of mankind. Witchcraft was persecuted by other forms of development from the same originals – particularly by Christianity and its theocratic systems. Later, it became ill-adjusted to new material conditions, and to the lessening of interest in non-material things, as men concentrated on what was called 'the conquest of Nature'. It had long been cut off from the higher thought behind its practices, and had parodied unpleasantly the religion which succeeded it. Its organization broken, it had become the individual habit of miserable or malevolent persons. Among the wealthy, who had inherited the cult from a knowledge of dualism, and of magical practices derived from higher sources, pockets no doubt continued, undetected until much later. As a parallel, cock-fighting is, nowadays, largely destroyed in Great Britain. Yet, occasionally, in Westmorland* or elsewhere, police fall upon groups of roughs holding a main. The law does not arrest the wealthy who – certainly until the 1930s – sometimes had private cock-pits in their homes. In the same way, the lower levels of witchcraft were split and destroyed, by prosecution or mockery – but the higher levels, in greater secrecy and with more resources, perhaps went on.

As with the Druids and most early peoples, including the first Christians, the secrets and rites of the witches were not committed to paper. This was not merely because of the illiteracy of the ordinary worshipper, but because of recognition that power evaporates from mysteries which are cheapened. The fact means, however, that the record of witchcraft is that set down by its enemies. It is as though, in a world

* As in 1938.

conquered by the Third Reich, all Jewish tradition and history had been destroyed – together with the Bible and all the Jews themselves – so that later generations knew of Jews only as portrayed by the men of Nuremberg. (In time, no doubt, sceptics would have asked whether such monsters had ever really existed at all.) That did not happen. Yet the orthodox story of witches and the scepticism of the humanitarians can only be checked by the evidences of folk-lore, by parallels in other parts of the world today, and by the realization that witchcraft was a poor relation of the higher magic and of earliest and ultimate experience.

The derivative survivals of the practice and fear of witchcraft in Europe, in the nineteenth century and today, would be another book. They are everywhere on the Continent, especially in Italy, and in the county histories and antiquarian proceedings of the whole British Isles. There was a trial involving witchcraft in County Down as late as 1871. Survival exists in America, and a charge was preferred in Delaware in 1950. It has been quoted in detail in the course of this essay. Everywhere you go you find it, and since I said that I was writing this book, dozens of people have told me, with tingling excitement, of wise women, witches, and marvels, up and down the English countryside. They also tell one of haunted houses, poltergeists, and improbable remedies, and of the whole tangle of half-faith in the mysteries and the supernatural which lies beneath a profound disinclination even to examine orthodox spiritual beliefs. I have met reputed witches in the Highlands and in the West Country. (In Dorset one was said to have paralysed and twisted a man's arm, so that 'the doctor broke his instrument trying to put it right' before the spell was taken off.) The witch of Dartmoor and the wizard of Maiden Newton are within memory. There was an old deaf and dumb eccentric who scared my boyhood in Wiltshire, and whose body was not discovered for a week after she had died, because everyone was too terrified to go into her house. It was much as when Richard Jefferies had written about the survival of the belief, in the same district, fifty years before. Anecdote could be multiplied indefinitely.

Throughout the early nineteenth century, lynching went on – and ducking, sometimes at the request of the accused, who wished to be cleared. By the twentieth century this went unrecorded, although individuals were bullied or sent to Coventry by the community. In 1924, a smallholder in Devon was prosecuted for wounding in the arm a woman he believed had bewitched him. In 1938, in a broadcast feature 'Abracadabra', which I wrote with Francis Dillon, we introduced Mr W. H. Paynter of Callington, who held the Cornish Bardic title of Searcher-out of Witchcraft, and who produced dozens of current examples of the craft – white, grey, and black. In Norfolk, in 1941, an army pensioner assaulted a Mrs Spinks, and declared in court: 'A witch has been in the witness-box. Many a time she has tied a bunch of flowers on my front gate and I have spat on them and thrown them away. You know that is going back to the witchcraft of the Dark Ages. I dare not tell you half the terrible things she has done to me. I have been tortured for five years.' Mrs Spinks, the report continues, denied she had practised witchcraft and said the trouble was due to her gathering parsley, which Sutton wrongly claimed to be in his garden. During the war, a group of men and women in Washington, in the district of Columbia (following a ritual, it was reported, advocated by Mr William Seabrook), set out to aid the war effort by sitting round in a ring and sticking pins, needles, and nails into a small image of Hitler. There are more recent examples.

The general belief in malevolent witchcraft, spells, the evil eye, and sympathetic magic (in its seventeenth-century form), therefore, clearly goes on in country districts, although it must be dying rapidly before the popular Press, popular education, a national health scheme, and the American Way of Life.

It is interesting to note evidences of the sort of behaviour inherent in the cult and continued until a late period by people clearly not remembering the early significance. The belief in the coven of thirteen, for instance, died very late. A Yorkshire clergyman is quoted in Henderson's *Folklore of the Northern Counties*, published in 1879, as saying that 'a woman who he knew always carried a stick of rowan in her pocket, as a safeguard from witches'. When he remarked that he thought that there were no witches nowadays, she observed quietly, 'Oh yes, there are thirteen at this very time in the town, but so long as I have my rowan tree safe in my pocket they cannot hurt me.' The true significance of the Haxey Hood Game (see page 121), with the lord, the fool, and the eleven boggens,* escapes most seasonal journalists. So does that of the Horn Dance at Abbots Bromley. It is recalled that sweeps are lucky, but not that it is because they are black – indeed in Yorkshire a sweep was known as a 'punk', and Punky Night or Spunky Night was the Night of All Souls. Ram-roasting was only ended by the last war, and a friend who visited a remote part of southern Ireland, during the thirties, tells me an extraordinary story of a village dancing round a goat with its horns and feet painted in gold, placed upon the third tier of an erection of wattles. This was on a Thursday, and the villagers told him that on the third day, the Sunday, the goat would be roasted and eaten, because 'they had done it always'. But we read of a calf being burnt as a scape-goat in Wales, in 1800, and, in 1850, an ox was sacrificed, in Morayshire, to the spirit of the murrain.

The bull, indeed, retained mysterious associations in many places. In the festival of the *black* Godiva at Southam near Coventry, old Brazen Face (the Sun, who is the Bull, who is the god) wore a mask of a bull's head, with horns. An article in the *West Countryman* of December 1949, speaking of the old-fashioned Christmas bull in Wiltshire, describes it with bottle eyes, large horns, and lolling tongue. It was personated by a man covered in sacking, and holding a broomstick which had the bull's head at one end, and its tail, a piece of rope, at the other. It all seems clear enough.

There is the Padstow hobby-horse and the Helston Furry dance. There are all the old country dances, traditional Morris dances, and immemorial plays, incorporating bits from the Crusades, the Napoleonic wars, and memories of local personalities, which went on all through Victorian times,

* Which incidentally must be a variant of Bog, who is god, and the Boh of my grandmother; and boggarts, who are fairies, and the boogaboo.

usually at Easter or at Christmas. As an example it is perhaps worth noting *The Peace Egg* – the Christmas mumming play recorded particularly by Mrs Ewing. I have not had opportunity to see original versions, and Mrs Ewing does not give one. She naturally observes that it is 'not fit for domestic performance', and it was usually a strictly oral and local tradition. But what she does give reveals a vast cross-section of the old witch ritual, existing in the country junketings of the nineteenth century. A certain amount of the significance she herself notices, when saying that 'the heathen custom of going about on the kalends of January in disguises, as wild beasts and cattle, the sexes changing apparel' was followed. The boys wore skirts and bonnets, the girls hats and greatcoats – as she remembered was also done at Hogmanay in Scotland. It was perhaps the death and revival of Osiris or of Mithras. It was the death and revival of the old year. It was more. There was Robin Goodfellow, Pan, Robin Hood, the Devil, crying 'I'll go put on my devilish robes – I mean my Christmas calf's skin suit – and then walk in the woods. . . . I'll put on my great carnation nose,* and wrap me in a rousing calf-skin suit, and come like some Hobgoblin.' There is no need to explain the eighteenth-century mummer who cried:

> 'My name it is Captain Calftail, Calftail
> And on my back it is plain to see
> Although I am simple and wear a fool's cap
> I am dearly beloved of a queen. . . .'

The mumming plays have the hobby-horse and the Old Tup – a ram's head impaled on a short pole used, Mrs Ewing says, 'as a sort of wooden leg'. The characters hopped along on it with back bent and covered in the hide of an animal. There was the devil with a besom – sometimes a girl – and maidens dancing in a circle. It was essential for the devil to have a good voice, and important adjuncts were the ribbons or 'points', which we have already noticed as part of the tradition. To cap everything, one character, in a tall beaver hat and blackened

---

* Scholars of Brasenose College may care to link this with the Brazen Nose which is the brazen-face of the sun, just mentioned.

face, was called Little Man Jack, who must be the Little John of the Robin Hood saga, and Jannicot of the witch legend. The enthusiast might like to tie him up with Janus. Mrs Ewing wrote it all down, without reference to the witch-cult and as entertainment for Victorian children, about a hundred years ago.

I have used examples from the British Isles, because these are the more accessible in the course of general reading. But there are parallels from all over Europe. In other parts of the world, of course, witchcraft is still a living thing, and said indeed to be on the increase in such places as West Africa. To adduce instances would merely be to set out a lesson in comparative anthropology. The theme could be illustrated, as I have tried to show, from Siberia, Tibet, North America, the lands of the Eskimos, Australasia, or India. The form in the West Indies is perhaps an obvious one, well quarried, and expounded by many journalists and autobiographical ex-Governors. Yet the parallels are so close that it is impossible not to remember them again. For the voodoo sabbat, degenerate as it may be from its African original, and incorporating, as it does, parodies of Christianity, is still very close to what we are told of the medieval European sabbat. It is held almost always in the open air or in cemeteries, and at the full moon. The music and the dance are described with a whole detail of similarity, including the devil whipping the laggards. He himself first, and then the rest, enter the state of possession. His voice and appearance change. If he is not wearing an artificial mask, his face is seen to twist into the '*masque voudourique*'. His breath becomes foetid. He speaks prophecies, and refers to his normal self in the third person. All the worshippers are infected, and can juggle with white-hot iron, dance in flames, smell ammonia, eat broken glass, and stir boiling water with their hands, without apparent pain or after-effects. Afterwards, and after the sacrifice of the god-substitute and the sexual orgy, there is no remembrance of what happened during the state of possession.

If the original primitive practices still pertain in different parts of the world, so does the esoteric tradition – the secret stream of magic and belief by which these primitive powers were kept alive among the adepts in the face of philosophies and religions which did not know them. It would, of course, be ridiculous to try to express, in a few generalizations, the fundamentals of man's profoundest experience. For the higher magic, the Secret Doctrine, must be an experience as well as a code. It provides, its seekers assert, the proper identification of self with the cosmos, and the powers that go with this – the ultimate religion. It involves the law of analogy, or equilibrium, by which it is seen that everything involves its opposite, so that ultimately both are the same. It is capable of realization through religion, through philosophy, and by physical means. It was the code of the Magi, of Zoroaster, of the Druids, the gnostics, and the cabbalists. It persists in many forms and places, and always must. Usually its teachings are heretical to any accepted religious orthodoxy. But they are actively malevolent, and so black magic, only where employed vulgarly for personal ends. For the physical manifestation of power – miracle-mongering or physical bewitchment – is reprobated by the true initiate.

This, the Grand Arcanum, the perennial philosophy, has its literature in every language, and its signs and expositions: pentacles, seals, circles, or tarots. Yet, even where not persecuted, it was to be held a secret, as being necessarily above the heads of the herd. For the herd needed a revealed religion, appreciated an anthropomorphic godhead, and were concerned with simpler ethic. Even if the great secret was profanely revealed it would mean nothing, since the search was itself part of the reward of the secret. To guard it, the steps to realization were shrouded in a profound symbolism of incalculable complexity. Often this degenerated into the most ridiculous mumbo-jumbo. The more dotty saw hermetic significance in everything, or slavishly pursued, in attempting necromancy or the raising of devils, elaborate and misunderstood formulas. Many were on the verge, or over the brink, of madness. Yet those who were not, followed, and follow, the essential truth of man's identification with nature. 'That which is above is equal to that which is below.' The truth implies control of nature, and those powers of hyperaesthesia, hypnosis, prevision, and so on, which came naturally to the earliest peoples and, for slightly later peoples, were generated in the group release of the dance.

All religions, in greater or lesser degree, stem from these truths, and incorporate them to taste. But popular religions, and the hierarchical leaders of these religions, must resist the complexity of a system which can only involve confusion for the majority. So that, whilst the mystics of all creeds and races seek the same goal, the priests and presbyters cannot. Since, to the adept, all things are ultimately and paradoxically identical, then black must be white. Which in turn means that if white (orthodox religion) is being stressed by a particular society, then due care must be paid to black, to restore harmony. Which is dualism, and any Church must therefore condemn. I will not labour an argument which leads directly into theology.

In the Christian Church, the earlier stream of belief was incorporated from history, from the presuppositions of many who adopted it, and, the gnostics claimed, from the secret teachings of its founder. The Apocalypse is seen by some as a symbolical document in the highest tradition of the magical teaching of the East, and together with an inner oral tradition, it was accepted by the neo-Platonists. It has continued all through the history of the Church, if only on the level that a belief in God presupposes necessarily a belief in the Devil. The power of one connotes the power of the other. Almost all theologians are led to this conclusion, and whilst some 'modern' churchmen accept a God of universal benevolence but reject a Satan, even a head of the Anglican community, the late Archbishop of Canterbury, William Temple, could write in 1935: 'Shelve the responsibility for human evil on a Satan if you will; personally I believe he exists and that a large share of that responsibility belongs to him and to subordinate evil spirits.' This may not be profound (it was written in a popular work) but I evidence it to show that the concept of active and actual evil forces – a form of dualism – does still exist in conventional Christian thought.

Outside the Church, and remote from conventional religious teaching, the early stream of belief was carried on by secret societies, and handed on by individuals – the non-Christian gnostics, the Cathari, the Rosicrucians, the Illuminati, and, in some respects, the Freemasons. The astrologers and the alchemists derived from it. The Yogis exercise it. It is represented today by some reputable and many earnest but somewhat pathetic organizations. These often operate to excess mere offshoots of the supreme mystery. Their followers become magnetists, theosophists, spiritualists, exponents of telepathy and telaesthesia, or professional clairvoyants. These forms mainly operate in Europe and America. In the East, acceptance of magic is even more common, although its operation is not necessarily more profound.

Magic and religion are co-terminous, therefore, in any given society. Both generate power. Wrongly directed, by any given convention, that power is Black Magic. Black magic, and dabbling in it, seeking to gain and not to give, to achieve and not to contribute, is what the addicts know as the Left-hand Path. They claim that it is very powerful, and (with the aid of the drugs and practices it imposes) practitioners indeed often end up out of their minds. They have been pushed by convention, or rather by their reactions from convention, over the edge of reason, and are the intellectual companions of the witches. Only sometimes are they charlatans as well.

This induction of ecstasy by physical means, and perverted play with the occult, which represented the worst of the old magic, also still exists. It is the black tradition, deriving from the grimoires and the heady writing of the romantics. It is the play of lonely minds, miserably seeking power. It is the pre-occupation of the over-sophisticated and the pervert. It germinates away in suburban covens and among the incense-ridden flats of the wealthy irreconcilables of every society. Rasputin (who himself was a dualistic occultist, in a tradition still existing in Russia) is a type of the centre round which interested people operate. They are the mad fringe of society. Montague Summers has blood-curdling stories of Black Masses in Paris and (indeed) Brighton, with the eating of babies and desecrations of the Cross. I do not doubt the occurrences, but the importance seems negligible. It is on the level of adolescent temptation towards cigarette cases made of human skin, or indeed books bound in human skin, which, in my day, could be ordered from a reputable bookseller in Oxford.* More recently, we have heard evidence of lampshades in human skin from Belsen. It is a revolt against reason and humanity. It is depravity. But it is not very interesting. Aleister Crowley, who died recently and has had a popular press, was a poet who developed this kind of interest, and had a deep reading of the occult. His disciples were mainly mental adolescents. It is to goat-orgies and suicide that the darker tradition of the earliest truths has declined.

It is sometimes asked whether witchcraft will revive: Dean Inge asked in an article in the *Fortnightly* in May 1949. As we know witchcraft, the answer is that it will not. For witchcraft, as a cult-belief in Europe, is dead. As a degenerate form of a primitive fertility belief, incorporating the earliest instructive wisdom, the practice is over. Conjurers, wisewomen, palmists, and perverts may be called witches, but it is using an old stick to beat a dead dog. In Europe the Church, and the Rationalist, have won, and, if the African and Asian continents still accept witchcraft, it is likely that this will be changed into something else as Western ideas penetrate and are absorbed. A raised standard of living and custom will mean a loss of psychic power.

The only likelihood of a return of witchcraft is if an authoritarian system is to succeed in acquiring power over Europe and the World. If this happened then there would again be a secret doctrine which would survive in cells, obscurely meeting to overthrow the hierarchy, celebrating its masses and providing its martyrs. There would be the herd celebrants, gradually dispersed and persecuted into acquiescence. There would be the initiates, secret and abstracted. The whole circle and cycle would begin again, and gradually the balance of human belief would be restored; the Divine synthesis retained.

* The skins came from the free hospital at Philadelphia, which somewhat dispelled the romantic overtones.

Science would be opposed by belief, and a new devil, a new god, would have been enthroned. But the witches would this time be Christian.

After all, each faith emerges from the purifying fires which destroyed its predecessors.

Or so it seems to me, some twenty-odd years after that silly evening in Oxford, in 1928.

*

And so it seems to me in 1964, in spite of anything that has happened since I wrote this book.

# Bibliography

THE study of witchcraft involves that of history, theology, anthropology, and folklore. I have not attempted to list in these subjects even the standard works which are relevant. I have not set out the pamphlet literature, nor that which deals with particular counties. I have mainly confined myself to works in English, or available in translation; which are comparatively accessible; or which have been specifically mentioned in this book.

ADY, THOMAS, *A Candle in the Dark*, London, 1656.

AINSWORTH, W. HARRISON, *The Lancashire Witches* (Nelson's Popular Library, London, and many other editions).

BAXTER, RICHARD, *Certainty of Worlds of Spirits*, London, 1916.

BODIN, JEAN, *De la démonomanie des sorciers*, Paris, 1580.
  *Le Fléau des démons et sorciers*, Nyort, 1616.

BOGUET, HENRY, *Discours des sorciers*, Lyon, 1608.

BOULTON, R., *Compleat History of Magick, Sorcery and Witchcraft*, 2 vols., London, 1725.

BRAND, J., *Observations on Popular Antiquities*, 2 vols., 1813.

BREWSTER, SIR DAVID, *Letters on Natural Magic*, London, 1842.

BURR, GEORGE LINCOLN, *Narratives of the Witchcraft Cases*, New York, 1914.

BUTLER, E. M., *Ritual Magic*, Cambridge, 1949.

BUTT-THOMPSON, F. W., *West African Secret Societies*, London, 1929.

*Calender of State Papers. Domestic, 1584*, London, 1865.

CAMPBELL, JOHN GREGSON, *Superstitions of the Highlands*, Glasgow, 1902.

CASTIGLIONI, ARTURO, *Adventures of the Mind*, London, 1947.

CHAMBERS, ROBERT, *Domestic Annals of Scotland*, Edinburgh, 1861.

*Collection of rare and curious Tracts relating to Witchcraft*, London, 1838.

CROWE, CATHERINE, *The Night Side of Nature*, 2 vols., 1848.

CUNNINGHAM, ALLAN, *Traditional Tales of the English and Scottish Peasantry*, London, 1874.

DALYELL, J. G., *Darker Superstitions of Scotland*, Edinburgh, 1834.

DAVIES, J. CEREDIG, *Welsh Folklore*, Aberystwyth, 1911.

DAVIES, R. TREVOR, *Four Centuries of Witch Beliefs*, London, 1957.

DE L'ANCRE, PIERRE, *Tableau de l'inconstance des mauvais anges et démons*, Paris, 1612.

*L'incredulité et mescréance du sortilège*, Paris, 1622.

DELRIO, MARTIN ANTON, S. J., *Disquisitionum Magicarum Libri Sex*, Louvain, 1599.

EWEN, C. L'ESTRANGE, *Witch Hunting and Witch Trials*, London, 1929.

*Witchcraft and Demonianism*, London, 1933.

FRAZER, SIR JAMES, *The Golden Bough* (and most of his other works).

FREUD, SIGMUND, *Totem and Taboo*, London, 1919.

GARDNER, GERALD B., *Witchcraft Today*, London, 1954.

GIRALDUS CAMBRENSIS, *Itinerary* (Bohn's edition), London, 1847.

DE GIVRY, GRILLOT, *Witchcraft, Magic and Alchemy*, London, 1931.

GLANVIL, JOSEPH, *Sadducismus Triumphatus*, London, 1681.

GODWIN, WILLIAM, *Lives of the Necromancers*, London, 1834.

GOLDSMID, E., *Confessions of Witches under Torture*, Edinburgh, 1886.

GUAZZO, FRANCESCO MARIA, *Compendium Maleficarum*, Milan, 1608. (Translated by E. A. Ashwin, with an introduction by the Rev. Montague Summers. London, 1929.)

HALE, SIR MATTHEW, *Collection of Modern Relations*, London, 1693.

HOLE, CHRISTINA, *Witchcraft in England*, London, 1945.

HOPKINS, MATTHEW, *The Discovery of Witches*, London, 1647.

HOWELLS, WILLIAM, *The Heathens*, London, 1949.

JAMES I, *Daemonologie*, Edinburgh, 1597.

KITTERIDGE, G. L., *Witchcraft in Old and New England*, Cambridge, Mass., 1929.

KLAATSCH, HERMANN, *The Evolution and Progress of Mankind*, translated by Joseph McCabe, London, 1923.

*Lady Alice Kyteler*, Camden Society, London, 1843.

LEA, HENRY CHARLES, *Materials towards a History of Witchcraft*, 3 vols., Philadelphia, 1939.

*History of the Inquisition*, New York, 1887; London, 1888.

LECKY, WILLIAM, *The Rise and Influence of the Spirit of Rationalism in Europe*, 2 vols., London, 1910.

# Bibliography

LEVI, ELIPHAS, *The History of Magic*, translated by A. E. Waite, London, 1922.

MACKAY, CHARLES, *Memoirs of Extraordinary Popular Delusions*, 3 vols., London, 1841.

MACKENZIE, SIR GEORGE, *Laws and Customs of Scotland*, Edinburgh, 1699.

MATHER, COTTON, *Wonders of the Invisible World*, London, 1862.

MATHER, INCREASE, *Remarkable Providences*, London, 1890.

MEINHOLD, WILLIAM, *The Amber Witch*, translated by Lady Duff Gordon, London, 1844.

MURRAY, MARGARET, *The Witch-Cult in Western Europe*, Oxford, 1921.
*The God of the Witches*, London, 1933.
'Witchcraft and its Suppression', article in vol. v, *Universal History of the World*, London, 1926.

NOTESTEIN, WALLACE, *History of Witchcraft in England*, Washington, 1911.

OESTERREICH, T. R., *Possession, Demoniacal and Other*, London, 1930.

PARRINDER, GEOFFREY, *Witchcraft*, London, 1958.

PERRY, W. J., *The Origin of Magic and Religion*, London, 1923.

PITCAIRN, ROBERT, *Criminal Trials*, Edinburgh, 1833.

POTTS, THOMAS, *Discoverie of Witches*, Chetham Society, Manchester, 1845.

REMY, NICHOLAS (Remigius), *Daemonolatria*, Hamburg, 1693 (and translated by E. A. Ashwin, with an introduction by the Rev. Montague Summers, London, 1930).

SCOT, REGINALD, *Discoverie of Witchcraft*, London, 1584.

SCOTT, SIR WALTER, *Letters on Demonology and Witchcraft*, Morley's Universal Library, London, 1883.

SEABROOK, WILLIAM, *Witchcraft, its Power in the World Today*, London, 1941.

SEYMOUR, S. JOHN D., *Irish Witchcraft and Demonology*, Dublin, 1913.

SPRENGER, JAMES, and KRÄMER, HEINRICH, *Malleus Maleficarum*, Nuremberg, 1494. (Translated by E. A. Ashwin, with an introduction by the Rev. Montague Summers, London, 1928.)

SUMMERS, MONTAGUE, *The History of Witchcraft and Demonology*, London, 1926.
*The Geography of Witchcraft*, London, 1927.
*Witchcraft and Black Magic*, London, 1946.
*The Werewolf*, London, 1933.
*The Vampire*, London, 1928.

# Bibliography

TAYLOR, JOHN, *The Witchcraft Delusion in Colonial Connecticut*, New York, n.d.

THOMPSON, R. LOWE, *The History of the Devil*, London, 1929.

WILLIAMS, CHARLES, *Witchcraft*, London, 1941.

WILLIAMSON, HUGH ROSS, *The Arrow and the Sword*, London, 1947.

WRIGHT, T., *Narratives of Sorcery and Magic*, 2 vols., London, 1852.

ROBBINS, RUSSELL HOPE, *The Encyclopedia of Witchcraft and Demonology*, London, 1959.

# Index

Abaddon, 115
Abelard, 65
Abyssinia, 137, 158
Addison, Joseph, 201
Adepts, the, 28, 175, 177, 204, 205, 214
Ady, Thomas, 200–201 n.
African cults, 17, 28, 31, 33–4, 50, 54, 72, 75, 78, 95, 102–3, 104–5, 106, 108, 110, 122, 135, 140, 141, 147, 148–9, 157, 158, 160, 166, 213, 217
Agape (love-feast), 43, 45, 67
Age of Faith, the, 59, 185, 197
Age of Reason, the, 197
Agriculture, 28, 29, 35, 52, 75, 196, 197
Agrippa of Nettesheim, 204
Ahriman, 105
Ainsworth, W. Harrison, 14, 188
Akhnaton, 27
Albertus Magnus, 86
Albigenses, the, 66, 67, 168 and n., 180
Albigensian Crusade, the, 67
Albrecht, Bishop of, 168
Alchemy, 31, 86, 204, 206, 216
Alexander Severus, mother of, 99
Allhallow Eve festival, 125
Alsace witches, 110
Ancestor-worship, 24
Ancyra, Council of, 166
Angevins, the, 81
Anglo-Saxon, the, 79, 149, 167
Animal Cults, 25–7, 33, 34, 35, 41, 49, 50 n., 54, 77, 105, 112, 114, 142, 157
Animals: and religious instinct, 21; and group, 22; and communication, 22 n.; and sex, 24 n.;

man's relationship with, 25–7, 29, 75, 81, 82, 112, 146, 156, 157, 158; as *totem*, 26, 28, 29, 81, 105, 112, 113, 153; of fairies, 77; as familiars, 112, 154, 155; medical treatment of, 146, 147; as pets, 155; as 'doubles', 156
Animism, 24, 35, 48
Anomalous Woman, the, 96
Anthropology, 12, 13, 14, 16, 21, 22, 145
Antichrist, 12, 178
Anti-phallicism, 46
Ants and communication, 22 n.
Apes, habits of, 21, 22 and n., 24
Aphrodisiacs, 40, 54
Aphrodite, 36, 37
Apocalypse, the, 52, 61, 215
Apollinaris, St, 49
Apollo, 36, 41, 49, 53
Apollyon, 115
Apostolic circle, 25, 120, 122
Apples in witch-cult, 80, 125
Apuleius, Lucius, 39, 40
Arabic influence, 62, 168, 202
Archaeology, 21
Ares, 36
Arian heresy, 64
Aristotle, 62
Ark, the Hebrew, 47
Armstrong, Ann (witch), 107, 120
Arras witches, 73 n., 176
Artemis, 36, 37
Arthur, King, 80, 120
Arydon, Ann (witch), 98
Asceticism, 43, 44, 46, 55, 60, 61, 63, 66, 73, 82, 83, 85, 86, 91, 104, 169, 180, 202
Asella, St, 61

223

# Index

# Index

Esbat of witches, 118, 119, 123, 126, 135

Eskimos, 25, 213

Essenes, the, 30

Ethiopian, *Book of Saints*, 104, 153

Etruscan culture, 36, 38

Eukidon, demon, 52

Evil eye, the, 148, 150, 151, 185, 205, 210

Ewen, C. L'Estrange, 138, 183 n.

Ewing, Mrs, 212

Exorcism, 13, 152 n., 204

Fairies: and the Dance, 23; and the Old Religion, 73, 86; nature of, 74 ff., 78; carried away by, 78, 93; sex of, 84; and salt, 140; end of the, 197–8; and dramatists, 206. *See also*, Little Folk, Witches

Fairy animals, 76, 77; mounds, 76 79, 123; trees, 76; circles, 76, 198; arrows, 78, 79; colours, 79; king and queen, 80–1; blood, 81; rings, 139; definition, 139 n.

Fakirism, 46

Familiars of witches, 50 n., 99, 112, 145, 153, 154–6, 190

*Farewell to the Fairies*, 198

Farnham, Wise Man of, 114

Faust, Doctor Faustus, 86, 98, 124, 154, 155, 188, 207

Fear: of personality, 23, 59; of animals, 26, 76; of Little People, 75

Feast of Fools, 111

Fens, the, 72, 186, 197

Fertility: cults, 16, 17, 23, 33–4, 35, 42, 48, 49, 50–1, 52, 53, 92, 96, 104, 105, 108, 111, 124, 128, 143; dance, 24, 25, 137, 142

Festivals, 26, 27, 29, 40, 61, 82, 95, 104, 105, 118, 124–5, 126, 137

Feudal system, the, 56, 83, 117

Fiacre, St, 50

Fiene, John, 117, 192–3

Finnen, Saint, 203

Fire: as symbol, 23, 84; ordeal by, 30; ritual, 122

Fireproof Lady of Bartholomew Fair, the, 30

Flagellation, 46, 61, 173

Fleming, Peter, 11, 18, 149

Florimond: *On Antichrist*, 178

Folklore, 12, 16, 27, 54, 73, 127, 159, 190, 205, 209

Food: as motivation, 22–4; at Sabbats, 140

Formorians, the, 110

France, 50, 52, 53, 63, 65, 66, 72, 75, 76, 92, 102, 107, 113, 118, 119, 124, 137, 139, 149, 158, 159, 173, 175 n., 176, 183, 184, 192

Francesco Prelati, 176

Francis of Abingdon, 203

Francis, St, 65, 130

Franciscan Order, 64, 65, 169.

Francken, Frans, 133

Frazer, Sir James, 17

Frederick II, of Sicily, 192, 202

Freemasonry, 95, 106, 216

Freud, S., 16, 29, 74

Freya, 52

Froissart, 57

Froude, J. A., 58

Galen, 203

Galgani, Gemma, 130

Garnier, Gilles, 184

Garter, the: of the Devil (points), 106, 107, 108–10, 212; Order of the, 109

Genesis, Book of, 80

George II, Act of, 191

Germany, 50, 66, 75, 97, 119, 125, 154, 166, 167, 168, 183, 184

Ghosts, 16, 21, 74, 192, 199

Gibbon, 46, 59, 165

Gipsies, 57, 81, 147, 191

Glanvil, Joseph, 199

Gnosticism, 65, 66, 82, 85, 166, 168, 170, 205, 214, 215

# MORE ABOUT PENGUINS
# AND PELICANS

*Penguinews*, which appears every month, contains details of all the new books issued by Penguins as they are published. From time to time it is supplemented by *Penguins in Print*, which is a complete list of all books published by Penguins which are in print. (There are well over three thousand of these.)

A specimen copy of *Penguinews* will be sent to you free on request, and you can become a subscriber for the price of the postage – 4s. for a year's issues (including the complete lists). Just write to Dept EP, Penguin Books Ltd, Harmondsworth, Middlesex, enclosing a cheque or postal order, and your name will be added to the mailing list.

Some other books published by Penguins are described on the following pages.

Note: *Penguinews* and *Penguins in Print* are not available in the U.S.A. or Canada

# Alchemy

## E. J. Holmyard

From Taoist China and medieval Islam to the European Renaissance, chemists, saints and charlatans spent their lives on history's strangest and most compelling search – the quest for the Philosopher's Stone which turneth all to gold. Like astrology and witchcraft, alchemy was an integral part of the scientific moral order, arousing the cupidity of princes, the blind fear of mobs and the intellectual curiosity of Aquinas and Newton. As a protection against persecution, alchemists often described their practices in enigmatic, allegorical language; and their search soon acquired a profound mystical significance and religious symbolism.

In this study of two thousand colourful years of naked greed, power politics, painstaking research and mystical experience, the late Chairman of the Society for the Study of Alchemy and Early Chemistry describes the ideas and methods of alchemists through the ages, and shows how their hopes were eroded by the gradual growth of a scientific method to which they themselves unwittingly contributed.

*In the Pelican Anthropology Library*
# Taboo
*Franz Steiner*

Ever since Captain Cook first used the word in his account of the Polynesians, the strange phenomenon of taboo has fascinated laymen and scholars alike. It has been absorbed into the language of psychology and has been applied, often carelessly, to a wide and varied range of human customs and beliefs. Franz Steiner's now classic study examines critically the taboo theories of Frazer, Freud, Lévy-Bruhl and others, and clears up much of the confusion surrounding a mysterious facet of human behaviour.

'His book will be found to be of great value to anyone interested in the idea of taboo and to those who in the future tackle once more the problems it raises ... it states in small compass, but with equal learning and wit, everything of any significance which has been written about taboo' – Professor E. E. Evans-Pritchard

*Also available*
KINSHIP AND MARRIAGE
*Robin Fox*

TOTEMISM*
*Claude Lévi-Strauss*

*NOT FOR SALE IN THE U.S.A.